The Wool-Hat Boys

The

Wool-Hat Boys

Georgia's Populist Party

❦

Barton C. Shaw

❦

Louisiana State University Press
Baton Rouge and London

To my parents,
Margaret Carr Shaw
Alvin L. Shaw

Copyright © 1984 by Louisiana State University Press
All rights reserved
Manufactured in the United States of America

Designer: Albert Crochet
Typeface: Linotron Plantin
Typesetter: G & S Typesetters, Inc.
Printer & Binder: Vail-Ballou Press

Publication of this book
has been assisted by a grant from the
Andrew W. Mellon Foundation.

LIBRARY OF CONGRESS CATALOGING IN PUBLICATION DATA

Shaw, Barton C., 1947–
  The wool-hat boys.

  Based on the author's thesis, Emory University, 1979.
  Bibliography: p.
  Includes index.
  1. Populist Party (Ga.)—History—19th century.
  2. Georgia—Politics and government—1865–1950.
  3. Populism—Georgia—History—19th century. I. Title.
JK2374.G4S52   1984   324.2759′027   83-19982
ISBN 0-8071-1148-1

Contents

Acknowledgments

Like most researchers, I have received help from many people. Although it is impossible to mention them all, a few must receive public recognition. In particular, I should like to thank Harriet E. Amos; Mary B. Eastland; Steven H. Hahn; Robert C. McMath, Jr.; James Z. Rabun; Robert H. L. Wheeler; and James Harvey Young, all of whom read the manuscript in whole or part and gave me valuable advice on topics that ranged from spelling to economics. Beverly Jarrett, the Assistant Director and Executive Editor of Louisiana State University Press, offered encouragement and patience. Trudie Calvert, my copyeditor, corrected the manuscript with great care. The Ford Foundation, Emory University, and Cedar Crest College, through the good offices of Dean Mark A. vanderHeyden, extended sorely needed research aid.

Two people must be singled out for special thanks. Dan T. Carter guided my work, providing ideas, good humor, and friendly criticism. I could not have wanted a more learned and helpful mentor. Finally, my wife, Diane Windham Shaw, was a source of unfailing support. She not only proofread every page, but she offered numerous suggestions from her own substantial knowledge of Georgia history. Many times she joined me as I scoured archives, tramped through graveyards, and explored the region that was once the "terrible Tenth." She made my years with the wool-hat boys a pleasure.

The Wool-Hat Boys

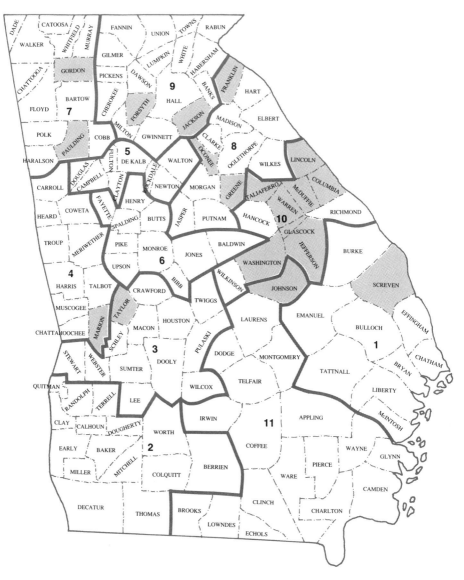

THE COUNTIES AND CONGRESSIONAL DISTRICTS OF GEORGIA IN THE 1890s.
Shaded areas indicate third-party strongholds.

Prologue

In Georgia the expression "wool-hat boys" is still occasionally heard. It refers to the folk who live outside Atlanta, who reside in the mountains, in the piney woods, and on the coastal plain. The wool-hat boys are farmers mostly, and the people who serve them in hundreds of country towns. The term goes back to the time of Andrew Jackson.[1] In those days it was said with a sneer and applied to rustics who wore hats of rough wool felt and who were likely to vote for Old Hickory. But the meaning of this phrase slowly changed until by the 1890s it had become an emblem of pride for the yeomen of Georgia. Indeed, they often divided the citizens of their state into two groups: the wool-hat boys and the silk-hat boys. The wool-hat boys were honest, thrifty, and industrious; people who lived by the Holy Bible and the sweat of their brows. The silk-hat boys were mostly city slickers, who existed not by work but by exploitation. They controlled government and business; they robbed the farmer in scores of artful ways. To destroy the power of these so-called parasites, the wool-hat boys helped create the Georgia People's party in 1892. This book is about the men and women who supported that rebellion. It will try to discover who they were, where they came from, and what they believed in. Because historians have usually considered the Georgia breed to be among the most radical of American Populists, their story is all the more compelling.

The nature of this movement has always been a controversial subject. If one is to believe their opponents, the Populists were at best confused and misguided farmers; at worst, communists. If one is to listen to the Populists themselves, theirs was a true uprising of the American peo-

1. Mitford M. Mathews (ed.), *A Dictionary of Americanisms on Historical Principles* (2 vols.; Chicago, 1951), II, 1889.

ple—an experiment in "primitive democracy" as one third-party man expressed it.[2] Historians have experienced similar difficulty in classifying this strange political party. Was it liberal or conservative, reactionary or radical? Populism fails to fit comfortably into any of our standard categories. Unquestionably, the movement provided its followers with remarkable insights about their nation; Populists believed, for example, that the economy was "rigged" to aid the rich at the expense of the poor. In its place, they called for a more humane and just economic order. Even so, the third-party vision was narrow. Many Populists were small planters and yeomen. While denouncing the evils of exploitation, such men often forgot their own treatment of sharecroppers, tenants, and cotton pickers. Nor were they able to understand the plight of city workers. In the end, they spurned this group for an alliance with the urban middle class. This does not mean, however, that Populists were uninterested in change. They demanded a number of important state reforms, and in the early twentieth century they usually rallied behind the progressive movement.

Most southern farmers refused to join the People's party. Consequently, scholars have wondered why the third party flourished in some places and failed in others. It might seem that hard-pressed regions would have gravitated to Populism; yet many of these areas remained solidly Democratic. Thus we must look for something besides poverty as a reason for Populism. In studies of various southern states, historians have offered several explanations. It has been argued that backwoods districts, far removed from towns and railroads, were most likely to join the third-party movement. Other scholars have pointed to Populist strongholds in regions with few blacks or many new settlers.[3] Yet none of these variables apply in Georgia. In this state, Populism was most successful in the northeastern cotton belt—an area that Georgians called the "terrible" Tenth Congressional District. The Tenth was a land of numerous blacks and few new settlers. True, the third party flowered in the more remote parts of this region. But physical isolation was not the paramount

2. Gracewood *Wool Hat*, May 26, 1894.
3. James Turner, "Understanding the Populists," *Journal of American History*, LXVII (1980), 354–73; Alex Mathews Arnett, *The Populist Movement in Georgia: A View of the "Agrarian Crusade" in the Light of Solid-South Politics, Economics, and Public Law* (1922; rpr. New York, 1967), 33 and maps facing page 184; Sheldon Hackney, *Populism to Progressivism in Alabama* (Princeton, 1969), 4, 26, and *passim*.

reason for Georgia Populism. Other out-of-the-way places—the lonely wiregrass country, for example—remained staunchly loyal to the Democratic party. Scholars have also hailed the Farmers' Alliance as the forerunner of Populism. This enormous organization, which reached its zenith in 1890, served as a school in which farmers learned to think and talk and read about the issues of the day. In particular, it tutored them on the advantages of cooperative stores and exchanges. One historian has argued that Populism generally flourished where these lessons—and especially the wisdom of co-ops—were best learned.[4] Yet in Georgia, Populism usually triumphed where the Alliance commanded only moderate support, and it often failed where the Alliance was strong and its cooperatives well established. Although the Farmers' Alliance played an important role in the coming of Georgia Populism, its activities fail to explain fully the success of Populism in the northeastern black belt.

So we are left with the same question: what was responsible for the rise of Georgia Populism? The roots of this movement burrow more deeply into the past than historians have realized. Long before the birth of the Alliance—indeed, stretching back to the days of the antebellum Whigs—the northeastern cotton belt was tutoring its citizens in political nonconformity. Such an education left little love for the Democratic party and a strong suspicion of corporations and railroad monopolies. As we shall see, it was this Tenth District school, which only later was aided by the Alliance school, that explains the strength of Populism in Georgia.

Besides the origins of the third party, other aspects of the movement are fascinating. For a time, the wool-hat boys vigorously tried to win blacks to their cause. Recalling that famous day in Thomson, Georgia, when Populists supposedly saved a black man from being lynched, C. Vann Woodward wrote in 1938: "Never before or since have the two races come so close together as they did during the Populist struggles."[5] Yet blacks gave Populism little support. Contrary to Woodward's findings, Georgia Populists were hostile to the former slaves, some occasionally donning the regalia of the Ku Klux Klan to intimidate them. A few wool-hat boys held Catholics, Jews, and foreigners in similar contempt.

4. Lawrence Goodwyn, *Democratic Promise: The Populist Moment in America* (New York, 1976), 110–53.
5. C. Vann Woodward, *Tom Watson, Agrarian Rebel* (New York, 1938), 222.

Three previous monographs have studied Georgia Populism and its leader, Tom Watson. In 1922 Alex Mathews Arnett published a brief history entitled *The Populist Movement in Georgia*. Since then two biographies of Watson have appeared: William W. Brewton's *Life of Thomas E. Watson* (1926), and C. Vann Woodward's *Tom Watson, Agrarian Rebel* (1938). Having known and admired Watson, Brewton produced an enlightening but one-sided portrait. As for Woodward's fine biography, its very excellence has tended to make readers forget that there was more to the movement than one leader. Since these three historians wrote, new documents have surfaced. These sources help to confirm and to contradict many of our earlier ideas.

Most Populists were unfamiliar with the conventions of letter writing and composition. Thus when moved to put their thoughts on paper, they often took extraordinary liberties with the rules of grammar, syntax, spelling, and punctuation. Crabbed penmanship was epidemic. Watson said that his attempts to decipher Populist correspondence had prepared him for the grave and "robbed death of its terror."[6] Sometimes messages were written to him on scraps of newspaper. Generally, however, these letters were intelligent and moving—obviously penned by citizens too busy with survival to bother about the finer points of style. To signal such errors with a string of *sics* would be unwarranted. Instead I have usually left the writings of the wool-hat boys undisturbed, trusting that what is lost in literacy is made up for in candor, immediacy, and charm.

6. *People's Party Paper*, July 10, 1896.

Shaking the Pillars of Property

A week before Christmas 1891, a winter storm rolled across central Georgia, encrusting the countryside in an armor of ice. As night fell the blizzard continued, and soon giant icicles hung from the eaves of barns and houses. By morning the storm had passed, leaving a slow, miserable sleet. It was impossible to keep warm. The chill drifted through overcoats and gloves; the water dripped off hat brims and down necks. On such a day most people would have stayed at home. Yet this morning men were already abroad, hitching their teams and venturing out upon the dangerous roads. Some were preparing for a twenty-mile ride. They were all to meet at noon in Thomson, the county seat of McDuffie County. There they planned to join a new political party.

By twelve o'clock the latecomers were still driving into town, covered with sleet, their nostrils and mustaches filled with frost. Most were farmers, but here and there was a lawyer or a townsman. Finally, a scholarly looking man, peering out from behind a beard and spectacles, rose and called the meeting to order. He was state senator Clarence H. Ellington. He reminded the men that they had come to support their congressman, Thomas E. Watson. "Anyone who endorses Tom Watson endorses the Third Party," Ellington said. "I tell you if there is any man whom his people ought to follow like a messiah it is Tom Watson. He is right, and to that extent he is like Christ." Ellington recalled that Watson had been the only Georgia congressman to give full support to the state's farmers. "It is the same old fight between the country and the towns," Ellington continued. "The people in the country are for him now stronger than ever." [1]

1. Scrapbook 5, pp. 79–82, in James C. C. Black Papers, Southern Historical Collection, University of North Carolina Library, Chapel Hill; Atlanta *Constitution*, December 20, 1891.

Next to speak was Mell Branch, a farmer from a neighboring county. Soon cheers answered his every sentence. "They tell us about the Democratic party," Branch cried. "It is controlled by a lot of gamblers and thieves in Wall Street and they want to see you placed in slavery. Vanderbilt once said 'the people be damned.' Politicians say 'the people be crushed' and the time is near when they will say 'the people be chained.' Are you ready to have these chains fastened upon you? It is time for the people to come together and send the politicians to the wall." [2]

The meeting then passed resolutions supporting Tom Watson and the Populist party. Just before the vote, a man rose and reminded them that this was no small thing they were doing. The old parties would never change, he said, and the farmers would have to remain loyal to their new organization for a long time. "We are in for the war," shouted voices from the crowd. [3]

Creating new parties, sending politicians to the wall—these were challenges not usually heard in backwoods Georgia after the Civil War. But on that raw December day the farmers were in earnest; they were in for the war. What caused men to leave warm beds, to ride through a storm to join a mutiny against the old customs, the old political ways? It had not been an easy trip, and the circumstances that brought it about were a long time in coming.

"I can make this march, and make Georgia howl!" wrote General William Tecumseh Sherman, and he did. In September, 1864, he captured and burned Atlanta. Then with scarcely any opposition, his soldiers tramped across the state, destroying plantations, uprooting railroads, and liberating slaves. From Macon, to Milledgeville, to Waynesboro his armies marched, slicing a gash across Georgia two hundred miles long and sixty miles wide. In late December, after he had captured Savannah, Sherman swung his armies north for an assault on South Carolina. He left behind $100 million in destruction and a lesson in modern warfare. [4]

Three months later the Civil War was over. The Yankees appointed a

2. Scrapbook 5, pp. 79–82, Black Papers.
3. *Ibid.*
4. William T. Sherman, *Memoirs of General William T. Sherman* (2 vols.; New York, 1875), II, 152; E. Merton Coulter, *Georgia, A Short History* (2nd ed., Chapel Hill, 1947), 344–45.

military governor, disfranchised the rebels, and marched in an army of occupation. The decade that followed, at least in the minds of white people, was the nadir of Georgia history. Yet the situation was never so dire as some had believed. By 1868 the federal government removed the last of its troops. At the same time, Georgia was quickly recovering from much of the destruction caused by the conflict. Enterprising men repaired railroads, cleared harbors, and built new factories. In some places business was booming. No Georgian was more optimistic than Henry Grady, the managing editor of the Atlanta *Constitution*. Grady believed that the war had been a blessing rather than a tragedy. It had swept away an antique system of plantations and slavery; it had given Georgia a chance to create a modern society based on diversified industry and agriculture. Much had yet to be done. But in a few years, Grady predicted, the South would become a capitalist's Eden, with huge factories, mighty railroads, and mammoth cities. For many businessmen, Henry Grady was an oracle, and his exuberant philosophy came to be called "the New South Creed."[5]

The seat of this faith was Atlanta. Burned during the Civil War, it soon rebuilt itself and became the leading southern metropolis. There its two newspapers, the *Constitution* and the *Journal*, trumpeted the coming new age. They differed only about how the millennium was to occur. Evan P. Howell, who controlled the *Constitution*, eventually came to favor a low tariff and an inflationary monetary policy, whereas Hoke Smith, the owner of the *Journal*, called for a high tariff and a deflationary policy. The *Constitution* also believed that Georgia's first order of business was to establish an adequate system of transportation. Consequently, this newspaper was often in league with the Georgia railroad interests. The *Journal* put more faith in manufacturing and objected to railroads receiving a free hand.[6]

But not every Georgian succumbed to the New South Creed. Many farmers viewed it as a will-o'-the-wisp that neglected the real needs of the

5. Roger L. Ransom and Richard Sutch, *One Kind of Freedom: The Economic Consequences of Emancipation* (Cambridge, 1977), 41–44; Paul M. Gaston, *The New South Creed: A Study in Southern Mythmaking* (New York, 1970).

6. Lewis Nicholas Wynne, "Planter Politics in Georgia, 1860–1890" (Ph.D. dissertation, University of Georgia, 1980), 386–87; Dewey W. Grantham, Jr., *Hoke Smith and the Politics of the New South* (Baton Rouge, 1958), 29–30, 37, 67–69.

state. Except for a few flush years in the late 1860s and 1870s, agriculture
had failed to recover after the Civil War. Prices fell each year. Farmers
believed that cotton could not be sold profitably for less than 8 cents a
pound; yet from 1875 to 1894 the price tumbled from 14.1 cents to 4.6
cents. At the same time the costs of farming were on the rise: fertilizer,
sacks, seed, mules, all were increasing in cost. The reasons for this agricultural depression became the subject of constant debate. Although
there was much disagreement, one fact was certain: emancipation had
left planters with serious labor problems. Their traditional field hands—
the men, women, and children of the Negro race—were no longer be-
having like slaves. Black men were refusing to work unreasonably long
hours; black women were finding jobs as domestics; and black children
were sometimes attending school. To add to their troubles, planters were
vexed by other difficulties. Credit was hard to come by. In 1863 Congress
had passed the National Banking Act, which made it more difficult for
banks to issue notes or receive a federal charter. Two years later a 10 percent tax was levied on state bank notes. Such regulations placed nearly
impossible burdens on southern lending institutions, many of which
were already crippled by the Civil War. In 1895 only 5 of Georgia's 137
counties possessed a bank.[7]

Thus the war had disrupted two vital components of southern agriculture—labor and credit. The planter had his land but no labor. The freedman had his labor but no land. By the 1870s, a compromise had been
worked out. The planter offered his fields to the landless blacks and in
return asked for a portion of the freedman's crop at harvest. If a freedman could contribute nothing besides his labor, the planter provided all
the needs of farming—mules, plows, tools, fertilizer, and a cabin. Under
such an arrangement, the black man became a sharecropper, and the
planter received 50 percent of the crop. If, however, the freedman owned
a mule or some tools, he might bargain for better terms. Called a tenant,
he could usually demand two-thirds to three-quarters of the crop. In
1890, 53.5 percent (or 91,594) of Georgia's farms were rented either to
croppers or tenants.[8]

7. Arnett, *Populist Movement in Georgia*, 66; Ransom and Sutch, *One Kind of Freedom*,
109–10; John D. Hicks, *The Populist Revolt: A History of the Farmers' Alliance and the People's Party* (Minneapolis, 1931), 40.
8. James L. Roark, *Masters Without Slaves: Southern Planters in the Civil War and Re-

Such was the system of labor and land tenure that came into existence after the Civil War. The planter was hardly pleased with such an arrangement; above all, it reduced his ability to control and exploit the freedmen's labor. High freight rates and exorbitant merchants' fees added to the troubles. Thus the planter's day was spent in farming and his nights in worry. As the price of cotton sank in the 1880s and 1890s, so did his profits. He tried in various ways to recoup his losses. Sometimes he diversified by raising cattle or colts or by planting a fruit crop. But mostly he grew more cotton. Land was cheap, and if he could find the labor, it was fairly easy to open new fields. Planters were also beginning to see the advantages of fertilizer, which had been used only rarely before the Civil War. When the farmer applied a mixture of phosphates, guano, and manure to the land, he found that fertility increased. Now sandy soil could grow cotton, and for the first time large numbers of settlers streamed into southwestern Georgia. The influence of fertilizer on postbellum cotton yields was extraordinary. In 1860 Georgia produced 701,840 bales; thirty years later this figure had jumped to 1,191,846 bales. But such an increase represented a bogus prosperity. With no corresponding rise in demand, the price of cotton fell even more rapidly.[9]

So the planter continued to cast about for a way to make ends meet. Some relief came as early as 1873, when the legislature granted landlords the exclusive right to supply renters. Not every planter took advantage of this privilege, but many did. If the tenant or cropper wanted cornmeal, pork, or other store-bought goods, he was required to shop at his landlord's commissary. The cost of these overpriced items came out of his share of the cotton crop. The landlord encouraged such purchases by confining his renters to plots of twenty to fifty acres so they would have little room for a vegetable garden and would need to make more trips to the commissary. Thus at harvest the renter often had little to show for his labor. Often he was still in debt to his landlord. Such a predicament

construction (New York, 1977), 111–209; Robert Preston Brooks, *The Agrarian Revolt in Georgia, 1865–1912* (Madison, 1914), 59–60.

9. Charles L. Flynn, Jr., "White Land, Black Labor: Property, Ideology, and the Political Economy of Late Nineteenth Century Georgia" (Ph.D. dissertation, Duke University, 1980), 85, 97, 202–203; M. B. Hammond, *The Cotton Industry: A Essay in American Economic History* (New York, 1897), 135–36; U.S. Department of the Interior, *Abstract of the Eleventh Census: 1890* (1895), 123.

forced him to work on the same farm during the next season to settle his old debt. This result was what many planters desired so they could retain their labor force.[10]

Yet few planters viewed tenancy and sharecropping as exploitive. Their own high costs and low profits justified the institution. As for the condition of their renters, planters offered a multitude of racist arguments proving that the former slaves were to blame for their own poverty. The blacks were either too lazy, careless, or stupid to profit from a free labor market. The whites, however, were forced to pay for the folly of the blacks. Every planter had horror stories about his "boys": how they beat his mules, broke his plow, mined his soil, ruined his cabin. In an odd contortion of logic, whites came to believe that they, rather than the former slaves, were the true victims of tenancy and sharecropping.[11]

Nevertheless, the planter's lot was not easy. Many were close to bankruptcy, and some would end up as tenants. So it was understandable that whites looked back to the antebellum age with a special fondness. Their stories about that lost time often became lyrical, as if the Old South had been nothing but a land of stately plantations and loving slaves. In those days gentlemen were invariably courtly, urbane, and dashing; ladies always beautiful, spirited, and chaste. An effortless charm and an unstudied dignity seemed to have permeated the planter class. How splendid that such a civilization should have dashed itself to pieces in the noblest of all wars. Out of such tales came the myth of the Old South. Like most mythology, such accounts contained an element of truth and an element of fantasy. Forgotten was the other side of plantation life— the unending routine of planting, housekeeping, sickness, and toil. Nor were the blacks in those days always as saintly as Uncle Remus, and deep in the minds of whites was the fear that one day they might rise up. It was also seldom noted that the gracious ladies and gentlemen of the antebellum age were sometimes less than gracious. The master of the plantation might be given to profanity, alcohol, or chewing tobacco; at dinner

10. Flynn, "White Land, Black Labor," 70–100.
11. Brooks, *Agrarian Revolt in Georgia*, 63–64; Roark, *Masters Without Slaves*, 111–209; Joseph D. Reid, Jr., "Sharecropping as an Understandable Market Response: The Post-Bellum South," *Journal of Economic History*, XXXIII (1973), 106–30; U.S. Department of the Interior, *Report of the Statistics of Agriculture in the United States at the Eleventh Census, 1890* (1895), V, 129.

his thoughts might turn to an evening rendezvous with one of his comely slaves. For the mistress, the plantation frequently offered few amenities. The "big house" was usually drafty in winter, broiling in summer, and crudely appointed. The isolation was sometimes unbearable.

Despite the reality of gentry life, the myth of the Old South remained. The antebellum planter had seemingly risen above the petty materialism of daily life. He professed to believe that such virtues as honor, breeding, and paternalism were more desirable than money. Trade was dismissed as the pursuit of shopkeepers—men who could measure human striving only in an account book. Of course, this code was often violated; nevertheless, it was venerated as the highest achievement of antebellum life. So it is easy to see why many southerners viewed the fall of the Confederate States of America as a catastrophe. For them the old order had slipped away, and a new age—graceless, hurried, and dominated by the sensibilities of shopkeepers—had arrived.[12]

But planters and renters were not the only farmers who lived in Georgia after the Civil War. Between these groups were wedged the "wool-hat boys"—the tens of thousands of white men who lived on small farms and who only had their families to help them in their toil. These people derived status from their race and from their ownership of land. In other respects their lives were more like those of black tenants than of the white planters. Normally their houses were built from logs or clapboard with the corners resting on little mounds of rocks. A porch and perhaps two or three dimly lit rooms provided the living space. In winter the family huddled around the fireplace as the wind whistled through windows and cracks. The opposite happened in summer. The heat would drive the inhabitants to the porch and yard, while the livestock often crawled under the house to find shade. Since there were no window screens, summer evenings were especially trying. Indeed, if mosquitoes failed to make the farmer's sleep wretched, the snorts of pigs beneath the floor usually would.[13]

12. On the Old South see Clement Eaton, *The Mind of the Old South* (Rev. ed.; Baton Rouge, 1967), 245–66; W. J. Cash, *The Mind of the South* (New York, 1941), 1–102; Anne Firor Scott, *The Southern Lady from Pedestal to Politics, 1830–1930* (Chicago, 1970), 3–120; Roark, *Masters Without Slaves, passim.*

13. There are a number of good primary and secondary sources on the life of the yeoman in Georgia. The description in these paragraphs was largely taken from the following

The dress of the wool-hat boy and girl was as crude as their dwelling. The man of the house usually wore a blue work shirt, trousers hanging from suspenders, and a pair of tough brogans. If he was lucky, he also owned a coat for winter work. Atop his head would rest a broad-brimmed hat fashioned out of rough wool felt. As he went about his chores he usually chewed on a plug of tobacco, and a dog or chicken that ventured too near might learn something about his legendary marksmanship. For outside work, the wool-hat girl usually donned a homespun dress and a bonnet. Besides helping in the fields during chopping and picking time, she reared the children, cleaned the house, sewed, washed clothes, kept the vegetable garden, and cooked. She was especially famous for creating a multitude of dishes out of the two staples of the southern diet—pork and corn. At the hands of a skilled cook, the pig could make a remarkable transformation for the better—the liver, heart, stomach, lungs, intestines, feet, ribs, ears, snout, tongue, brain, jowls, skin, and tail all providing excellent dishes. From corn would come ash cakes, crackling bread, cornbread, corn pone, cornmeal mush, and other concoctions. Vegetables in summer and preserves in winter also appeared on the table. Finally, the forests offered honey, nuts, and berries, as well as rabbit, squirrel, possum, turkey, and deer.

Besides his hogs, the wool-hat boy owned other animals. Almost always there were a milk cow and a brood of chickens, which were allowed to forage for themselves. The farmer had only to throw out a little corn to keep them nearby. There were also draft animals. Most yeomen kept a mule or two. A destitute farmer had to make do with oxen—inexpensive beasts renowned for their strength and indolence. (When inspired, an ox would trudge down a field row at two miles an hour.) In addition, it was a

works: Floyd C. Watkins and Charles Hubert Watkins, *Yesterday in the Hills* (Chicago, 1963); Arthur F. Raper, *Tenants of the Almighty* (New York, 1943); James C. Bonner, *Georgia's Last Frontier: The Development of Carroll County* (Athens, 1971); Steven Howard Hahn, "The Roots of Southern Populism: Yeoman Farmers and the Transformation of Georgia's Upper Piedmont," (Ph.D. dissertation, Yale University, 1979); K. Thompson (ed.), *Touching Home: A Collection of History and Folklore from the Copper Basin, Fannin County Area* (Blue Ridge, Ga., 1976); Eliot Wigginton, *The Foxfire Book* (Garden City, 1972); Gavin Wright, *The Political Economy of the Cotton South: Households, Markets, and Wealth in the Nineteenth Century* (New York, 1978); Willard Range, *A Century of Georgia Agriculture, 1850–1950* (Athens, 1954); Ransom and Sutch, *One Kind of Freedom*; Flynn, "White Land, Black Labor."

rare house that failed to have a hound or a flea-bitten mutt skulking about, always ready to snarl at a stranger or go on a hunt.

In early spring the wool-hat boy, his sons, and his mules repaired to the fields, and soon the air rang with the sounds that signaled the rebirth of nature: "Gee! Mule!!! Dad blast your hide, why don't you gee-e EE!" [14] After the land was plowed, it was harrowed and planted, mostly with corn, clover, and alfalfa. The yeoman might also raise a small patch of cotton to provide what little money was needed for taxes and store-bought goods. Formal agricultural training was almost unheard-of. A father simply taught his son what he knew about planting and reading the "signs." The cry of the raincrow warned of rain, the song of the whippoorwill meant fair weather was approaching. The boy learned that only a fool would castrate a hog without consulting the moon. There were also home remedies to be mastered. Catnip tea would hush a bawling infant, lady's slippers would soothe the nerves, fresh cow manure would cure athlete's foot. The farmer told his son always to open the stomach when gutting a deer. On rare occasions he would find inside a porous little rock called a "mad stone." When placed on a wound caused by a rabid dog, the stone was said to draw out the poison.

The days passed slowly on such farms, and the dates that modern people find so vital had little importance. The baby was born two years ago. Or was it three? Uncle Hiram died before the big snow. But when was the big snow? The times of births, deaths, and marriages grew blurry in the mind. When queried about his age, one piedmont farmer said: "Well, I don't know just exactly how old I am. I am between 37 and 38 years old; somewhere along there." Another man, when asked the same question, seemed baffled and finally confessed: "I haint very good at figgers." [15]

But if the life of the wool-hat boy was hard, it was not wretched. It was, in fact, an existence that provided many satisfactions. The small farmer lived close to nature, owned his own land, and was sustained by

14. Quoted in Scrapbook 1, p. 46, in William J. Northen Papers, Georgia Department of Archives and History, Atlanta.

15. "G. W. Burnett vs. J. G. Camp: Contested Election from Douglas County—Evidence for Contestant, [1892]," 3, 57, typescript in Georgia Department of Archives and History, Atlanta.

his Bible, his folklore, and his family. If his farming methods were un-
scientific, they still worked well enough to keep him fed and out of debt.
Yet the times were changing, and by mid-century modernity was already
abroad. The wool-hat boy knew something was changing. Indeed, he
could read the "signs"—the distant rumble of the locomotive, the far-off
shriek of the factory whistle, the glinting wares of the traveling man.

The change had begun in 1861. From out of the hollows and sticks of
Georgia, the wool-hat boys had trooped. With the sons of the planters,
they marched off to fight in foreign places named Virginia, Maryland,
and Pennsylvania. Those who returned four years later found their fields
in weeds and their farms broken down. Few had any money to rebuild.
But there seemed to be a way out of this predicament. During the conflict the world had starved for southern cotton. When peace came and the
federal naval blockade was lifted, the demand for cotton soared. Before
the war, most wool-hat boys had been subsistence farmers who grew
mostly corn. Now there was reason to plant as much cotton as possible so
they could replace their stock and reconstruct their farms. Even though
they would have to give up food crops and would go into debt, it seemed
like a good risk.[16]

But where could they get credit? With most banks ruined by the war,
there was usually only one possible source—the local storekeeper. After
some haggling over terms, the merchant would agree to provide the yeoman with his needs. In return, the farmer was to pay him back with interest at harvest time. To protect his investment, the merchant received a
lien on the farmer's future cotton crop. And so the wool-hat boy began
his venture in commercial farming. Since he was growing mostly cotton,
he relied increasingly on the merchant. Besides the usual seed, fertilizer,
and plow tips, the farmer found he was buying more and more food.
Down from the store's shelves would come lard, flour, cornmeal, pork,
molasses—goods the farmer had once produced at home. The costs of
these items was often extraordinary, averaging from 20 to 50 percent
above the retail price. Sometimes markups soared as high as 100 or even
200 percent. Often when the wool-hat boy finally sold his cotton and set-

16. Wright, *Political Economy of the Cotton South*, 100–101, 164–76, 181–84; Hahn,
"Roots of Southern Populism," 37.

tled his account, he had little left. And if the crop failed to "pay out," he was likely to end up owing money to the merchant, in which case the storekeeper placed a new lien on the farmer's next crop, and so the cycle would continue. As the years rolled by, most yeomen found they could not escape debt. When they had sunk too deeply into arrears, the merchant foreclosed, and the land and other property were sold at auction. Such bankruptcies became more and more common as the century wore on. In 1892 an editor lamented that an "epidemic of distress warrants and foreclosures [is] sweeping over the state. . . . The doors of every courthouse in Georgia are today placarded with the announcements of [sheriff's] sales." The public auction was a heartbreaking moment for the dispossessed yeoman. "When they were bidding the land off at App- ling," one ruined farmer wrote in 1894, "and I found it would be sold so cheap *I felt so bad I could hardly stand it,*—to think some of our best land was sold." Afterward, he wrote: "I could not keep from crying when I read to-day where every thing [else] we have is to be sold." [17]

It is easy to see why the merchant was despised in the Georgia coun- tryside. Few storeowners enjoyed this reputation. They protested that their risks were great and that their own mortgage, wholesale, and ship- ping costs were heavy. Farmers seldom found such arguments convinc- ing. To them the merchant's lien and markup were larcenous, and the merchant himself a man to be feared and loathed. Backwoods stories and songs told of his villainy. In the cool half-light of the country store he seemed to lie in wait—his easy smile and ready credit always at the ser- vice of the farmer, his soft, white hands only too willing to draw up the necessary papers. Yet once the advance had been made, there was little chance of escape. The storekeeper's lien, which year after year coiled slowly about the yeoman, was dubbed the "anaconda mortgage." The merchant was simply "the Man." [18]

17. Ransom and Sutch, *One Kind of Freedom*, 122–23, 130; Arnett, *Populist Movement in Georgia*, 56, quotations from Lawton B. Evans Scrapbooks, Vol. 9, p. 2, in Manuscripts Division, University of Georgia, Athens; and Jordan Hill to Mary Camak, December 6, 31, 1894, in Camak Family Papers, Manuscripts Division, University of Georgia, Athens.

18. Arnett, *Populist Movement in Georgia*, 11; Michael Schwartz, *Radical Protest and Social Structure: The Southern Farmers' Alliance and Cotton Tenancy, 1880–1890* (New York, 1976), 39; Thomas D. Clark, "The Furnishing and Supply System in Southern Agricul- ture Since 1865," *Journal of Southern History*, XII (1946), 24–44; Goodwyn, *Democratic*

As the years passed, the fear of bankruptcy bore down upon the wool-hat boy, but he continued to farm and hope that his luck might change. Such men were the backbone of the Georgia Democratic party. If the politician seldom aided the small farmer, he at least paid him court. The Dahlonega *Signal* recorded what happened when a Georgia congressman descended upon a picnic in 1892: "Carter Tate was there. He came just in time for the fun, and he lit out of his buggy, and just such a time as he had going through the crowd, with both hands extended: 'Howdy, John, hello Bill, by george Jack, hello Bony, why Dave you're as gray as a rat, Captain howdy, and how's your family, how are all the folks up in town, hello, Dan, and here's Joel, well I'll declare, I must go and see Mrs. Howel Randa and the children,['] and he soon returned, bought a load of watermelons, and the crowd devoured them in a few minutes." The wool-hat boy seldom missed a political rally. "Once there," one man remembered, "he was ready to swap lies with the town lawyer, pitch horse shoes with the squire, or engage in a tussle with *any* man who might think he understood the rough science of a country wrestle." What always followed was a "hair-pulling, ear-biting, nose smashing" fight.[19]

In return for such pleasures, the wool-hat boy was expected to be a good party man who would, as the old quip put it, vote "early and often" for any Democratic candidate. A cynic wrote that the political acumen of the small white farmer went no further than one sentence: "I'm a Democrat, because my daddy was a Democrat, and I'm g'wine to vote agin the nigger!"[20] Whether or not this statement was true, his party had little use for him except on election day. Planters, merchants, and lawyers usually dominated county politics, and such men were reluctant to share their power with yeomen farmers. Usually they held nominating conventions at times and places inconvenient to country people. Thus on election day the wool-hat boy could cast a ballot for either the "picked" Democratic candidate or a Republican. For most whites, the latter choice was un-

---

Promise, 28. For a different view of the postbellum southern economy, see Stephen J. De-Canio, *Agriculture in the Post-bellum South: The Economics of Production and Supply* (Cambridge, 1974); Robert Higgs, *The Transformation of the American Economy, 1865–1914: An Essay in Interpretation* (New York, 1971); Robert Higgs, *Competition and Coercion: Blacks in the American Economy, 1865–1914* (Cambridge, 1977); Reid, "Sharecropping as an Understandable Market Response," 106–30.

19. Dahlonega *Signal*, September 9, 1892; Atlanta *Constitution*, March 22, 1891.
20. Rebecca Latimer Felton, *"My Memoirs of Georgia Politics"* (Atlanta, 1911), 6.

thinkable, and so they reluctantly voted for men who had little sympathy for their problems.

Such an ironbound system was resented in the backwoods. Frequently it was whispered that "cliques" and "rings" ruled state and local politics. "The Georgia Democratic party was a great big wheel that turned any number of smaller wheels," one country woman later wrote. "It worked like it was well greased and so it was! A button, when pushed in Atlanta moved another smaller wheel in nearly every courthouse in Georgia; and in every courthouse was a . . . miniature Tammany Hall!"[21] If this was an overly simple view of Georgia politics, it contained a measure of truth. In the late 1860s and 1870s Atlanta had been the scene of a confrontation between the planters and a coalition of urban industrialists, railroad owners, and New South men. The business interests were largely victorious. A friendly legislature soon endorsed the bonds of numerous railroads, granted special favors to corporations, and failed to create even a weak railroad commission. Planters angrily complained about such favoritism, fearing that new factories would lure away tenants and worsen the labor shortage. They likewise feared railroads. Although they had no objections to trains that would haul their cotton to market, planters worried about high freight rates and demanded a railroad commission.[22]

Thus many large farmers welcomed the convention in 1877 to write a new constitution for Georgia. Their leader was General Robert A. Toombs, a wealthy planter from Wilkes County. With a great, rolling belly and a wild mane of hair, he had played a prominent role in southern affairs for thirty years—first as a United States congressman and senator, then as the first Confederate secretary of state, and finally as a brigadier general. For many, Bob Toombs was a man from out of the past—a

21. *Ibid.*, 6–7.
22. Wynne, "Planter Politics in Georgia," 211, 220–22, 238–42, 454. The nature of postbellum leadership, both in Georgia and across the South, continues to be a controversial subject. C. Vann Woodward has argued that after the Civil War leadership passed from the planters to urban, middle-class "New Southmen," who were mainly interested in industrialization. Recently historians have begun to reconsider this view, arguing that power largely remained in planter hands. See Woodward, *Origins of the New South, 1877–1913* (Baton Rouge, 1951), 1–21; Woodward, *Tom Watson*, 52–72; Wynne, "Planter Politics in Georgia"; Jonathan M. Weiner, *Social Origins of the New South, Alabama, 1860–1885* (Baton Rouge, 1978); Dwight B. Billings, Jr., *Planters and the Making of a "New South": Class, Politics, and Development in North Carolina, 1865–1900* (Chapel Hill, 1979); William J. Cooper, *The Conservative Regime: South Carolina, 1877–1890* (Baltimore, 1968).

planter-bohemian in the tradition of John Randolph of Roanoke. Always the prima donna, Toombs could be generous, charming, arrogant, and vain. He never doubted his own abilities, and he honestly believed that the Confederacy would have triumphed if it had elected him its president. Both in and out of his cups, he was never at a loss for words. During the war, an English reporter had asked him for the location of the Confederate State Department. "In my hat, sir; and the archives are in my coat pocket," he growled. His candor, like his repartee, was legendary. When a caucus announced to the state Democratic convention of 1855 that it had selected an unknown north Georgian as its candidate for governor, Toombs reputedly bellowed: "Who in the hell is Joe Brown!" Everywhere the general traveled he was surrounded by young men eager to hear his imperial pronouncements. He was constantly queried about the past. The Confederate cabinet—"A queer crowd [with] . . . a queer history." President John Tyler—"Great at a female seminary commencement or a cow show." General Zachary Taylor—"The most ignorant [p]resident of them all." On one occasion a man asked Toombs why he stayed at the Kimball House, an Atlanta hotel owned by one of the great pirates of Reconstruction. "By God," the general sputtered, "the money with which it was built was stolen from the treasury of Georgia, and that gives every Georgian an interest in it."[23]

But there was more to Robert Toombs than Olympian conceit and a ready quip. As a politician, he represented the old plantation country located between Augusta and Atlanta. As early as 1845 the Georgia Railroad had transversed this section, and within three decades it had built a good system of trunk lines and spurs. The cost of this progress had been heavy. The Georgia Railroad often watered its stock, granted rebates, and charged exorbitant freight rates. By the 1870s the farmers of the region—which later became the Tenth Congressional District—had been taught a lesson about how a corporation might abuse its power. Fortunately for them, they had little need for more track, and so they could afford to challenge the railroads. In particular, they demanded that

23. For biographical details about Robert Toombs, see Ulrich Bonnell Phillips, *The Life of Robert Toombs* (New York, 1913); William W. Brewton, *The Son of Thunder: Epic of the South* (Richmond, 1936). Quotations are from William Y. Thompson, "The Toombs Legend," *Georgia Historical Quarterly*, XL (1957), 344, 340, 343, 338; and James F. Cook, *Governors of Georgia* (Huntsville, 1976), 150.

Georgia establish a railroad commission. At the constitutional convention, Robert Toombs reflected this sentiment perfectly. "Shall Georgia govern the corporations or shall the corporations govern Georgia?" he roared to the delegates. "Choose ye this day whom ye shall serve." At length the convention elected to serve Georgia—or, more accurately, Georgia's planters. In the final document the legislature lost the power to grant corporations special privileges and tax advantages. Nor could a corporation buy stock in another company if by doing so competition would be reduced. Finally, the new constitution prohibited rebates and provided for a railroad commission. The finished document was a triumph for Robert Toombs. Of all his important proposals, only his demand for the legalization of dueling had been defeated.[24]

A year later General Alfred H. Colquitt, a planter from Baker County, was elected governor. In some ways he resembled Robert Toombs. He, too, had sat in Congress and had served as a Confederate general; he, too, was descended from an old and wealthy family. But in other respects there was little similarity between the two men. Whereas Toombs had been forced to leave the University of Georgia for playing cards, Colquitt had faithfully completed his studies at Princeton; and although Toombs seldom turned down a friendly glass, Colquitt was a leader of the Georgia Sunday school movement. Their Civil War records were likewise dissimilar. Colquitt was celebrated for his victory at Olustee, Florida; Toombs was remembered for having challenged his commanding general, D. H. Hill, to a duel. Colquitt was almost everything Toombs was not—steady, sober, pious, and dull.[25]

But Colquitt and Toombs differed in more fundamental ways. Colquitt hailed from southwestern Georgia, a region only lately settled. Its lands had yet to be exhausted from years of cultivation, and fertilizer had opened even its sandy soils to cotton. Unlike the old plantation country, southwestern Georgia still needed railroads; consequently, its planters

24. Quoted in Pleasant A. Stovall, *Robert Toombs, Statesman, Speaker, Soldier, Sage* (Richmond; 1892), 349, see also 340, 350; William Y. Thompson "Robert Toombs and the Georgia Railroads," *Georgia Historical Quarterly*, XL (1956), 56–64; Wynne, "Planter Politics in Georgia," 288–314.

25. For biographical details about Alfred H. Colquitt, see *Biographical Directory of the American Congress* (Washington, D.C., 1971), 769; I. W. Avery, *The History of the State of Georgia from 1850 to 1881* (New York, n.d.), 515–17.

wanted to do nothing that would thwart the laying of more track. General Colquitt heartily concurred with this view. One of his first acts as governor was to champion the state endorsement of Northeastern Railroad bonds. Nor was it surprising that among Colquitt's closest friends was Joseph E. Brown, the president of the Western and Atlantic Railroad, the Dade Coal Company, and the Walker Iron and Coal Company. Brown had served as governor from 1855 to 1865, but his popularity had collapsed after he had allied with the Republicans during Reconstruction. When General John B. Gordon suddenly resigned from the Senate in May, 1880, to become general counsel of the Louisville and Nashville Railroad, Colquitt appointed Brown to Gordon's vacant seat. Many Georgians, including Robert Toombs, were outraged by the appointment. They were sure a deal had been struck ahead of time: Brown had used his influence to obtain a lucrative position for Gordon with the railroad; in return, Brown had gone to the United States Senate. Colquitt's reward came when he sought another term as governor a month and a half later. Brown and Gordon warmly endorsed him, as did Henry Grady of the Atlanta *Constitution*. Colquitt had skillfully married the interests of the new planters of western Georgia with those of the railroads and the New South men. The farmers of eastern Georgia, with their fears of railroad monopolies, had been left out.[26]

Few citizens realized that a new political alignment was forming. They saw only three men boldly dominating the affairs of Georgia. The scandals that had permeated Colquitt's first administration added to their indignation. His commissioner of agriculture had resigned during an investigation, and his comptroller general had been convicted of extortion and bribery. Colquitt, however, appeared to be innocent of any wrongdoing, and he retained much of his popularity. At the state Democratic convention in July, 1880, a majority of the delegates supported him; nevertheless, Colquitt needed a two-thirds vote to obtain the nomination for governor. Various enticements were offered to win over the necessary delegates. But his opponents, mostly from the coast counties and the old plantation country, refused to bolt. After thirty-two ballots the governor

---

26. Wynne, "Planter Politics in Georgia," 315–16; Walter G. Cooper, *The Story of Georgia* (4 vols.; New York, 1938), III, 11–19; Avery, *History of the State of Georgia*, 558–64.

was still 14 votes shy of the 234 needed for nomination. The convention was deadlocked. At length, a majority of the exhausted delegates "recommended" Colquitt as the Democratic candidate for governor. With this endorsement, Colquitt was easily reelected. Afterward the legislature elected Brown to a full six-year term in the Senate, and in 1882 it sent Colquitt to the Senate. Four years later John B. Gordon was elected governor. The position of Colquitt, Brown, and Gordon now seemed impregnable, and the newspapers soon dubbed them the "Georgia Triumvirate." Their supporters from the cities and the new plantation country had long been called "Bourbons."[27]

The power of the Triumvirate did not go unchallenged. During the 1870s, groups left out of the Bourbon alliance rebelled against its rule. Occasionally the aging Robert Toombs took part in these fights; but for the most part the leadership was devolving to a younger man, William H. Felton of Bartow County. In 1875 Felton successfully ran for Congress as an independent. A number of other men who became prominent in the 1890s also took part in the struggles. In the Bourbon camp were Leonidas F. Livingston and William L. Peek; among the anti-Bourbons were Thomas E. Watson, Sam W. Small, Charles E. McGregor, and James K. Hines.[28] Within a few years, however, the uprising was exhausted, and in 1880 Felton failed to win reelection. For the first time in years, a peace had settled over Georgia politics. Now there was room for magnanimity. When Robert Toombs died in 1885, even his enemies mourned. For them, a vastly amusing but essentially irrelevant figure had passed from the scene. He clearly had no place in a hardheaded age of railroads and industry. Others were not as certain. As the price of cotton continued to fall and rumors swept the state of corporate scandal and railroad fraud, Toombs's ideas seemed strangely pertinent. Some even remembered his words at the constitutional convention of 1877: "Better shake the pillars of property than the pillars of liberty."[29]

27. Avery, *History of the State of Georgia*, 546–52, 568–86.
28. For the Bourbon records of Livingston and Peek, see Atlanta *Constitution*, November 11, 12, 1880, and November 15, 1882; Avery, *History of the State of Georgia*, 580, 584, 600. For the anti-Bourbon records of Watson, Small, McGregor, and Hines, see Atlanta *Constitution*, November 15, 1882; Avery, *History of the State of Georgia*, 588, 593; Woodward, *Tom Watson*, 74–83, 104–105, 121.
29. Quoted in Cooper, *Story of Georgia*, III, 262.

◆◦II◦◆

The Alliance Moses

By the mid-1880s the power of the Georgia Triumvirate had reached its zenith. But the peace that had fallen over state politics was not to last. Every farmer, whether he was a sharecropper or a planter, was alarmed by the sinking price of cotton. In 1886 the price fell to a mere eight cents a pound, and a growing number of foreclosures and sheriff's sales added to the discontent. Everywhere the question among growers was the same: what was wrong with southern agriculture? Some believed the problem was overproduction. Before the Civil War the South had served as the earth's principal cotton-growing region. Now Egyptian, Brazilian, and Indian cotton was swelling the world's supply. Since there had been no corresponding increase in demand, it was obvious that the price should fall. To survive, the South needed to reduce its cotton yields and diversify its agriculture. Many critics also deplored the shoddy farming methods common to Georgia. Diversification, self-sufficiency, and scientific agriculture was their formula for prosperity.[1]

A leading exponent of modern agriculture was William J. Northen, the president of the Georgia State Agricultural Society. A grave and scholarly man with a rich auburn beard that tumbled down his chest, Northen had served as headmaster of Mt. Zion Academy, one of Georgia's most prestigious private schools. By the 1880s he turned to planting, and soon his eight-hundred-acre farm in Hancock County became noted for its progressive operation. Rather than raising cotton, Northen specialized in dairying and breeding horses and pigs. His remarkable success convinced him that scientific farming was the answer to Georgia's

---

1. Arnett, *Populist Movement in Georgia*, 66; Range, *Century of Georgia Agriculture*, 90–117, 123.

plight. Thus Northen was attracted to the Georgia State Agricultural Society, a planter organization dedicated to modern farming methods. The members of the organization elected him president in 1886. They were not disappointed by their new leader. Early on, one member described Northen as a "splendid man who is . . . taking hold with a vim." A brilliant coup came when Northen convinced Jefferson Davis to attend the state fair of 1887. A prominent Macon citizen called Northen the finest president the agricultural society had had in twenty-five years.[2]

But wool-hat boys sometimes scoffed at Northen and his theories. Although he had much to say about scientific methods, he never seemed to address the question of debt. Many farmers even doubted that the South was producing too much cotton. Did the poor really have too many cotton shirts to wear? Rather than overproduction, they believed the problem was an economic system that allowed nonproducers—such as merchants, bankers, and lawyers—to steal the earnings of those who worked. With such ideas, these farmers were unlikely to join the Georgia State Agricultural Society. Instead, they turned to the National Farmers' Alliance and Industrial Union—or, as it was more commonly called, the Southern Farmers' Alliance, which had been founded in Texas in 1877. Among other demands, its St. Louis Platform of 1889 called for free silver, the government ownership of the railroads, and cooperative purchasing by farmers. The Alliance at first met with little success. But as the price of cotton fell in the late 1880s, it began to grow at an extraordinary pace. Within a few years it could boast of three million members—a figure that did not include the Colored Alliance with possibly 1.2 million followers, or the Northern Alliance, located above the Ohio River, with thousands of additional members.[3]

Alliance organizers first entered Georgia in 1887. Within a year the order had enlisted 30,000 supporters, and two years later its ranks had swelled to 85,000. To the outrage of merchants, the Alliance established

2. Quoted in Scrapbook 1, p. 1, Northen Papers. For biographical details about Northen, see Northen Papers; A. B. Caldwell, "William J. Northen," in William J. Northen (ed.), *Men of Mark in Georgia*, IV (7 vols.; Atlanta, 1907–12), 285–86; James Calvin Bonner, "The Gubernatorial Career of W. J. Northen" (M.A. thesis, University of Georgia, 1936); Hancock County Tax Records, 1892, Georgia Department of Archives and History, Atlanta.
3. Robert C. McMath, Jr., *The Populist Vanguard: A History of the Southern Farmers' Alliance* (Chapel Hill, 1975); Schwartz, *Radical Protest and Social Structures*.

a state exchange where members could buy supplies at reduced prices. Any farmer and his wife were eligible to join the new organization, as could the natural friends of the grower—country doctors, schoolteachers, preachers, and mechanics. Those in nonagricultural pursuits—such as lawyers, bank cashiers, store clerks, cotton mill agents, grain merchants, and warehouse operators—were excluded. Most Alliancemen appear to have been small planters and yeomen, and it is likely that the more prosperous tenants and sharecroppers also joined. Few large planters became members although some such as William J. Northen enlisted once the order had gained strength. Although the Alliance was active all over Georgia, it was especially vigorous in places that only lately had been settled. Thus the majority of Alliancemen lived in the piedmont and the western blackbelt.[4]

The leader of the Georgia Alliance was a small planter from Newton County named Leonidas F. Livingston. Popularly known as Lon Livingston, he sported a goatee and fancied that he resembled Uncle Sam. One man wrote that he was as "plain as an old shoe." Indeed, Livingston's talents became apparent only when he spoke. An excellent if somewhat ungrammatical orator, he seemed to delight in debate, his repartee never more deadly than when he was comparing an opponent to a chicken, a jackass, or some other barnyard creature. This gift helped win him a seat in the legislatures of 1876, 1880, and 1882. There he specialized in farm affairs, and at various times served as chairman of the House and Senate agricultural committees. In 1884 he was elected president of the state agricultural society, and four years later he became head of the Georgia Farmers' Alliance.[5]

Almost the instant he entered office, Livingston was faced with a crisis. Earlier the national jute-bagging manufacturers had created a trust that was forcing up the cost of burlap. Since cotton was shipped in burlap sacks, the farmers of the South were directly affected. When the price of bagging doubled in late summer 1889, Alliances from Georgia to Texas

4. Robert C. McMath, Jr., "Mobilizing Agrarian Discontent: The Rise of the Farmers' Alliance in Georgia," Paper presented at the annual meeting of the Southern Historical Association, Atlanta, 1973, p. 9.
    5. For biographical details about Livingston, see A. B. Caldwell, "Leonidas Felix Livingston," in Northen (ed.), *Men of Mark*, IV, 168–71; Thomas W. Loyless (ed.), *Georgia's Public Men, 1902–1904* (Atlanta, n.d.), 246–47.

demanded action. It had been a black year for cotton prices, and the jute trust threatened to wring another $2 million from southern growers. After deciding to substitute cotton bags for those made from jute, the national Alliance declared a boycott. Livingston led the cause in Georgia, and even the state agricultural society and the Atlanta *Constitution* endorsed the movement. A New York wholesaler was soon complaining that he was unable to sell his bags in Georgia and that even to mention the word "jute" was like "striking a match to a powder magazine." By fall more than half the state's cotton had been wrapped in cotton sacks. In response, the jute trust rapidly cut the price of burlap in half.[6]

The success of the jute-bagging boycott endeared Livingston to Alliancemen. But the agricultural depression worsened, and Livingston continued his search for a remedy. In December, 1889, he attended the national Alliance convention in St. Louis, where he sat on the Committee on Monetary Systems. Among his colleagues were Leonidas L. Polk, the national president, and C. W. Macune, the former president and founder of the Southern Alliance. Macune presented an idea he had been working on for some time. Called the subtreasury plan, it promised to bring almost immediate relief to farmers. Livingston heartily supported the new idea, and the convention quickly endorsed the scheme.[7]

Macune's plan demanded that the federal government aid the tillers of the South. Farmers picked their crop in late summer, so the price of cotton was invariably low at that time. According to Macune's plan, the government would build a large warehouse (called a subtreasury) in every county that grew more than half a million dollars worth of agricultural produce a year. Rather than sell his crop when the price was low, the farmer could store it in the warehouse and wait for the market to improve. The subtreasury would also issue him greenbacks worth 80 percent of his cotton's value; for example, if his crop was worth $1,000, the farmer would receive $800 in paper money. His cotton would stand as his collateral, and he could use the greenbacks to settle his debts with his merchant or landlord. For such a service, the government would charge a modest storage fee and an annual interest of 1 percent. Corn, wheat, and

6. Athens *Banner*, August 20, 1889; McMath, *Populist Vanguard*, 54–59.
7. Hicks, *Populist Revolt*, 119–21.

tobacco farmers could also take advantage of the subtreasury under roughly the same terms.[8]

Word of the new idea spread quickly among the wool-hat boys. For the first time, the government would directly aid the farmers of the South. Talk of the scheme grew more and more impassioned. Within one growing season, many predicted, the depression would end and the chains of the furnishing merchant would be burst forever. But some expressed doubts. Men who had a stake in a stable economy darkly warned of the consequences. Governor John B. Gordon and William J. Northen argued that the plan would create wild inflation at harvest time. If the entire cotton, corn, wheat, and tobacco crop was worth $1 billion, then $800 million in paper money would suddenly flood the country. When the farmers settled their debts, the money supply would instantly contract. Such expansion and contraction had to cause financial anarchy, it was argued. Nor would all farmers benefit from the scheme. Only a quarter of southern counties enjoyed yields large enough to qualify for a warehouse. Moreover, many tenants and sharecroppers were contractually bound to sell their cotton to their landlords at harvest. They, too, would be left out. Upon reflection, most farmers were willing to admit that the subtreasury plan had flaws. Still they refused to be dissuaded. Thousands continued to clamor for the new scheme or, as they put it, "something better."[9]

Despite Livingston's support of the subtreasury plan, he did not favor every Alliance principle. In particular, he objected to the demand for government ownership of the railroads. Thus when the national leaders of the order gathered in Ocala, Florida, in 1890, Livingston lobbied for a new platform. By the end of the meeting, the Alliance had dropped its demand for government ownership of the railroads in favor of government regulation. Having changed the philosophy of the national organization, Livingston returned to Georgia and tightened his hold over his own Alliance. To head the state exchange, he selected his friend William L. Peek of Rockdale County. Within a year Peek's operation had

8. McMath, *Populist Vanguard*, 90–91.
9. John D. Hicks, "The Sub-Treasury Plan: A Forgotten Plan for the Relief of Agriculture," *Mississippi Valley Historical Review*, XV (1928), 355–73; Thomas E. Watson, *Life and Speeches of Thomas E. Watson* (Thomson, 1911), 92.

saved Alliancemen $200,000 in fertilizer costs. Such success won Livingston thousands of additional supporters, and he was soon dubbed the "Alliance Moses." [10]

But Livingston had also created enemies. Alliancemen who favored government ownership of the railroads said that he and his cohorts had betrayed the order. But there was little that was hypocritical about Livingston—at least at this point in his career. His farm and Peek's rested on the northern edge of the new plantation country. It was a matter of public record that both men were allies of Alfred Colquitt. Livingston had served as one of Colquitt's strongest supporters during the state Democratic conventions of 1880 and 1882. And while members of the legislature, both Livingston and Peek had voted to send Colquitt and Joseph E. Brown to the U.S. Senate. The majority of Georgia Alliancemen probably favored Livingston's service to the railroad interests. Most members lived in the piedmont and the western cotton belt—regions still in need of tracks. Therefore they wanted to do nothing that would discourage more railroad construction. Indeed, some piedmont farmers were beginning to say that Livingston would make a fine governor and Peek an excellent congressman. [11]

Such talk worried Democratic leaders, many of whom were enemies of the subtreasury plan. They advised the Alliance to stay out of politics. Despite this warning, in April, 1890, the state Alliance Executive Committee drew up a list of eight principles by which it asked Alliancemen to judge political candidates. Did the candidate endorse railroad reform, the subtreasury plan, better schools, lower taxes, prison reform, and an end to national banks, trusts, and speculation? [12] If not, the committee urged farmers to vote against him. Even the dullest politician understood the power of the Alliance, and hundreds hastily agreed to the eight demands. It appeared certain that Georgia's next chief executive and perhaps all of its congressmen would be Alliancemen or public advocates of Alliance doctrine.

10. Range, *Century of Georgia Agriculture*, 142; McMath *Populist Vanguard*, 107–109.
11. Atlanta *Constitution*, November 11, 12, 1880, November 15, September 2, 1882; Atlanta *Journal*, August 18, 1892; Wynne, "Planter Politics in Georgia," 240; Avery, *History of the State of Georgia*, 580, 584, 600.
12. Lewis Nicholas Wynne, "The Alliance Legislature of 1890" (M.A. thesis, University of Georgia, 1970), 30.

Northen and Livingston became the main contenders for the governorship. Bourbons such as Governor John B. Gordon and Evan Howell of the Atlanta *Constitution* gave Northen their enthusiastic support. In addition, Northen's strength came mostly from urban businessmen, cotton-belt planters, and farmers from small counties that would not be qualified for a subtreasury. Livingston's followers were generally small planters and yeomen living in the piedmont and western cotton belt. Like Livingston, they refused to believe that overproduction was responsible for the decline in cotton prices. Instead, they argued that the economy was "rigged" in favor of the rich and that only the subtreasury plan would free them from the lien system. Because their part of Georgia was still in need of trunk lines and spurs, they also agreed with Livingston's stand against government ownership of the railroads. But except for the endorsement of William L. Peek, who was running for Congress in the Fifth Congressional District, Livingston failed to gain the support of many prominent politicians.[13]

In early August, 1889, Northen announced his candidacy for governor. He openly admitted to strong reservations about the subtreasury plan. Declaring that overproduction was Georgia's most pressing problem, he advised farmers to diversify and to adopt scientific farming methods. Northen also denounced monopolies (but suggested no remedy for them) and called for the free coinage of silver, a lower tariff, better schools, and improved race relations. He argued that transportation was not a serious difficulty because the railroads would soon penetrate the backwoods and every farmer could get his produce conveniently to market. But on all of these issues—money, the tariff, monopoly, and transportation— Northen's comments were usually perfunctory. To his mind, the agricultural crisis would be won or lost depending on how extensively the farmer employed thrift, diversification, and scientific methods. Hard work, rather than political agitation, was the key to prosperity. Nothing was more repulsive to Northen than the thought of class struggle: "Whatever builds up, legitimately, the efforts of industry, builds up also the prosperity of the commonwealth; whatever encourages the peace and conciliation of the classes, makes a united society and an impregnable

13. Wynne, "Planter Politics in Georgia," 315–16.

state." In most areas, Northen could see no need for serious reform. "The strengths of our government must be found in the conservative intelligence of the people," he said.[14]

The friends of Lon Livingston were quick to reply. "This old cry is all bosh," one newspaper wrote of Northen's call for more economy. As opposition unified in the spring of 1890, many questions were put to Northen. Why were so many anti-Alliance newspapers supporting him? And why, while he was a member of the Georgia Senate in 1885, had he voted to emasculate the state railroad commission? It was whispered that Northen favored the corporations, that his Civil War record was less than honorable, that he was not even a planter. "He knows no more about farming than a mule does about the Samoan difficulty," one newspaper sneered. The crowning insult came when it was rumored that Northen was a Yankee. "This deep schemer . . ." declared the Henry County *Weekly*, "like effete monarchs of Europe, believes he is entitled to succeed . . . Governor Gordon by Divine right. Foolish man!"[15]

Rather than trying to win over his enemies, Northen took the offensive. He proudly admitted that he had reservations about the subtreasury plan. And although he favored a railroad commission, he said that railroad companies should have the right of judicial appeal. Finally, Northen proclaimed that he was "not the candidate of a single class, but the champion of the rights of all." The Atlanta *Constitution* and other city newspapers mounted a vitriolic attack on Livingston, and by late May it was apparent that Northen was pulling into the lead. In early June, Livingston allowed William L. Peek to meet with Northen in Atlanta. When the parley was over, they had agreed that Livingston would leave the gubernatorial contest and run for Congress in place of Peek. Livingston had clearly underestimated the strength of the Bourbons, and Northen was inaugurated in November, 1890.[16]

After the gubernatorial race came the congressional elections. In the Fifth District, Livingston easily defeated his opponent. In the "terrible

14. Scrapbook 1, p. 5, Northen Papers.

15. *Ibid.*, ii, 5, 11, 14 (McDonough *Henry County Weekly*, n.d.), 17; with the exception noted, all are unidentified newspaper clippings.

16. Quoted in Arnett, *Populist Movement in Georgia*, 104–105; see also 102–12; Scrapbook 1, p. 21, Northen Papers.

Tenth," Thomas E. Watson gained Alliance support and was victorious. The Alliance also endorsed four incumbents who campaigned without opposition. In the five other congressional races Alliance candidates won. Thus every Georgia congressman was an Alliance member or a public advocate of Alliance doctrine. In the legislative elections, the organization's victories were equally spectacular—or so it seemed. The Atlanta *Constitution* reported that out of 219 seats, the Alliance captured 182. But events would prove that many of these legislators had almost no loyalty to the order.[17]

In early November, 1890, the "Alliance legislature" met for the first time, and the House elected Clark Howell, the son of Evan Howell of the Atlanta *Constitution*, its Speaker. Because the old triumvir, Joseph E. Brown, had announced his retirement, the General Assembly was also required to appoint a new United States senator. Immediately Governor John B. Gordon declared his candidacy. But Gordon's opposition to the subtreasury plan had won him enemies. So into the field came a host of pro-subtreasury candidates. Among them were Thomas M. Norwood, a former United States senator from Savannah; James K. Hines, a circuit court judge from Washington County; and Patrick Calhoun, a railroad attorney from Atlanta and the grandson of John C. Calhoun. Even parties from outside the state were active. Leonidas L. Polk, the president of the Southern Farmers' Alliance, campaigned for Norwood, and C. W. Macune, the founder of the organization, supported Calhoun. But when the General Assembly balloted, Gordon was triumphant, followed by Norwood, Calhoun, and Hines. Many farmers were dumbfounded. How could the "Alliance legislature" have sent an enemy of the subtreasury plan to the United States Senate? Rumors swept the state that the election had been stolen, and an Alliance investigation later discovered that Calhoun had given Macune free railroad passes and a $2,000 loan. Nevertheless, Gordon had entered the struggle with considerable support, especially among delegates from the cities, black belt, and sparsely populated counties that had nothing to gain from the subtreasury plan. In short, Gordon had done well among the same groups that had supported

17. McMath, "Mobilizing Agrarian Discontent," 12 and *passim*.

Northen in his race for governor. Their victories demonstrated how badly the Alliance was divided over the subtreasury question.[18]

But another issue was also helping to sunder the Alliance. In 1890 few Alliance members desired government ownership of the railroads, and Patrick Calhoun, the railroad lawyer, had received much farm support in his campaign for the Senate. Among his followers were Lon Livingston and legislators including Clarence H. Ellington, John A. Sibley, William R. Gorman, I. A. Hand, and A. W. Ivey.[19] Why had they endorsed Calhoun? And why did most of them later become leaders of the Georgia Populist party?

Patrick Calhoun was a member of the Atlanta law firm of Calhoun, King, and Spaulding. The firm's principal client was the Richmond and East Point Terminal Company. The Richmond Terminal, as the company was commonly called, was the largest railroad in the South, its tracks stretching from Virginia to the Mississippi River. Calhoun was a friend of the company's president and served as its general counsel. He would appear an unlikely candidate for Alliance support. But as we have seen, most Georgia Alliancemen were friendly to the railroad interests. In addition, Calhoun had publicly defended the subtreasury plan and had advocated government regulation of the railroads, which along with his lofty position in southern society made him an instant candidate for the Senate. For the first time the subtreasury plan had been given a respectability it had never experienced. Thus it was not surprising that Calhoun gained a strong Alliance following.[20]

But Calhoun's Alliance support did not last. In early July farmers were astonished to learn that the Central of Georgia Railroad, which had earlier leased the Georgia Railroad, had leased itself to the Richmond Terminal. Once the papers had been signed, almost every important trunk line in the state was controlled by the same company. Soon it was reported that one of the men behind the takeover was Patrick Calhoun. The scheme, however, had strained the Terminal's already overextended

18. Atlanta *Constitution*, November 19, 1890; Arnett, *Populist Movement in Georgia*, 118–20; Wynne, "Alliance Legislature," 85–89.

19. Atlanta *Constitution*, November 6, 16, 19, 1890.

20. Maury Klein, *The Great Richmond Terminal: A Study in Businessmen and Business Strategy* (Charlottesville, 1970), 33; Atlanta *Constitution*, October 17, 1890.

resources. To recoup some of the losses, its directors watered the Central's stock and drove up freight rates. Melon and vegetable growers were nearly bankrupted. At about the same time, the New York *Herald* ran an exposé detailing the Terminal's hidden debts and fraudulent bookkeeping practices. By the end of the month Central of Georgia stock had fallen from $1.20 a share to 88½ cents and stock in the Georgia Railroad had tumbled from $2.05 to $1.85.[21]

Many legislators were appalled, and Robert L. Berner of Monroe County authored a bill to empower the railroad commission to cancel leases and begin suit against any railroad monopolies in Georgia. But the delegates from the old plantation country—and especially those from the Tenth District—were most incensed by the Richmond Terminal monopoly. In the House, W. R. Kemp of Emanuel County introduced legislation to outlaw the watering of railroad stock; in the Senate, Clarence H. Ellington of McDuffie County demanded a complete investigation of all Georgia railroad companies to see if any had violated their charters or the state constitution. Word of such proposals alarmed Wall Street and further depressed the value of Terminal stock. Lobbyists led by Patrick Calhoun descended upon the capitol. Their labors were not in vain. The Berner bill passed through the House but was tabled in the Senate. The Kemp bill died in the lower chamber by a vote of 92 to 32. To deal with the Ellington proposal, the General Assembly agreed to appoint an investigative committee with Senator Ellington as its chairman. At length Ellington reported that the Central of Georgia had no legal right to lease itself to the Richmond Terminal and that such an action had violated the state constitution. With this knowledge, the Senate voted to postpone indefinitely any deliberation on Ellington's report.[22]

Despite his defeat, Ellington had made himself the leader of the anti-Terminal legislators. Although his spectacles and beard gave him the air

21. Klein, *Great Richmond Terminal*, 225, 230–34; *People's Party Paper*, June 29, July 13, 1894; Atlanta *Constitution*, August 26, 1891.

22. Atlanta *Constitution*, October 7, 9, 10, 1891; *Journal of the Senate of the State of Georgia* (1891), 46 (hereafter *Georgia State Senate Journal*); Georgia General Assembly, Joint Committee on Railroad Leases, *Majority and Minority Reports, with Exhibits of the Joint Committee on Railroad Leases* (Atlanta, 1891); see also Tom Watson's account of this affair in his *People's Party Campaign Book. Not a Revolt; It Is a Revolution* (Washington, D.C., 1892), 206–10.

of an intellectual, he had left school when he was only fifteen. He was
hard-driving and ambitious. Starting as a hired hand, Ellington eventually rented a one-horse farm and after six years had accumulated
$3,000. In about 1880 he bought a 1,140-acre plantation in McDuffie
County. Within a decade he could boast of eleven tenant families, two
gins, and an annual operation that produced 125 bales of cotton, 2,000
bushels of corn, and a large fruit crop. The local press hailed Ellington as
one of the outstanding planters of the county, and the farmers elected
him president of the Thomson Sub-Alliance and chairman of the Mc-
Duffie Alliance Exchange. In 1890 he successfully campaigned for the
state senate. For a man who had begun his career as a hired hand,
Ellington had much to be proud of. He was only forty years old, yet he
had clearly become an influential man. He hobnobbed with the local
squirearchy and numbered among his friends Congressman Thomas E.
Watson.[23]

But if outwardly Ellington affected the quiet composure of a planter,
inwardly he knew little peace. Because the declining price of cotton
threatened his prosperity, as a legislator he devoted himself to the problems of agriculture. He was also a student of railroad issues. In part this
interest was personal: he, Tom Watson, and a few other men were trying
to build a railroad line in their part of Georgia. It was only a spur, but the
promoters grandly dubbed their enterprise the Thomson and Lincolnton
Railroad Company. Even after the venture failed for want of capital,
Ellington's interest in railroads continued. In 1890 he nominated Patrick
Calhoun for the United States Senate, an act he would soon regret. A few
days after the lease of the Central, Ellington called for his investigation of
Georgia's railroads. He eventually came to believe that only the federal
government could tame a colossus like the Terminal. He had also given
up hope that the Democrats would champion such a cause. A new political party was needed.[24]

23. For biographical details about Ellington, see Atlanta *Constitution*, November 23,
1890; Randolph Dennis Werner, "Hegemony and Conflict: The Political Economy of a
Southern Region, Augusta, Georgia, 1865–1895" (Ph.D. dissertation, University of Virginia, 1977), 259.
24. Werner, "Hegemony and Conflict," 251; see also Ellington's bill to incorporate the
Thomson and Lincolnton Railroad Company, *Georgia Senate Journal* (1891), 69.

But in the fall of 1891 few Georgians were willing to follow him. The idea, however, was catching the imaginations of hard-pressed farmers in the Midwest. In May they held a convention in Cincinnati, with a gaggle of organizations and individuals attending. "I think if anyone would sprinkle a few hayseeds on his coat he would be admitted to the floor and have a right to vote," one man said.[25] Of the 1,417 delegates present, only 36 were from the South. Charles Cyrel Post of the Union Labor party represented Georgia. Lon Livingston, who attended as an observer, urged that rather than creating a third party, the convention should wait and see if the Democrats would bring about reform. But the delegates had not journeyed all the way to Cincinnati to be told to wait, and they quickly formed a new political organization called the People's party. The convention granted each state three members on the national executive committee. Charles Post represented Georgia. Later Clarence Ellington and Assistant Alliance Lecturer J. L. Gilmore were secretly added.[26]

Charles C. Post was Georgia's first Populist. That he had been born a Yankee and had only recently immigrated to the South was an irony that did not escape his enemies. At forty-nine years of age Post was tall and gaunt with, it was said, a "lean and hungry look." A congenital nonconformist and crusader, he possessed an optimist's faith that the world might be made better. While living in Indiana, Post had worked as a reporter and later as editor of the Terre Haute *Express*. His editorials gained national attention, and in 1876 he served as secretary to the Greenback party's national convention. Eight years later Post made an unsuccessful race for Congress. In 1886 illness forced him to move to the warmth of Georgia, where he had bought a 350-acre farm near Douglasville. As he regained his health, Post went back to his old ways. He became a county Alliance lecturer, a friend of the Georgia labor movement, and a founder of a School for Mental Healing. At the same time, he devoted himself to the writing of books and articles, among them one entitled *Metaphysical Essays*. Although this work was published three years after he had lived in Georgia, it is probable that Post was formulating the ideas he expressed in it while living in the state. The book lam-

25. Hicks, *Populist Revolt*, 212.
26. Atlanta *Constitution*, May 20–22, 1891.

basted the notion that a personal God was the prime mover of the universe; instead, Post believed that energy ruled the cosmos. Since individual particles came together to create forms, their attraction (or love) was the fundamental characteristic of energy. And because energy was everywhere, Post believed love was everywhere. There could be no evil. All the afflictions of the human race, whether crime, sickness, poverty, or old age, were simply inventions of the mind.[27]

While attempting to solve the mysteries of the universe, Post was also trying his hand as a storyteller. His first novel, *Driven from Sea to Sea* (1884), was dedicated to the laborers of America. An immense success, the book sold fifty thousand copies and as late as 1892 was still enjoying excellent sales. Under the cloak of fiction this work exposed the frauds of the Southern Pacific Railroad Company. Post's second novel, *Congressman Swanson*, appeared in 1891. A plea for the subtreasury plan, free silver, and social reform, the book demonstrated the influence of John Stuart Mill on Post's thinking. The work also condemned the North for carpetbag "outrages" during Reconstruction. Nor did Post find the South blameless during this period. Reformers and their ideas had never been welcome in Dixie. "[The first] reform speaker sent South, was run out of [his] state . . . under threat of personal violence," Post wrote in *Congressman Swanson*.[28] Little did he know that these words could eventually describe his own experience in Georgia.

Post and Ellington were slow to organize their party. Post, in particular, wanted to see if the Democrats might bring about reforms that would make a new political organization unnecessary. But events were quickly overtaking him. The Richmond Terminal crisis and the declining price of cotton had stunned the state. There was open talk about the Populist party, and John A. Sibley, a member of the legislature, publicly endorsed the movement. A few farmers were growing militant. Most ominous was a resolution from the hills of Pike County, signed by the members of the Mountain Gap Sub-Alliance, which attacked "our dear brother—W. J.

27. For biographical details about Post, see Atlanta *Constitution*, May 22, 1891; Woodward, *Tom Watson*, 182. Among his writings was an able defense of the subtreasury plan, "The Sub-Treasury Plan," *Arena*, V (1892), 342–52. See also Charles C. Post, *Metaphysical Essays* (Boston, 1895), 5, 122–23, 125.
28. Charles C. Post, *Congressman Swanson* (Chicago, 1891), 250, 258.

Northen." The governor had failed to invite any Alliancemen to the convention that had planned Georgia's part in the World's Fair of 1892. "Therefore said convention must have consisted of ayowed [avowed] enemies of the Alliance," the resolution proclaimed. Arguing that the fair would only aid the rich and "those who sek [seek] to oppress labor," the document warned that "we, the taxpayers of Pike county, will defend our public treasury with Winchester rifles before it shall be robbed for such purposes."[29]

Rumors flew everywhere that Livingston, rather than Ellington and Post, was the puppeteer behind this third-party drama. At Cincinnati he had apparently told party leaders that he favored Populism but needed another year to lead the Georgia Alliance into the new organization. His support of the People's party seemed confirmed when General James Baird Weaver and Congressman "Sockless" Jerry Simpson of Kansas toured the state in July. Both were champions of the movement, and Livingston introduced them when they spoke. In August the state was invaded by another Populist, Mary Elizabeth Lease of Kansas. Her caustic assaults on the Democratic party infuriated Georgians. Some newspapers even forgot their famed southern manners. The Sparta *Ishmaelite* referred to Mrs. Lease as a "watery-eyed, garrulous, ignorant and communistic old female from Kansas." It went on to say that "the world will have to welcome . . . the millennium before the murky shadows of hoodlumism . . . which have [fallen] upon the eyelids of the Leaseites . . . and the Livingstonites will have passed entirely away."[30]

By September it was clear that secession from the Democratic party was near. Almost everyone believed that Livingston was about to mutiny. There was also reason to think that Tom Watson might join him. As early as March, Watson had written to his fellow Georgia congressman, Charles F. Crisp, about the latter's chances of being elected Speaker of the House during the next Congress. Watson noted that he had read that Crisp was a member of the high-tariff wing of the Democratic party. "I say to you . . . that I would not vote for my father for a high federal office if he had been a Randall or Gorman or a Pat Walsh Democrat," he

29. Sparta *Ishmaelite*, June 5, 1891.
30. *Ibid.*, August 14, 1891.

warned.[31] Yet to refuse to vote for Crisp, who was the probable Democratic candidate for speaker, was political treason. It left Watson only two choices: to support the Republican nominee, which was political suicide, or to cast his lot with the handful of recently elected Populists in the House.

The thirty-five-year-old congressman who faced this dilemma hailed from Thomson, Georgia. At first glance, Tom Waton cut an unimpressive figure: he weighed only 120 pounds, his features were rawboned and homely, and a shock of red hair constantly tumbled down his brow. "He is small," an acquaintance wrote. "He is meagre in flesh, and what there is seems laid on grudgingly as if nature hesitated to make the man at all." But if Watson was small of stature, few cared to provoke him. His temper and deadly sarcasm could explode at the smallest slight. "Watson can talk like the thrust of a bowie knife," one reporter wrote.[32] Indeed, he would soon prove to be one of the most brilliant orators Georgia had ever known.

Although Watson spent his boyhood in poverty, his grandfather had been a wealthy planter and slaveholder. Thus his family remained on good terms with their distinguished neighbors, Alexander H. Stephens, the former vice-president of the Confederacy, and Robert Toombs. Both men became the heroes of Tom Watson's youth. In 1872 Watson's father managed to find enough money to allow his son to attend Mercer University for two years. Afterward Watson became a schoolteacher and later an attorney. In 1882 McDuffie County elected him to the Georgia House of Representatives, but Watson soon tired of the legislature and returned to his law practice. Well known as a skilled defense lawyer, he quickly became one of the wealthiest men in his part of Georgia. In 1887 twenty-one tenant families worked his land, and five years later he owned three thousand acres and was worth $17,000. When the jute-bagging boycott came the next year, he led the fight in his district. Although Watson was a lawyer, Alliancemen had been impressed by his devotion to their cause.

31. Scrapbook 5, p. 13, Black Papers. Arthur Pue Gorman was a United States senator from Maryland; Samuel Jackson Randall was a congressman from Pennsylvania; and Patrick Walsh was editor of the Augusta *Chronicle* and later a United States senator from Georgia.
32. New York *World*, n.d., quoted in Atlanta *Journal*, July 28, 1896.

In 1890 they nominated him for Congress, and after a strenuous campaign Watson defeated his more conservative opponent.[33]

Such was the man who was now edging toward Populism. Still, there was reason to think that Watson might not join the wool-hat boys. In July he said that he attacked the Democratic party only "to reform it, not to desert the ranks."[34] Earlier he reminded a member of the press that he had never advocated a new party. Watson's indecision was probably not calculated. His political career was at stake, and a wrong move could mean his end. But by September he had made up his mind. During a speech in Bamberg, South Carolina, Watson was asked what he would do if the Democrats refused to endorse the Ocala platform. "Sufficient unto the day are the evils thereof," he said. "This is as far as my people authorize me to speak. If that means a third party, it is all right. My people are my bosses." On separate occasions Larry Gantt, the editor of an important Alliance newspaper, and Lon Livingston were asked the same question. Both gave the same reply: "Sufficient unto the day are the evils thereof."[35]

Despite Livingston's service to Populism, many reformers were growing suspicious of him. For all his rantings against the Democratic party, he still insisted that he was a loyal Democrat. When the Clayton County Alliance and a Douglas County suballiance endorsed the Populist movement, they angrily complained that "our leaders are trying to keep the Alliance in the Democratic party, to our ruin."[36] Livingston was undoubtedly the target of this outburst. It was also rumored that Livingston would support for Speaker of the House Congressman Charles F. Crisp—a man who had failed to endorse completely the Ocala demands. But most reformers believed that Livingston was suffering only a momentary loss of nerve. In the end, they predicted, Lon Livingston would become a Populist.

During the last days of the General Assembly, third-party members made their first attempt to compel Georgia congressmen to support the subtreasury plan and other Alliance principles. John A. Sibley presented

33. Woodward, *Tom Watson*, 1–216; McDuffie County Tax Records, 1892, Georgia Department of Archives and History, Atlanta.
34. Unidentified newspaper clipping, July 26, 1891, Scrapbook 5, Black Papers.
35. Macon *Telegraph*, September 23, 1891.
36. *Ibid.*, October 21, 1891; see also Calhoun *Times*, May 12, 1892.

a resolution urging congressmen, when deciding on a Speaker, to vote only for a man who fully endorsed the Ocala demands. The moderates quickly forced a compromise, which called on Georgia congressmen and senators to vote merely for "legislation which will correct the evils complained of by the National Farmers' Alliance . . . in convention at Ocala." [37] This wording was sufficiently vague to suit the moderates, and it passed through the House by a vote of 138 to 5. After such a defeat there seemed only one alternative left for Georgia Populists. The Supreme Council of the Southern Alliance was holding its annual meeting in Indianapolis. Perhaps something could be done there to forbid Alliance congressmen from entering the Democratic caucus and voting for Crisp.

In mid-November a thin Georgian, sporting a small mustache, boarded the train for Indianapolis. He was forty-four years old and a member of the official delegation that was to attend the meeting of the Supreme Council. His name was Mell I. Branch, and in his pocket was a document that would shatter the Farmers' Alliance. Branch hardly seemed the man for such a task. Outwardly he was bluff and jovial, a lover of jokes, especially when they were on him. Although Branch had political foes, they nearly always admired him as a man, sought out his company, and delighted in his joshing and storytelling. "He is one of the boys," a Democrat declared. Perhaps part of his appeal was his modesty. Branch was uninterested in gaining high political office. Instead he preferred the quiet of the committee room, where he might wield his charm, his intellect, and his ability as an organizer. These gifts would shortly make him one of the most powerful Populists in Georgia and a force in the national organization.

Born in 1849 in Petersburg, Virginia, Mell Branch was the son of Thomas Branch, a wealthy businessman who had founded the Merchant's National Bank of Richmond. In 1863 fourteen-year-old Mell joined the Confederate army, and within a year he was appointed to the Virginia Military Institute. Still a cadet at the close of the war, Branch remained at VMI to graduate in 1868. He then traveled to Augusta,

37. Minutes of the Farmers' Alliance Caucus, 1890–91, October 13, 1891, MS in Graves Family Papers, Southern Historical Collection, University of North Carolina Library, Chapel Hill.

Georgia, to become a businessman. He moved again in 1876 to Columbia County, helping to found the town of his residence, Berzelia—a name he selected. Here Branch farmed and eventually became a watermelon grower. By 1892 he owned thirteen hundred acres and was worth $6,175. He also joined the Alliance. Farmers soon found that behind Branch's cheerful façade was a man both thoughtful and angry. Newspapers sometimes called him "hell-raising Mell," and a few of his neighbors incorrectly believed him to be a socialist. As the Populist movement gathered strength, Branch founded a third-party weekly called the Harlem *Farmers' Light*. He seemed particularly incensed by the Richmond Terminal monopoly, an organization in which his father had been an original stockholder. It is unknown if there had been a falling out between father and son. Indeed, all that is certain is that Mell went to Georgia to raise watermelons and his brother became a shareholder in the Terminal, a member of the New York Stock Exchange, and president of his father's bank.[38]

Whatever the reason for his reform zeal, Branch was a devoted third-party man. Before leaving for Indianapolis, he met with his friend Tom Watson, and they drew up two proposals that Branch was to show to "Sockless" Jerry Simpson. One resolution instructed all Alliance-elected congressmen only to enter caucuses in which an endorsement of the Ocala demands was a requirement for membership. The other proposed that government ownership of the railroads become a part of the Ocala platform. Branch was the only Populist among the Georgia delegates attending the meeting. The rest were controlled by Livingston, who seemed to be growing more and more hostile to the third party. To help lobby for the Populists, Watson, Ellington, and Gilmore also left for Indianapolis, although none could officially take part in the meeting.

When Branch arrived at his destination, he met Jerry Simpson and showed him the proposals. Simpson said that he would be delighted to present them in the council. But at the last minute, the Kansas delegation failed to elect Simpson as one of its members. Now the unknown

38. For biographical details about Mell I. Branch, see "M. J. [*sic*] Branch," *Memoirs of Georgia* (2 vols.; Atlanta, 1895), I, 512; U.S. Congress, House, *Contested Election Case of Thomas E. Watson vs. J. C. C. Black* (Washington, D.C., 1896), 690. For the Branch family's connections to the Richmond Terminal Company, see "John Kerr Branch," *National Cyclopaedia of American Biography*, VIII, 99; Klein, *Great Richmond Terminal*, 86, 202.

Branch could do nothing except offer the resolutions himself. But a number of forces were working in his favor. The president of the Southern Alliance, Leonidas L. Polk, was sympathetic to the third party. In addition, the Committee on Demands was filled with Populists and chaired by the third-party leader, General James B. Weaver. On the second day of the meeting Branch surprised the delegates by suddenly introducing his proposals. They "appeared like a clap of thunder in a clear sky," he later recalled. Jerry Simpson said they produced "acres of hell." Branch asked the chairman to send the resolutions to the Committee on Demands. By this time, Livingston was on his feet hotly denouncing his fellow Georgian. His protest, however, had little effect. After listening to Livingston's arguments, the chairman immediately ordered the proposals to Weaver's committee.[39]

The next day the Committee on Demands reported favorably on the first resolution. But for some unexplained reason it decided against the demand for government ownership of the railroads. During the discussion that followed, a delegate inquired if the first resolution was an order or a request. Weaver answered that it was a request, thus giving Livingston a way out. When Livingston returned to Atlanta, reporters asked him about the Branch resolutions. Livingston quoted Weaver, adding that any Alliance congressman could enter the Democratic caucus because the Ocala demands were "pure Democracy." Livingston was opposed to turning the Alliance over to the Populists. "We have no right and no business to do that," he declared. "The Alliance can discuss political questions, but it is not a political party."[40]

Just before Congress was to elect a new Speaker, all the Alliance congressmen met for a last time. Eighteen, including Livingston, were determined to join the Democratic caucus. Seven, including Watson, supported the Branch resolutions. As the meeting progressed, tempers exploded, and a half-dozen congressmen were needed to prevent Livingston from physically assaulting Watson. The Alliancemen who supported the Branch resolutions then nominated Watson as the Populist candidate

39. For details about the Indianapolis convention, see Atlanta *Constitution*, November 17–24, 1891; Atlanta *Journal*, November 18–24, 1891; *People's Party Paper*, November 26, 1891; *National Economist*, November 28, 1891; Woodward, *Tom Watson*, 186–87.
40. Atlanta *Constitution*, November 24, 1891.

for Speaker. When the House convened, its members gave Crisp 228 votes, Thomas B. Reed of Maine (the Republican candidate) 83 votes, and Tom Watson 8 votes. If there was any hope that Livingston would join the third party, it vanished when he cast his ballot for Charles F. Crisp.[41]

In 1890 Georgia possessed more than 170,000 farms and hundreds of thousands of farmers.[42] With such numbers, it was natural that disagreement should have arisen about how the state was to solve its problems. As we have seen, one group, led by William J. Northen, favored scientific agriculture and maintained strong links to Bourbonism. Another faction, led by Lon Livingston, differed from its opponents on a number of issues, including the subtreasury plan. While these two camps battled for control of state politics, the Richmond Terminal abruptly leased the Central and gained a monopoly over the trunk lines of Georgia. From out of the Livingston ranks came a new group, which demanded the subtreasury plan and government ownership of the railroads. Its principal strength lay in the "terrible Tenth"—a land that already possessed a strong anti-Bourbon tradition. Indeed, the spirit of Robert Toombs was still abroad in this region. Watson's speeches and writing often referred to the general and his struggle against monopolies.[43] But Toombs had called only for government regulation of the railroads, never for government ownership. What had happened to change the thinking and the temper of this region?

Part of the answer involved the land. After more than a century of cultivation, its soil was weary from scores and scores of plantings. In the 1870s fertilizer had offered a rejuvenation of sorts, but cotton profits were at best marginal. To increase their earnings, many farmers grew fruit as well as cotton. As early as 1877, Augusta shipped sixty thousand watermelons to the North.[44] Tom Watson, Mell Branch, and Clarence Ellington were all cotton and fruit farmers. It was a risky enterprise. Un-

41. Woodward, *Tom Watson*, 190–93; *Congressional Record*, 52nd Cong., 1st. Sess., 23, 7–8.

42. U.S. Department of the Interior, *Report of the Statistics of Agriculture in the United States at the Eleventh Census: 1890*, V, 128.

43. See, for example, *People's Party Paper*, June 29, 1894.

44. Range, *Century of Georgia Agriculture*, 112.

like cotton, fruit could stand little rough treatment from the weather or during shipment. Moreover, once the fruit had been picked, it had to be sent to market immediately, which gave the railroad companies an enormous advantage over the fruit farmers. In 1885 the Georgia Railroad, which transversed the region, leased itself to the Central of Georgia. Thus when the Central came under the sway of the Richmond Terminal six years later, the fruit growers suddenly became the victims of soaring freight rates. "Shippers of melons, fruits, lumber and vegetables were almost driven from the market," Tom Watson later wrote.[45] The Richmond Terminal had given men with an antirailroad heritage only two choices: to pay or to let their fruit rot. There was little the farmers could do. They paid the shipping costs, sent their fruit to market, and joined the Populist party.

There were other reasons for the rise of Populism in Georgia. The Farmers' Alliance played an important role. Its lectures helped yeomen take a more discerning look at politics and economics; its victories gave its members a sense of pride and self-reliance; its exchanges taught them the advantages of cooperative buying and action. In some places the Populists would use the sub- and county alliances as the bases of their own organization. Yet it is possible to overstate the importance of the Alliance as a forerunner of reform. The main strength of the order lay in the piedmont and western black belt—regions that largely failed to join the Populist crusade. Southern Georgia, where local exchanges were especially common, likewise spurned the third party.[46] Indeed, Populism was strongest where the Alliance had had only moderate strength—the old plantation country.

By summer 1891, the Georgia Farmers' Alliance was barring the way of Populism. Most Alliancemen had little use for an organization that demanded government ownership of the railroads and threatened to split the Democratic party. The showdown came in August at the state Alliance convention in Atlanta. By this time Livingston's position was clear: he had denounced the Populist party, fought the Branch resolu-

45. *People's Party Paper*, June 29, 1894. See also Gracewood *Wool-Hat*, July 8, 1893.
46. McMath, *Populist Vanguard*, 48–63, 151–52; Goodwyn, *Democratic Promise*, 123. See also Stanley B. Parsons *et al.*, "The Role of Cooperatives in the Development of the Movement Culture of Populism," *Journal of American History*, LXIX (1983), 866–85.

tions, voted for Charles F. Crisp, and lobbied with Patrick Calhoun to weaken the antirailroad bills before the Georgia legislature. Ellington traveled to the convention determined to prevent Livingston's reelection as president. But when he arrived, the hall thundered with cheers for his opponent. Convinced that he had no chance, Ellington refused to allow his own nomination. Instead, he announced that he would accept the vice-presidency. He was convincingly defeated.[47]

Despite his triumph, Livingston had lost some of his popularity. Loyal Democrats were angered and baffled by his flirtation with Populism, a liaison that Livingston had also found uncomfortable. But he was an ambitious man. In 1891 he probably still dreamed of becoming governor, and occasionally he had been mentioned as a possible third-party candidate for vice-president of the United States. These were heady visions for a backcountry politician. So during the second half of 1891, he did exactly what Watson was doing: he tested the political waters. If the Alliance was about to join the Populist party, Livingston did not want to be left behind. Finally, he decided that most farmers would remain Democrats. It was a shrewd political judgment. And, unlike Tom Watson, Livingston would remain in Congress for the next twenty years.

The Populists had been outraged by Livingston's indecision. For months he seemed to be edging toward Populism. Suddenly, however, he had turned and attacked the movement. His name became anathema in third-party circles. Most Populists would have heartily agreed with a resolution passed by one suballiance that condemned "Benedict Arnold Judas Iscariot Livingston." Calling him a "loathsome piece of disease," the proposal called on the Alliance to remove its president immediately and "with a pole long enough to keep the odorous dead cat from our nostrils . . . gently lift it over the garden wall, and consign it to its proper sphere—among the scum and Wall Street pimps of the so-called Democratic party."[48]

47. Atlanta *Constitution*, August 19, 1891.
48. Scrapbook 2, p. 30, Northen Papers.

✦III✦

Gideon's Band

The defection of Lon Livingston left the third party without a leader. Tom Watson was eager to take charge of the organization, but this was no easy task. Populists believed most of their support would have to come from former Alliance members. Because Watson had never joined the Alliance, he had little direct influence over that order. His power was certainly unequal to that of Lon Livingston and William L. Peek, the manager of the state Alliance exchange. Watson's ambitions were further confounded when Peek announced in December, 1891, that he had become a Populist. Many reformers believed that Peek rather than Watson was the logical man to lead the Alliance into the Populist camp. Peek wasted little time in trying to achieve this end. In early December his son-in-law, Mark Irwin, bought a controlling interest in the *Southern Alliance Farmer*.[1] Although serving as the official organ of the Georgia Alliance, the *Farmer* suddenly began a thunderous assault on Livingston. It was an open secret that Peek was behind this attack, and overnight it appeared the Populists had gained a new hero.

William L. Peek was every inch a farmer. The sun had deeply burnished his face and neck, and like most men who spent their days in the fields, he was given to wearing black, wide-brimmed hats.[2] At fifty-four years of age, Peek was a God-fearing Presbyterian, who hated alcohol

1. Atlanta *Constitution*, December 5, 1891.
2. For biographical details about Peek, see *Georgia's General Assembly, 1880–1881* (Atlanta, 1882), 292; Biographical Questionnaire on William L. Peek, Biographical Data File, Georgia Department of Archives and History, Atlanta; Scrapbook 2, p. 103, Northen Papers; H. W. J. Ham, *Representative Georgians* (Savannah, 1887), 139; Winder *Jackson Economist*, March 2, 1899; Atlanta *Constitution*, August 6, 1896; Conyers *Solid South*, July 24, December 18, 1886; Rockdale County Tax Records, 1892, Georgia Department of Archives and History, Atlanta.

and loved politics. He had started life with only a common school education, served briefly in the Civil War, and then returned home to create a
model farm near Conyers. Peek worked diligently to diversify his six
hundred acres. He was the first planter in his county to terrace his land,
and on one occasion he produced more corn per acre than any farmer in
the state. Such success won him considerable acclaim, and in 1886 the
Russian government sent a family to observe his operation. By 1892 he
was worth more than $9,000. From 1877 to 1882, Peek served in the
Georgia house, and four years later he was elected to the state senate. As
a legislator he had been a friend of the Bourbons and the railroads.[3] He
was also deeply concerned about controlling the supply of cheap labor. In
1887 he introduced the so-called Peek slave bill—a proposal that would
have jailed tenants who failed to fulfill all their contractual obligations to
their landlords. The bill was defeated after senators complained that
such legislation would reestablish debtors' prisons in Georgia. Once Peek
had declared himself a Populist, his enemies resurrected the memory of
the slave bill. Third-party leaders were hardly shocked; indeed, some of
them, including Charles McGregor and Tom Watson, agreed with such
antitenant legislation.[4] Nevertheless, the Democratic press argued that
Peek was simply an opportunist eager to fill the vacuum left by Livingston—as he may well have been. But such a judgment failed to consider
that in the Northen-Livingston race for governor in 1890, Peek had settled the controversy by encouraging Livingston to run for Congress in
his place. Such a sacrifice hardly seemed the act of a self-serving man. It
was certain, however, that he had been one of the most useful and enthusiastic Alliancemen in Georgia—a man with plenty of "git up and git,"
as one friend put it. Upon becoming a Populist, Peek first hoped to campaign for Livingston's congressional seat, but he soon decided instead to
run for governor against William J. Northen.

Some third-party men were unhappy at these developments. Until

3. Atlanta *Constitution*, November 11, 12, 1880, November 15, September 2, 1882; Atlanta *Journal*, August 18, 1892; Wynne, "Planter Politics in Georgia," 240; Avery, *History
of the State of Georgia*, 580, 584, 600.
4. *Georgia Senate Journal*, 1887, p. 10. This proposal was modeled after a similar bill
introduced by Senator W. W. Tutt in 1883. Although the Tutt bill was eventually defeated
in the House, William L. Peek, Charles McGregor, and Tom Watson voted for it. Seaborn
Wright fought the measure. See Georgia *Senate Journal*, 1883, pp. 6, 204–209; *Georgia
House Journal*, 744–45; Atlanta *Constitution*, August 30, 1883.

Peek's conversion to Populism, Watson, Ellington, and Post had expected to gain control of the party after Livingston's disgrace. Planning
to appoint Post as permanent chairman, they hoped to run Ellington for
governor and Watson for Congress. It was whispered that if elected,
Ellington would appoint Watson to the United States Senate.[5] This
speculation seemed confirmed when Watson and Post established the
People's Party Paper in October, 1891. Why, Georgians asked, would
Watson found a statewide weekly if he fostered no statewide ambitions?
Peek, with the aid of the *Southern Alliance Farmer*, now threatened to
disrupt these designs. But not all was lost for Watson. He had already
established himself as the third party's finest orator; and Post, at least for
the moment, was still temporary chairman. Thus it remained to be seen
whether Peek or Watson would finally rule the infant organization.

Before anyone could campaign for governor, these leaders had to organize a party. Post sent out messages urging Populist sympathizers to form
county organizations. In his letter he announced Tom Watson's support
and encouraged his followers to "consult with such staunch friends of the
cause you deem best." He requested that a man be appointed to organize
each militia district. Another letter was enclosed from the members of
the temporary state committee—Post, Ellington, and Gilmore—asking
for a list of all white voters and their parties. The committee hoped that
literature could be sent to those who were undecided. "Do not show the
list or give any intimation of what is being done to any but true friends of
the cause," the letter warned. "Beware of the politicians. Keep your own
council."[6]

The wool-hat boys usually organized their counties after a self-
appointed committee placed an announcement in the local newspaper.
The notice gave the time, the place (generally the courthouse), and the
purpose of an organizational meeting. On the appointed day those who
attended elected a county executive committee, as well as committees to
handle the militia district campaigns. Although beginning a new party in
rural Georgia might seem to have been an onerous task, in some areas it
was fairly simple. Every county had an Alliance and local suballiances. In

5. Macon *Telegraph*, December 2, 1891. See also, Dawson *News*, December 2, 1891.
6. Sparta *Ishmaelite*, December 25, 1891.

places where the Populists had gained control of these organizations, they could easily turn them into county executive and militia district committees.

Newspapers also aided the coming of Populism. Two statewide weeklies eventually endorsed the new party: the *Southern Alliance Farmer* and the *People's Party Paper*. The first was the official organ of the Georgia Alliance. Its outspoken editorials did much to convert farmers to the movement. But financial troubles constantly harried its editors, and by the end of 1892 the publication was bankrupt. Afterward the Alliance tried to finance a new paper, *Living Issues*. Within a short time this journal also collapsed. More successful was the *People's Party Paper*. Founded by Tom Watson, Charles Post, and Eliam Christian, it began publication on October 1, 1891. Like the *Southern Alliance Farmer*, this weekly was bedeviled by business reverses. Within a year Watson had lost $3,600. Undaunted, he bought Post's and Christian's interests and became sole owner. Although Watson eventually transformed the *People's Party Paper* into one of the leading third-party journals in the country, its existence was assured from its early days. Post, with his rich experience in journalism, could make certain that the scores of tiresome but necessary newspaper chores were carried out. In turn, Watson could provide his money and his skillful pen. As a propagandist he had few equals. His prose was straightforward and plain, charged with the energy of a man who knew the truth, or at least thought he did. Readers delighted in his sometimes crude but always effective assaults on the Democratic party. Governor Northen was a "long-whiskered imbecile" whose "brains are chronically stagnant." "Trim your beard, William," Watson advised. "Too much whiskers will capsize a heavier brain than yours ever was." Watson also possessed the traditional gifts of the southern writer. In an instant he could conjure up the old antebellum days—the perfume of the magnolia, the rustle of hooped skirts, the songs of the slaves. Such humor and nostalgia helped make the *People's Party Paper* immensely popular among reformers.[7]

7. Robert W. Smith, "*The People's Party Paper* and Georgia's Tom Watson," *Journalism Quarterly*, XLII (Winter, 1965), 110–11; Letters, Scrapbook 18, Thomas E. Watson Papers, Southern Historical Collection, University of North Carolina Library, Chapel Hill (hereafter Watson Papers, UNC); quotation in *People's Party Paper*, September 23, 1892.

But the importance of Watson's newspaper should not be overemphasized. Although the journal would eventually claim a circulation of more than twenty thousand readers, it was not the only Populist weekly in Georgia. In 1896 twenty-five third-party papers were in business, with such picturesque names as the *Wool Hat*, the *Plowboy*, and the *National Headlight*. Some, like the Glascock *Banner* and the Carnesville *Enterprise*, were more reform-minded than the *People's Party Paper*. Small-town editors knew they were writing for country folk, and so their columns rang with a frankness and wit that farmers could understand: "Today there is no more difference between the two old parties than there is between one hog with its nose in a pail of milk and another that wants to get his nose in it."[8]

Running a small, third-party press was a risky venture. The most successful had existed before the rise of Populism. Relying on former subscribers, they could sometimes survive when Democratic merchants withdrew their advertising. But many reform newspapers were poorly capitalized and edited and went out of existence in a short time. Perhaps no third-party newspaper had a more unpromising beginning than the Gracewood *Wool Hat*. Sometime in May, 1892, William J. Henning, a Gracewood farmer, tried to publish a letter in the Augusta *Chronicle*. When he was refused, the indignant Henning bought some old type and on his porch constructed a type case out of cigar boxes. On June 1 he published his first edition. Although it contained only one sheet with two columns, the *Wool Hat*'s lead editorial rose above the crudeness of the typeface and layout: "[A] mighty struggle [is occurring] . . . between the working masses who produce and the favored parasites who prey and fatten upon the toil of others." Henning promised that he would fight the people's fight "till the wrongs of oppression are righted, or [till] we tenant our last narrow home." Unlike most Populist newspapers, the *Wool Hat* was a success and eventually became a daily called the Augusta *Tribune*.[9]

In the midst of organizing the new party, word came from Washington

8. Smith, "*People's Party Paper*," 110–11; Louis Turner Griffith and John Erwin Talmadge, *Georgia Journalism, 1763–1950* (Athens, 1951), 120; quotation in Dahlonega *Signal*, June 10, 1892.

9. Dorothy Haynie Murray, "William John Henning, the Man—the Publisher," *Richmond County History*, II (Winter, 1970), 7–12; Gracewood *Wool Hat*, June 1, 1892.

that the Democratic Congress, with a majority of 150 members, had failed to pass the Bland silver bill. Georgia Democrats had hoped this inflationary measure might bring relief and head off the Populist uprising. Even the conservative Atlanta *Constitution* was stunned and blamed the defeat on "Wall Street Clevelandism and eastern goldbugism." A few days later the *Constitution* suffered another shock. In a letter to the editor, Congressman Thomas E. Winn of the Ninth District observed that nobody could now expect the Democrats to pass a subtreasury bill or dissolve the national banks of issue. Thus, Winn wrote, he was joining the Populist crusade. "This is too much," the Savannah *Press* wailed. "The trail of the devil and Tom Watson is over them all." [10]

And so it seemed. The party that Democrats had mocked was nearly a reality. In March the *Southern Alliance Farmer* polled the state's sub-alliances, asking them if they endorsed the St. Louis demands of 1889. Out of about sixteen hundred responses, only three were opposed. Although this figure was probably inaccurate, it sent a chill through the Democratic ranks. "The Alliance is going into the third party," Mark Irwin, the editor of the *Farmer*, cheerfully gloated. Many Democratic newspapers remained confident, but some were beside themselves. The Savannah *Press* counseled Democrats to stay calm, then burst into a nearly hysterical plea for somebody to do something. "The country is bearing the standard of revolt," the *Press* shrieked. "There is not a day to spare to arrest this tide." The newspaper urged Democrats to send speakers to every crossroads and militia district. "The odds are all against us," the *Press* continued. "The other side has numbers and drill, and a spirit of opposition that has been burning like a prairie fire. It is time to act. Delay is dangerous. It means defeat, disaster." By fall some Democratic leaders were also becoming apprehensive. "If the damned Alliance, or the People's Party should carry Kansas this year," Congressman Charles Crisp said to a friend, "all hell can't hold the Alliancemen of the South [in the Democratic party]." [11]

Many Democrats darkly murmured that Lon Livingston and other Al-

---

10. Atlanta *Constitution*, April 1, 2, 1892; Savannah *Press*, April 2, 1892.
11. Irwin quoted in Atlanta *Constitution*, March 22, 1892; Savannah *Press*, April 2, 1892; Crisp quoted in Peter H. Argersinger, *Populism and Politics: William Alfred Peffer and the People's Party* (Lexington, 1974), 116.

liance leaders had earlier created a secret organization called Gideon's Band. The purpose of this cabal was to draw the Alliance into the Populist movement. Only a few men in each county could join the band, and they identified each other by lolling their tongues—as did the followers of Gideon in the Bible (Judg. 7:5–7). A Democrat described this society as "one of the most corrupt machines . . . that was ever concocted on American soil." How close he came to the truth was unclear because the members of Gideon's Band were sworn to secrecy. Some people even doubted the brotherhood's existence. Later, however, Tom Watson wrote that Gideon's Band had functioned for a time and that Lon Livingston was one of its founders. Georgia Democrats sometimes referred to Populists as Gideons, although most third-party men had never belonged to the secret order.[12]

The Democrats were quick to fight back, and Charles Post became their main target. "He is a carpetbagger from the city of Chicago," charged former Congressman Allen Candler. Livingston accused Post of being an atheist and a spiritualist and stated that his wife was a friend of anarchists. But William J. Northen delivered the most vindictive assault. Angry citizens had sent word to him that Post was a freethinker who shoveled manure on the Sabbath. Enraged, the God-fearing Northen publicly called Post an "infidel," an "anarchist," and a "cur." He too claimed that Post's wife was an atheist and that she had sent money to the anarchists charged with the bombing of Chicago's Haymarket Square in 1886. Northen added that Mrs. Post had "unsexed herself" and no longer qualified as a lady. Charles Post pronounced the governor a liar. While rumors spread that Democratic thugs were searching for Post, third-party men seethed. "When the governor of this state—these old doughfaced demagogic leaders, any of them—attack a lady just because she has written letters against the infamous thieving and democratic party, they should be taught a lesson," one Populist warned. The rancor that would scar Georgia politics for nearly a decade was quickly spread-

12. Atlanta *Constitution*, May 26, 28, June 1, 1892; Conyers *Hale's Weekly*, June 4, 1892; Dawson *News*, November 9, 1892. For the operation of Gideon's Band in other states see Roscoe C. Martin, *The People's Party in Texas: A Study in Third Party Politics* (Austin, 1933), 158–59; Hicks, *Populist Revolt*, 254–55. See also *People's Party Paper*, December 2, 1892, January 27, 1893, March 23, 1894; Vol. 17, p. 95, in Watson Papers, UNC.

ing. Mark Irwin and Lon Livingston, once close friends, were rumored
to be no longer speaking. Denying the charge, Irwin declared, "Why, I
would speak to a dog." And the Rome *Tribune* hardly rose above the passions of the hour when it referred to the less-than-beautiful Mrs. Lease as
a "hermaphrodite." [13]

In this rancorous climate, the Populist leaders prepared to christen
their party. At the Ocala meeting of 1890, Alliance delegates had decided
that one year hence they would call together a great assembly of farm and
industrial brotherhoods in St. Louis. There they planned to draw up a
list of demands and consider ways of enforcing them. If third-party men
could gain control of this meeting, they could win the Alliance over to
their cause. Many Populists in different parts of the country considered
Georgia to be critical. "We will break the back of the damn democracy in
that state, and other states will follow," one reformer maintained. [14]

At the same time, Livingston's power was slipping away. In 1890 the
Georgia Alliance claimed a membership of eighty-five thousand; now its
ranks had been thinned to sixteen thousand. Some farmers left in disillu-
sionment, convinced the order had failed to bring the promised millennium. Others departed because hard times made it impossible for them
to pay their dues of fifty cents a year. But most walked out for political
reasons. For those in the Northen wing, the Alliance had clearly grown
too radical; for those in the Ellington faction, it had become too conservative. Livingston's short brush with Populism had driven thousands of
his supporters from the order. The defection of so many Northen and
Livingston people changed the nature of the Alliance. Now a larger per-
centage—perhaps even a majority—of the remaining members were
Populists, and they were determined to wrench the organization from
Livingston's grasp. But when time came to select men for the St. Louis
convention, Livingston adroitly packed the delegation with his friends.
E. L. Richardson, the leader of the state's Colored Farmers' Alliance,
did the same in his brotherhood. Thus all seventeen delegates from

13. Atlanta *Constitution*, April 21, May 29, June 2, 1892; Scrapbook 2, pp. 87–88, 92,
Northen Papers; Woodward, *Tom Watson*, 227–28; McDonough *Henry County Weekly*,
June 3, 1892; Knoxville *Crawford County Herald*, May 27, 1892.
14. Washington (Ga.) *Chronicle*, April 4, 1892.

Georgia were enemies of the People's Party.[15] Despite this setback, the Populists were still determined to send spokesmen to the national Alliance convention. They did so through a simple ruse. Ellington, Gilmore, Branch, and Post appeared in St. Louis claiming to represent a nonexistent organization called the Citizens' Alliance.

When the meeting convened an acrimonious struggle erupted in the credentials committee. So many conflicting delegations demanded seats that it took hours to sort them out. Finally, the committee reported that it had settled all contests except the one involving the Georgia delegation and the Citizens' Alliance. It asked that the convention as a whole consider this difficult question. After the debate started, it became obvious that the Populists had control of the convention. Livingston's words were met with hoots and groans; he could do little to head off the rush to Populism. Indeed, the most dramatic anti-Populist speech was made not by Livingston but by Charles Moses, a young Georgia congressman elected by the Alliance in 1890. Climbing onto a chair, Moses spoke to thousands of menacing faces. Amid the uproar his words could hardly be heard.

"[Ellington] does not represent a dozen Alliancemen in Georgia, so far as my knowledge goes," he declared.

"Sit down! Sit down!" voices bellowed from the throng.

"If you don't want to hear me, take me off my feet."

For a moment the crowd was taken aback and the din subsided.

"Is it a crime to be a democrat?" Moses asked. "Then hang me, if you want to, but I am an Allianceman, too."[16]

Quickly Post was on his feet, hotly denouncing Moses and Livingston amid a storm of cheers. Called the "fiercest" address of the convention, Post's speech ended when he declared that Livingston had virtually no support in Georgia. Suddenly Mell Branch climbed onto a chair and cast a thirty-foot roll of paper out over the heads of the delegates. On it, he cried, were four hundred Georgia Alliance resolutions endorsing Tom Watson. Next he held up a two-foot roll containing resolutions of support

15. See Congressman Charles Moses's letter in *ibid.*, April 4, 1892.
16. Atlanta *Constitution*, February 23, 1892.

for Livingston. The convention then clamorously voted to seat the representatives of the Citizens' Alliance as part of the Georgia delegation.[17]

Even though Livingston had lost the battle, he appeared to have won the war. His partisans still outnumbered the third-party men in his delegation. In an instant, however, this situation changed. Although he was a white man, J. L. Gilmore announced that he was a Colored Allianceman and had the authority to vote as a proxy for all the Colored Alliance delegates from his state. Flabbergasted blacks demanded to know what was occurring. To their chagrin, they learned that Gilmore was in fact a member of their brotherhood. And, to their horror, they learned that he indeed had the right to vote as a proxy for the black Georgians. The extraordinary news passed from delegation to delegation. Soon blacks throughout the hall were told that J. H. Humphrey, a white superintendent of their order who was friendly to Populism, had quietly appointed Gilmore a proxy shortly before the convention. Enraged, all ninety-seven delegates sent by the Colored Alliance walked off the floor. With astonishing insouciance, Humphrey then appointed Gilmore proxy for the entire Colored Alliance. Thus the meeting witnessed the spectacle of a white Georgian, who had only recently immigrated from England, casting ninety-seven votes for the 800,000 Colored Alliancemen of America.[18]

As the meeting progressed it became apparent that the Populists had won the day. As a climax, Leonidas L. Polk, the president of the Southern Alliance, dramatically joined the movement. Hastily, the delegates endorsed the Ocala platform and the demand for government ownership of the railroads. Although a Populist party had been founded in Cincinnati in 1891, this body had never pretended to be much more than a sectional party. The time had come to prepare for a national organization. But the Populists had to be cautious. Rather than risk a walkout by the conservatives, they decided to make arrangements for their new party after the convention. The instant the proceedings ended, C. W. Macune

17. Woodward, *Tom Watson*, 201–202; *People's Party Paper*, March 3, 1892.
18. For details about the Gilmore episode, see *National Economist*, March 5, 1892, p. 395; Atlanta *Constitution*, February 26, 1892. For a Democratic exposé of the incident, see Congressman Charles Moses's letter in the Washington (Ga.) *Chronicle*, April 4, 1892. For Gilmore's explanation of his activities, see *People's Party Paper*, March 17, 1892. See also William F. Holmes, "The Demise of the Colored Farmers' Alliance," *Journal of Southern History*, XLI (1975), 190.

called for a mass meeting. At Post's suggestion, the remaining delegates selected a committee to ask the American people to send representatives to a great national convention in Omaha. To plan this gathering, they created a Committee of Fifteen and appointed Mell Branch as one of its members.[19] When the mass meeting ended, many well-known Populists assembled on the stage. Among them was Branch, who became so moved that he joyously embraced the famous reformer from Minnesota, Ignatius Donnelly. For Branch, over a year of work had at last brought forth a new political party. In five months the Populists would meet in Omaha and nominate presidential and vice-presidential candidates. Then the Georgians would return home and begin their crusade.

Two months before the Omaha meeting was to be held, Leonidas L. Polk died, depriving Populism not only of one of its most eloquent champions but also of its strongest candidate for president. When the Georgia delegation departed for the national convention in early July there was some talk of nominating Watson or Ellington for president or vice-president. But this suggestion was not serious. Watson was determined to run for Congress, and Ellington was too obscure. Even so, there were to be honors for the Georgians. When they arrived in Omaha, party leaders selected Ellington as temporary chairman and appointed Branch to preside over the resolutions committee.[20]

With Polk dead, the contest was reduced to three men: General James B. Weaver of Iowa, Judge Walter Q. Gresham of Illinois, and United States Senator James H. Kyle of South Dakota. Most Georgia Populists were friendly toward Weaver, probably because of his visit to their state in 1891. Nevertheless, southerners generally disliked him. Weaver was a former Union general, whom many believed had sacked Pulaski, Tennessee, during the Civil War. Judge Gresham was an attractive candidate, but there was uneasiness about his recent conversion to Populism. "We do not want a man to come to us at the last hour of the day," one Georgia delegate said. Therefore, southerners tended to support Senator Kyle, a reform-minded Allianceman. Post and Mark Irwin agreed and convinced most of their colleagues to abandon Weaver in

19. Hicks, *Populist Revolt*, 438; *National Economist*, March 5, 1892.
20. Atlanta *Constitution*, July 2, 3, 1892.

favor of Kyle. Indeed, the Georgia delegation was the first to endorse the
senator from South Dakota.[21]

Meanwhile, Branch was quietly at work as chairman of the resolutions
committee. His main concern was that it pass a resolution condemning
any federal interference in southern elections; surprisingly, his resolution
met little opposition. Next he urged that the graduated income tax plank
be explained more fully. Again he was successful, although this time he
had to apply some of his celebrated charm to the more reluctant members. Another issue that interested him was the demand that former
Union soldiers and sailors receive a generous pension, an idea that was
popular in the North but unpopular in the South. The committee worked
out a compromise whereby the pension demand would be published with
but would not technically be part of the platform. As usual, Branch had
played a vital, if quiet, role behind the scenes. Some Populists were so
impressed with his ability to run a committee to suit his own ends that
they nicknamed him the "General."[22]

The convention began while "General" Branch was at work. Clarence
Ellington delivered the opening address; otherwise, the first day was
taken up with preliminary business. By the next morning the meeting
was tense with excitement. Judge Gresham had withdrawn his name, and
supporters of Kyle and Weaver were frantically trying to win over the
dispossessed delegates. At three o'clock in the afternoon the resolutions
committee reported. The hall now sweltered, and many delegates, tired
and edgy, had stripped off their coats. Nevertheless, as Branch read the
proposed platform, each plank drew explosive applause. Most popular
were the demands for free silver and government ownership of the railroads—the latter being greeted by a demonstration led by the Georgia,
Texas, Kansas, and Nebraska delegations. When Branch finished, the
convention joyously adopted the proposed platform. Then for twenty
minutes the delegates reveled. Hats sailed through the air, men waved
their coats, and "Dixie" and "Yankee Doodle" thundered from the

21. *Ibid.*, July 6, 9, 1892; Hicks, *Populist Revolt*, 234; E. A. Allen, *Lives of Weaver and Field and Achievements of the People's Party* (N.p., 1892), 82–83.
22. Hicks, *Populist Revolt*, 444; Atlanta *Constitution*, July 6, 9, 1892.

band. Several Populists rushed Branch, hoisted him onto their shoulders, and paraded him about the hall.[23]

The convention, however, was not over. As evening fell, the Kyle and Weaver factions still struggled to capture delegates. The voting began after midnight. On the first ballot Weaver captured 995 votes to Kyle's 275. Knowing that the senator from South Dakota was beaten, Post rose and asked the convention to endorse Weaver unanimously. It did. The last order of business was the selection of a vice-presidential candidate. Because Weaver was a northerner, the party needed a southerner to balance the ticket. Several men approached the Georgians about entering Tom Watson's name, but they refused. Perhaps the delegates sensed that the Populist ticket could not win in 1892, or possibly they feared that Watson was the only third-party man who could successfully run for Congress in his district. The nomination eventually went to General James G. Field, a one-legged Confederate veteran from Virginia. Those with a sense of symmetry liked the idea of Yankee and rebel generals running on the same ticket; others fancied that the pair would give credence to the third-party theme that the old Civil War hatreds must end. Nevertheless, it was doubtful that the unknown Field added much strength to the ticket.[24]

Well after one o'clock in the morning, James B. Weaver entered the hall and delivered his acceptance speech. Overcome with excitement, Weaver described the convention, and presumably his own nomination, as the "grandest moment of our civilization."[25]

A few months before the Omaha convention, Charles C. Post, William L. Peek, Mell Branch, Clarence Ellington, and two other Populists met in Douglasville, Georgia. There they signed a circular calling prominent reformers to Atlanta to create a temporary state organization. From then on, Populists always considered Douglasville to be the home of Georgia Populism, and third-party gubernatorial candidates usually de-

23. *National Economist*, July 9, 1892; Allen, *Lives of Weaver and Field*, 100; Hicks, *Populist Revolt*, 234.

24. Atlanta *Journal*, July 6, 1892; Hicks, *Populist Revolt*, 236.

25. Allen, *Lives of Weaver and Field*, 119.

livered their first addresses there. On March 30, Post called the organizational meeting to order in Atlanta. The twenty or thirty Populists present established a temporary executive committee and appointed Peek, Ellington, Branch, Gilmore, and others as members. They also formed a campaign committee to work when the executive committee was not in session. Post served as chairman. Finally, they selected July 20, 1892, as the date for a state convention.[26]

As the day of the convention approached, it seemed more and more likely that Peek would win the gubernatorial nomination. Rank-and-file Populists could only speculate about why Ellington's star had fallen so suddenly. He was undoubtedly the choice of Watson, Branch, and Post. But there were other considerations. The party chiefs did not want an ugly convention struggle that might shred the organization before the campaign began. The Peek faction had the power to create a split. Although Peek's *Southern Alliance Farmer* was firing its editorial ordnance at the Democrats, it could just as easily turn its guns on Ellington, who in turn would have to be defended by the *People's Party Paper*. Perhaps to make his withdrawal more palatable, Ellington was urged to run for the presidency of the Georgia Alliance.[27]

A few days before the convention, delegates began to pour into Atlanta. Their red convention badges, sunburned faces, and cracker drawls made them easily recognizable. Since most were apparently novices to politics, they were not a politically sophisticated group. Nevertheless, the Democrats noted uneasily that Branch was calling for more "hell raising," that Peek wanted to destroy the Democratic party, and that Watson's latest book was entitled *It Is Not a Revolt, but a Revolution*. Just before the convention, a delegate named "Blue" Fred Wimberley said, "Be not deceived. Socialism, anarchism, communism and nihilism in Europe is but a phase of the Alliance in America. Those men in Europe are desperate because they have lost all hope in life." But what angered Democrats most was the presence of two black delegates, John Mack and

26. Atlanta *Constitution*, April 1, 16, 1892, July 13, 1898; Scrapbook 2, pp. 44–45, Northen Papers; *People's Party Paper*, March 31, 1892.
27. Atlanta *Constitution*, July 19, 1892; Macon *Telegraph*, July 20, 1892.

R. J. Mathews. Mack was "Peek's nigger," the Macon *Telegram* sneered, and referred to Mathews as a "nigger co-laborer."[28]

At ten o'clock in the morning the convention opened in the house chamber of the state capitol. Post stepped to the podium, pounded the gavel three times, and called the meeting to order. Silence fell over the hall, broken only by the ticking of the clocks on either side of the chamber. Reporters were present, eyeing the scene. "Plug hats, patent leather shoes, standing collars and store-bought clothes were conspicous [*sic*] by their absence," one wrote. Another said that "every face was sunburned, and there were none of the kid-glove variety of human beings present."[29]

Post introduced the temporary chairman, Mell Branch, who delivered the opening address. The convention then elected Post permanent chairman and appointed Post, Ellington, Branch, and others to the platform committee. Afterward this group considered a number of ideas, including a dry plank proposal submitted by the Reverend Sam Small of the Georgia Prohibition party. Although this suggestion was seriously considered, the group eventually decided against it. During the afternoon the committee presented its final report, which was enthusiastically endorsed by the delegates. In seventy-nine words it praised the Omaha demands, repudiated the state's leasing of convict labor to private individuals, and called for lower taxes whenever feasible.[30]

The delegates then selected a state ticket. Without opposition, Peek was nominated for governor and seconded by John Mack and others. The convention also picked James Barrett of Richmond County for commissioner of agriculture; William R. Gorman of Talbot County for secretary of state; J. A. B. Mahaffey of Jackson County for attorney general; A. W. Ivey of Thomas County for comptroller-general; and J. E. H. Ware of Fayette County for treasurer.[31] Branch was not added to the ticket because he had already decided to run for the Georgia House of

28. Sparta *Ishmaelite*, July 22, 1892; Atlanta *Constitution*, July 10, 1892; Macon *Telegraph*, July 27, 1892.
29. The best descriptions of this convention are in the Atlanta *Constitution*, July 19–23, 1892; Atlanta *Journal*, July 19–23, 1892; and Augusta *Chronicle*, July 21–22, 1892.
30. Atlanta *Journal*, July 21, 1892.
31. *Ibid.*, July 19, 1892.

Representatives. Nor did the delegates nominate Post, whose now-famous "atheism" made him an unattractive candidate.

Just as the convention was about to adjourn, a number of Populists clamored for an address by the Reverend Sam Small. A former alcoholic and an ardent prohibitionist, Small had been saved after hearing a sermon by the famed evangelist, Sam Jones. Many thought he planned to run for Congress against Lon Livingston. He was not, however, a typical member of the Atlanta clergy. Some months before the convention he had participated in a barbershop brawl in which a saloonkeeper had kicked out one of his teeth. The resulting lawsuit took up much of his time during the meeting; but now with shouts of "Speech! Speech!" sounding in his ears, he had a chance to play a dramatic role. After lambasting the Republicans and the Democrats, he lit into Grover Cleveland for dining with the black leader, Frederick Douglass, and his white wife: "Grover Cleveland invited that leader of niggerdom, Fred Douglass, to his dinner table. I might excuse him for getting the nigger into his house for supper, but when he invited the low wife to go there, it is more than I can stand." And so his harangue continued, until even the reporter from the racist Atlanta *Constitution* was offended and called the speech "unprovoked," "vindictive," "terrifying," and "ugly." [32]

But the emotional high point of the gathering came just before Small's address. Post asked the soloist to sing "We'll Get There," a song especially written for the coming campaign. This number seemed to capture the spirit of Georgia Populism, and as the words rolled out across the hall, one stanza in particular sent hats into the air and drove the convention wild:

> When Watson led the people out,
>   They marched thro' flood and flame;
> Old Livingston tried to turn them back,
>   But they got there just the same. [33]

The words to "We'll Get There" may have rankled party leaders. They, too, had "led the people out"; yet the names of Peek, Post, Ellington, Branch, Gilmore, Sibley, and Irwin were strangely missing.

---

32. Atlanta *Constitution*, July 21, 1892.
33. *Ibid.*

Indeed, Watson's efforts to dominate the movement had largely failed. Peek had crushed Ellington's candidacy for governor, and most of the men on the state ticket were members of his faction. The words of this song left unanswered other questions about Georgia Populism. Who were the "people" who had been so bravely led? And was the Georgia Populism really a democratic uprising—an uprising of the common man? In some ways the happenings at the state convention suggested that it was. Newspapers were agreed that the delegates were not politicos; that they did not represent the railroads or the corporations. Rather, an atmosphere of backwoods innocence—part revival, part gander pull— pervaded the meeting. No one thought it inappropriate that the proceedings be stopped so a delegate, known in his parts as a champion shouter, could deliver several splendid bellows. Likewise, the brevity and forthrightness of the platform gave the meeting an air of a simple, God-fearing yeomanry taking back their government in the name of great Jehovah and Thomas Jefferson. Delegates often said that Populism was the people's way of returning to the wisdom that once had poured from Monticello. And when the gathering adjourned with the singing of "Old Hundred," the words of that doxology must have had a special meaning for many delegates. In this sense the convention in Atlanta was an assembly of the common man.

Yet in other ways it was not. Although ordinary men attended, the convention was anything but democratic. Party leaders had agreed upon the candidate for governor ahead of time; not one man on the state ticket was challenged by an opponent. The delegates accepted the platform without discussion; there were no floor fights and virtually no disagreement. Beneath the speeches, the singing, and the cheers, an eerie, almost mechanical ambience hung about the hall. But the meeting had other questionable qualities. The Gilmore fraud, perpetrated upon the Georgia Colored Alliance, made it clear that some Populists were not above trickery. Indeed, the views of third-party members about the former slaves were unknown. At one convention they had risked political ruin to allow two black delegates to attend; at another they had stolen the votes of the entire Colored Alliance. That the Georgia convention ended with the hate-filled rantings of the Reverend Small was equally disturbing to blacks.

Whatever the answers to these questions, Populist leaders had proved themselves remarkable men. At convention after convention they had played vital roles. Their early advocacy of the subtreasury plan and government ownership of the railroads seemed to place them among the most radical of American Populists. Why Georgia, a state hardly noted for reform, should have produced such men was a question that perplexed conservatives. But it was not a question that troubled Populists in July, 1892. There was a campaign to wage, a state to win. The wool-hat boys were on the march.

◄❧IV❧►

"The Damnedest Sight I Ever Saw"
The Georgia Elections of 1892

A week after his nomination, William L. Peek was nearly assassinated in Quitman, Georgia. Earlier in the day he had delivered his first campaign address in the town square—an effort that was constantly interrupted by catcalls and insults. When Charles Post tried to speak, the heckling swelled, and a Democratic brass band marched up to add to the din. Not until third-party men in the audience had chased the musicians from the square could Post continue. After the rally, Peek, Post, and a few others walked to the train station, where a dozen men lounged about. To Peek's surprise, a knife fight abruptly broke out between two of the bystanders. Although onlookers made several attempts to separate the opponents, every time this was done the scuffling men drew nearer the Populists. Suddenly, all the bystanders drew knives and tried to surround Peek. The third-party men hurried toward the waiting train, at the same time trying to protect Peek from flying stones and eggs. Boarding the train with their assailants close behind, the Populists prepared for a fight. But the Democrats, on seeing their enemies ready with raised canes, decided that the situation was becoming dangerous and quickly withdrew. As the locomotive puffed from the station, they bade farewell by shattering the train's windows with rocks.[1]

It had not been a happy beginning for the Populist campaign. A rock had struck and paralyzed Peek's arm, and a year would pass before the candidate regained full use of his hand. Yet Peek was tenacious. "Nothing can stop me in whooping up the state," he declared.[2] The

1. *National Economist*, August 20, 1892; Atlanta *Constitution*, July 31, 1892; Dawson *News*, August 10, 1892.
2. Atlanta *Constitution*, August 6, 1892.

Populists, however, needed more than pluck to defeat the Democrats, and their weaknesses were becoming apparent.

One problem was the state ticket, which was composed of politically inexperienced farmers and lawyers. As a group they seemed to have but one helpful qualification: they were surprisingly well-educated. With one exception, all had attended college and two seemed especially cultivated. The candidate for attorney general, J. A. B. Mahaffey, was an Emory College graduate, a lawyer, and a man known for his love of classical literature. William R. Gorman, running for secretary of state, had attended the University of Georgia and Harvard. Although initially trained for the bar, he eventually became a mill owner.[3]

But the member with the most unusual background was James Barrett, the candidate for commissioner of agriculture. Outwardly he seemed a reputable Georgia planter, and like Gorman and Mahaffey, he could boast of substantial education. As a youth he had studied for two years at the University of North Carolina, then joined the Confederate army and rose to the rank of captain. For much of his military career he served at the Confederate prison camps in Richmond, Virginia, Andersonville, Georgia, and Florence, South Carolina. After the war he left the United States for Germany, where he married and continued his studies at several German universities. In about 1869 he returned to Georgia, eventually taking up farming near Augusta.[4]

This at least was the image of James Barrett that appeared in the newspapers. There existed, however, another James Barrett—a darker, less attractive man whom many regarded as little less than a monster. At the close of the Civil War, the United States government selected Barrett as one of ten Confederates to be tried as war criminals. "The testimony fixes upon [him]," wrote Judge Advocate General Joseph Holt after his investigation, "not only a series of cruel and inhuman acts of neglect, abuse, assault, robbery, etc., but a considerable number of well established homicides." Undoubtedly, this was Barrett's reason for his hasty depar-

3. *Ibid.*, July 21, 1892; A. W. Cozart and Jno. J. Strickland, "Memorial of James Alexander Benceer Mahaffey," *Report of the Thirty-Seventh Annual Session of the Georgia Bar Association, May 22–29, 1920* (Atlanta, 1920), 268; *Brief Biographies of the Members of the Constitutional Convention, July 11, 1877* (Atlanta, 1877), 63–64; *Georgia's General Assembly*, 51; *People's Party Paper*, June 1, 1894.
4. *People's Party Paper*, June 1, 1894.

ture to Europe at the close of the war. By the 1890s Barrett's past had largely been forgotten, at least in Georgia, but former prisoners still remembered the deeds of this Confederate officer. Every so often one would write his memoirs, and invariably the opinion was the same: Barrett was a fiend who delighted in suffering. One former prisoner remembered him as a "rough, green, conceited brute, who never spoke without blasphemy, and never gave a civil word, or did a kind deed for any prisoner—a man with as few of the elements of good in his nature as I ever knew." Another soldier, who had been imprisoned under both Barrett and Henry Wirz (the only Confederate tried and executed for the murder of Union prisoners), considered Barrett the more vicious of the two because he had "a little more brains . . . and this extra intellect was wholly devoted to cruelty." On one occasion Barrett became convinced that the prisoners were digging a tunnel out of the Florence stockade. For three days he cut off rations to his thirteen thousand captives. "Air ye're hungry enough to give up them God damned sons of bitches yet?" he demanded of the federals. Finally, the prisoners dug a tunnel (the one Barrett believed existed was imaginary), and four men "confessed." Tying their hands behind their backs, he hung these soldiers by the thumbs, crippling at least one for life. As they shrieked and begged to be shot, Barrett exclaimed, "By God, I'll learn these Yanks to be more afeard of me than the old devil himself. They'll soon understand I'm not a man to fool with. . . . Just hear 'em squeal won't yer?"[5]

Obviously, Barrett was not a typical Georgia Populist, nor was it surprising that a movement as large and varied as Populism should have attracted a great variety of people. Nevertheless, one wonders why the third party had selected for high office a man who was, at least according to former Yankee prisoners, a sadist. Some Populist leaders undoubtedly knew of Barrett's sordid past when they nominated him for commissioner of agriculture. And although this information did not become gen-

---

5. *The War of the Rebellion: A Compilation of the Official Records of the Union and Confederate Armies* (130 vols.; Washington, D.C., 1880–1901), Ser. II, Vol. VIII, 783; Warren Lee Goss, *The Soldier's Story of Captivity at Andersonville, Belle Isle, and Other Rebel Prisons* (Boston, 1868), 225–26; John McElroy, *Andersonville: A Story of Rebel Military Prisons* (Toledo, 1879), 526, 532–34; Robert H. Kellogg, *Life and Death in Rebel Prisons* (Hartford, 1866), 341.

erally known during the election of 1892, five years later the Democrats would use it in their attempts to discredit the Populists.

As Peek's campaign struggled through its hapless beginnings, Populists across the state were meeting to pick candidates for Congress. In the "terrible" Tenth Congressional District, the nominating convention selected Thomas E. Watson without opposition. But in other places these meetings failed to go as smoothly. In the Ninth, Thomas E. Winn, the congressman who had lately joined the People's movement, posed a problem. For many his defection from the Democratic party smacked of opportunism. Shortly before declaring himself a Populist, Winn had written a letter to the Atlanta *Constitution* lauding the Democrats. Consequently, a fierce opposition arose at the nominating convention, with his enemies supporting Thaddeus Pickett, a former Republican and independent. When it appeared that the meeting was about to nominate Winn, Pickett's supporters stormed out of the hall, organized a rump, and nominated their man for Congress. As angry charges and counter-charges shredded the Populists in the Ninth, it remained for the members of the state executive committee to pick the legitimate candidate. When they finally selected Pickett, many Winn supporters swore they would vote Democratic. Just after Pickett was declared legitimate, the Atlanta *Journal* published an article proving that Pickett had been a deserter during the Civil War.[6]

A similar struggle occurred at the Fifth District convention, where Sam Taliaferro defeated the Reverend Sam Small by one vote. Taliaferro then commenced a breathtakingly dull campaign. To make matters worse, the colorful Small decided to run for Congress as a Prohibitionist, thereby splitting the reform vote and making Lon Livingston's election a certainty. In desperation, the state executive committee gathered during the last days of the contest to try to convince Taliaferro to withdraw in favor of Small. Taliaferro's representatives refused to consider such an idea and stalked out of the room. Then the committee nominated Small, thus giving the Populists two candidates for Congress in the Fifth. Al-

6. Atlanta *Constitution*, July 28, 1892. For the Populist candidates for Congress and their opponents, see Robert A. Diamond (ed.), *Congressional Quarterly's Guide to U.S. Elections* (Washington, 1975), 667.

though Taliaferro later withdrew, many of his supporters apparently voted Democratic.[7]

But the most unusual development in the early days of the contest was Charles Post's abrupt exit from the state. Just before the Quitman incident, the *People's Party Paper* announced that Post was leaving for three weeks to help the Populist campaign in Michigan.[8] The newspaper implied that his departure was temporary. Yet Post never returned. Some believed he had fled because he feared for his life. Others wondered if Populist leaders had decided that an alleged atheist was too much of a liability in God-fearing Georgia. Whatever the reason, Mark Irwin took over Post's duties as chairman of the party. Peek's victory over Watson was now complete.

Even as the campaign commenced, the Populists had suffered some damaging setbacks. Many party members were disturbed that they had attracted a number of mentally ill, eccentric, or unorthodox leaders. Post's so-called atheism, Small's barbershop brawl, and Pickett's Civil War record had upset a considerable number of Populists. The organization had even gained a few radicals. Most notable was J. B. Osborne, a one-eyed socialist, who led the party's efforts to win the labor vote. Especially among Watson's followers, there was a growing sense of embarrassment and apprehension. Still, the prospects were not completely bleak. Earlier the state executive committee had asked the national party headquarters to send some leading Populists to stump the state.[9] They must have felt gratified that General Weaver, General Field, and Mary Elizabeth Lease all agreed to campaign in Georgia.

The task of organizing Georgia Democrats in their fight against the third party was left to William Yates Atkinson, the state Democratic chairman. At thirty-six years of age, he had previously served in the General Assembly. He realized that his political future depended on a convincing defeat of the Populists. This, however, was no simple task. In many counties the Democrats had not waged a serious campaign since

7. Atlanta *Constitution*, February 6, July 29, August 21, 26, 31, 1892; Atlanta *Journal*, September 7, 1892. See also Diamond (ed.), *Guide to U.S. Elections*, 667.
8. *People's Party Paper*, July 29, 1892.
9. Atlanta *Constitution*, September 24, 1892.

Reconstruction. With Weaver and Lease about to invade the state, Atkinson worked swiftly to prepare his party for war. Nevertheless, he had reason for confidence. The Democrats had nominated the popular Northen for a second term as governor, and at a moment's notice Atkinson could cover the state with dozens of impressive speakers. Senator Gordon and Congressman Livingston seemed to be everywhere, alternately chiding the Populists and crying for a Democratic victory. For humor, Atkinson could dispatch H. W. J. Ham, a candidate for the state legislature from Hall County. Behind a folksy and bluff demeanor, Ham possessed a caustic wit. Of Mary Elizabeth Lease, he declared: "She's got a face that's harder and sharper than a butcher's cleaver. I could take her by the heels and split an inch board with it. She's got a nose like an ant-eater, a voice like a cat fight and a face that is rank poison to the naked eye." [10]

The state Democratic press also did its part. The Waynesboro *True Citizen* called General Weaver a "foul mouth poltroon" and a "dirty wretch." The Sparta *Ishmaelite* devoted itself to attacks on "Jack Cade Peek, the wild ass of the 5th district." Describing one of Peek's speeches, the *Ishmaelite* said, "He made without the slightest proof one assertion after another, and after each one belched out a nasty joke and smiled the grisly smile of an idiot who thinks he has done something very grand." Still, the *Ishmaelite* professed pity for "Magnus Asinus"—its nickname for Peek. "To be ignorant and weak witted is a misfortune rather than a crime," the newspaper declared. "Candidate Peek can't help being a fool." About other Populist leaders, the *Ishmaelite* was more moderate. Mell Branch was simply a "vicious ignoramus"; Clarence Ellington, a "mouthing demagogue." [11]

When their campaign transcended name-calling, the Democrats were forced to improvise. The state platform endorsed nothing except "time honored Democracy" and the national Democratic platform. Moreover, with Post absent from the state, they could no longer rail against the

10. Clark Howell (ed.), *History of Georgia* (4 vols.; Chicago, 1926), IV, 226–28; Macon *Telegraph*, July 20, 1892; Ham quoted in Atlanta *Constitution*, September 25, 1892.
11. *True Citizen*, n.d., quoted in Sparta *Ishmaelite*, September 16, 1892; Scrapbook 2, p. 110, Northen Papers; Sparta *Ishmaelite*, September 16, April 18, May 27, October 28, 1892.

forces of atheism. A new issue was needed. Quickly Democrats pounced on the Omaha convention's pension resolution. Why should Union veterans receive such largesse, they demanded.[12] And why should Confederate veterans have to help pay for it? At the same time, Democrats continued to stress that timeworn but important issue—black rule. They implored voters to contemplate the horrors that would befall Georgia if the white vote should divide. The Augusta *Chronicle* warned that a People's party victory would "destroy white supremacy," bring "death to our civilization," and spread "socialism, communism, and anarchy." On the same issue, the Vienna *Progress* claimed to have discovered new verses to a Populist song:

> We first could only brother with,
> The ploughman and the digger
> But now we'll take—Lord, anything
> The donkey or the nigger.[13]

But soon even these issues were eclipsed by one that would have the entire state trembling with excitement—General Weaver's war record. About a month before Weaver was to campaign in Georgia, the Atlanta *Journal* published an exposé on his Civil War occupation of Pulaski, Tennessee. There Weaver had supposedly instituted his own reign of terror—executing Confederate soldiers and robbing, imprisoning, and insulting civilians. The *Journal* reported that Weaver later referred to Democrats as a "hungry, rebellious, man hating, woman-selling gang corporated under the name of democracy, a name so full of stench and poison that it should be blotted from the vocabulary of civilized man." Georgia Democrats were beside themselves with rage. "If I had a yellow dog that would dignify Weaver by association, I'd kill it," H. W. J. Ham roared at a meeting. And from the audience came cries of "the rebel-hanging scoundrel" and "that man Weaver ought to be hung with the rope he hung his rebels with."[14]

In such an atmosphere General Weaver, his wife, and Mary Elizabeth

12. Atlanta *Constitution*, August 11, 1892, July–November 1892, *passim*.

13. Augusta *Chronicle*, October 1, 1892; Vienna *Progress*, n.d., quoted in Atlanta *Constitution*, August 4, 1892.

14. Atlanta *Journal*, September 2, 1892; Atlanta *Constitution*, August 4, September 15, 1892.

Lease entered the state in mid-September. Weaver claimed he had been misquoted but added lamely that he had probably said things equally as harsh. Georgia Democrats were hardly pacified. The General was coolly received in Waycross; at Albany he was met by a "howling mob"; at Columbus a fist fight nearly erupted on the speaker's platform. The evening appointment in Macon was, according to Weaver, "simply disgraceful, beyond words." Shortly before the general was to speak, the Macon Young Men's Democratic Club gathered to listen to the harangues of Du-Pont Guerry, a prominent politician. "If you should break every ancient egg in town on Gen. Weaver's filthy carcass you could not make him stink the worse in the nostrils of decent people," Guerry declared. Hundreds of shouting Democrats then rushed down the street into the crowd that was waiting for Weaver to speak from a hotel balcony. Pandemonium erupted, the throng turning angry and boisterous. As Weaver's party stepped onto the balcony, they were greeted with boos and catcalls. Suddenly, an egg flew from the crowd, striking Mrs. Weaver on the head. When the general tried to speak, the jeering swelled until he was forced to shout above the din. Never, he bellowed, had anyone refused him a hearing. At these words the crowd went wild, driving the Populists from the balcony with a barrage of eggs and insults.[15]

Nor was Macon the only city in Georgia alive with mobs. In Cordele the abuse from hecklers was so great that James G. Field, the Populist candidate for vice-president, was forced to seek protection from the mayor. When Tom Watson tried to deliver an address in Atlanta, a Democrat wrote that "the scene has never had an equal in the history of this city." The snarling mob literally shouted Watson down, and police were needed to see him safely through the crowd. The next night General Weaver was to appear at the same hall, but after learning about Watson's experience, he declined. Canceling his remaining engagements, Weaver, his wife, and Mrs. Lease boarded a train for South Carolina. The national Populist campaign committee declared the situation so dangerous that it was sending no more speakers into the state.[16]

15. Atlanta *Journal*, September 24, 1892; Macon *Telegraph*, September 23, 30, 1892; *People's Party Paper*, September 30, 1892; Atlanta *Constitution*, September 23, 24, 1892.
16. Atlanta *Constitution*, September 24, 25, October 1, 1892; Macon *Telegraph*, September 23, 30, 1892.

Recounting her experiences in Georgia, Mary Elizabeth Lease said that the "lower regions seemed turned loose." [17] It was an apt description. The eggs that flew at General Weaver and his wife smashed like bombs in the Populist press. Third-party newspapers screamed that Democrats had rotten-egged an old lady, that they had debauched the southern code of chivalry. Suddenly, all the venom that had not been seen in Georgia politics since Reconstruction came flowing to the surface. Reports from all over the state told of shootings and fist fights. Rumor had it that if Peek were elected he would "die the death of Garfield and Lincoln." [18]

In the Tenth District, the situation was growing especially dangerous. When speaking in Thomson, Watson's opponent, Major James C. C. Black, charged that Charles Post "was so obnoxious to the new party that he was sent away." Suddenly, Clarence Ellington, who was in the audience, jumped to his feet. "And we are not ashamed of it," he cried. Bedlam resulted, with Democrats and Populists in the crowd grabbing pistols and knives from their pockets. For one terrifying moment they stood glaring at each other. It was a miracle, a witness reported, that no one was killed. The next day a Democrat attacked Ellington on the street in Thomson. Just as they were separated, another Democrat assaulted John T. West, a prominent Populist and former law partner of Tom Watson. Three hundred third-party men gathered at Harrisburg, resolving that in the future they would resist with arms any Democratic attempts to disrupt their meetings. It seemed to many that the state was on the brink of calamity. Mark Irwin believed Georgia was like France before the Revolution. "The Times are ominous," he wrote. "There will be bloodshed or death unless there is change." [19]

Election day was filled with reports of shootings and intimidation at the polls. In a brawl at Ruckersville, Democrats killed one black and wounded four others. In Augusta the secretary of a local Populist club shot a deputy sheriff.[20] In all, possibly fifteen citizens had been killed since the beginning of the campaign. Nor did this bloodletting help the

17. Scrapbook 2, p. 157, Northen Papers.
18. *People's Party Paper*, October 7, 14, 1892.
19. Augusta *Chronicle*, September 22, 23, 25, 1892; *People's Party Paper*, September 30, 1892.
20. Woodward, *Tom Watson*, 204.

Populist cause, for when the ballots were counted Northen received 140,432 votes to Peek's 68,990.[21] The results were just as dismal in the legislative races—the Populists had elected only sixteen members. Furious third-party men charged that their opponents had often cheated, bribed, and coerced voters. Meanwhile, the Democrats gleefully celebrated their triumph, seemingly oblivious to the election's cost. Families and friendships, churches and political parties had been split. The state seemed awash in loathing and recrimination. Mark Irwin's prediction of "bloodshed or death" had become a reality, and the federal elections were still to come.

Peek's defeat stunned not only Georgia Populists but Populists everywhere. "The people's party leaders in this community are thunderstruck at the result of the Georgia election," one Kansan wrote. "Quite a number here have renounced their allegiance [to Populism]."[22] It was certain now that General Weaver could never capture Georgia in the presidential election. Still, the situation was not totally bleak. Some Georgia Populists argued that electing a president was unimportant because he would be ground between the Democrats and Republicans—"pulverized finer than the face powders used by prostitutes," as one Populist expressed it. More critical were the congressional elections. In the Tenth, Peek had received more votes than Northen, suggesting that Watson might very well defeat his opponent, Major James C. C. Black. Populists also felt optimistic about the mountain districts. In the Seventh, John Sibley was riding his bicycle from gathering to gathering. "Everything is lovely and the goose hangs high," he said, while his opponent admitted that the "signs are none too good." In the other mountain district, the Ninth, Thaddeus Pickett was fighting a quiet but effective campaign despite the growing knowledge that he had deserted the Confederate army.[23] In only one other district was there hope for the Populists. In the Fifth, the Reverend Sam Small had married the Populists and the Prohibitionists in a colorful struggle against Lon Livingston. And because so many voters—both Populist and Democrat—now distrusted Livingston, there was reason to think Small might defeat him.

21. *Georgia House Journal*, 1892, p. 5.
22. Quoted in Argersinger, *Populism and Politics*, 119.
23. Carnesville *Enterprise*, April 15, 1892; Atlanta *Constitution*, November 3, 1892; Dahlonega *Signal*, October 7, 1892.

The most important issue of the congressional campaign was the Lodge election bill. Dubbed the "Force Bill," this Republican legislation would have provided supervisors for federal elections. Although Congress had defeated the measure in 1890, some Populists now began to see its value. But such an idea challenged the doctrine of states' rights, as well as the plank in the national Populist platform that Mell Branch had authored. Consequently, Branch and other third-party figures fought the idea. "We had supervisors during Reconstruction and they were made drunk and bought off," Reverend Sam Small said. Many Populists disagreed. Three hundred men signed a petition in Augusta demanding supervisors, and to the chagrin of the Democrats, the federal courts upheld their request. Populists in at least eight counties likewise asked for and received supervisors at the polls.[24]

As election day approached, all the horrors of the earlier contest reappeared. The Tenth turned into an armed camp as Democrats and Populists engaged in a vitriolic struggle. John B. Gordon, William Y. Atkinson, Lon Livingston, Hoke Smith, Augustus O. Bacon, Charles Crisp, Joe James, H. W. J. Ham—virtually every Democrat of any consequence—hurried into the district to aid the campaign. In many counties local party members were determined to win the election whether by bribes, whiskey, or Winchesters. Nor was it difficult for them to justify their acts. "Watson has gone mad," one newspaper shrieked.[25] The Populist leader's appeals to the blacks—his assertion that they should have political rights—was unthinkable heresy to most Democrats. Anything would be justified in defeating this affront to Anglo-Saxon supremacy.

At the same time Populists were at work. Watson spoke every day, sometimes to crowds of more than a thousand, while bands of his followers rode the countryside at night frightening Democrats and trying to win more black votes. "I am living in an extreme dark corner of Lincoln County and nothing but negroes for miles around," one Democrat wrote. "In some way the third partyites got to work at night and formed clubs and have terrified the negroes so that they are afraid of one another." Often there was bloodshed. A shootout in La Grange killed a Populist

24. Atlanta *Constitution*, November 5, 1892. For more details about the question of supervisors, see Macon *Telegraph*, November 4, 1892; Carnesville *Enterprise*, August 19, 1892; Dahlonega *Signal*, November 9, 1892; Atlanta *Constitution*, November 4, 1892.
25. Quoted in Woodward, *Tom Watson*, 240.

and wounded a Democrat. Citizens fearfully wondered what was afoot. On October 23, Mell Branch's Harlem *Light* gave them an answer: "There is no wiping out the fact that this is a revolution, and it depends upon the action of the enemy whether it shall be peaceful or a bloody one. To be candid about the matter we believe it will be the latter." [26]

The next evening a rider tore out of the village of Thomson with news that Branch's terrible prophecy seemed to be coming true. By morning many Populists had gotten word: the Democrats had murdered Tom Watson. At other places reports were not so grave. Rumor had it that Watson was alive but that a Democratic mob was threatening his house. When word reached Lincolnton the scene "beggar[e]d all description," a Democrat later said. "The third partyites were wild; they were furious." Men ran in every direction, collecting rifles and saddling horses. Soon they had a force of seventy farmers, both black and white. Quickly mounting up, they galloped out of town, headed for Thomson. All over the district the scene was the same. By the next day possibly two thousand Populists, armed with shotguns and Winchesters, had poured into Thomson. There they found their leader protecting Seb Doyle, a black third-party minister whom the Democrats had threatened to whip. The farmers stacked their rifles on Watson's veranda, built little fires, and prepared their food. "They didn't go up to the house," one man recalled, "and they didn't talk with Tom. They just slept in their wagons on some old quilts or sat hunkered around, talkin'." Some stayed for two days, guarding Watson's house. Then they went home. Fifty years later a townsman remembered the incident, calling it "the damnedest sight I ever saw, and one to chill your blood, and one that smelled of death though there was no death in it." [27]

But if there was no death that day in Thomson, death was still abroad in Georgia. A Populist was murdered in Louisville, and a week later another man was killed. Watson's last campaign speech turned into a near riot. A shot was fired, and several times men in the crowd threatened each other with pistols. "I have never seen such a state of feeling," one

26. Augusta *Chronicle*, November 8, 1892; Harlem *Light*, October 23, 1892, quoted in Augusta *Chronicle*, October 23, 1892.
27. Augusta *Chronicle*, October 26, 1892; U.S. Congress, House, *Contested Election Case of Thomas E. Watson vs. J. C. C. Black* (Washington, 1896), 575–81; Ralph McGill, *The South and the Southerner* (Boston, 1963), 127.

citizen in the Tenth District reported. "We are here in the hands of a howling mob. Life is in danger." Terrified Democrats moved their families out of Thomson, fearful that the Populists would burn the town if they lost the election. Governor Northen ordered the Augusta militia to be prepared to march at a moment's notice. In Atlanta special locomotives stood ready, their boilers fired night and day. If necessary, they, too, would rush troops from the capital into the "terrible" Tenth."[28]

Election day was as chaotic as had been feared. Although it was unnecessary to call out the militia, shootings, fist fights, bribery, and fraud accompanied the voter to the polls. And as in the earlier contest, the Populists were crushed. Grover Cleveland, the Democratic candidate for president, captured the state as well as the nation. The Democrats won every congressional seat in Georgia. Charging that his opponents had stolen the election, Tom Watson bitterly announced that he would contest the results in the United States House of Representatives.[29]

The Georgia elections of 1892 are most famous for their violence and fraud. Although Peek was certainly not swindled out of a victory, it is possible that Watson was. Many responsible Georgians, both Populist and Democrat, argued about the frauds, trying to determine their extent and who was responsible. In some places the Democrats had undoubtedly used underhanded methods. In Peek's county they had truly turned out the electorate, even enlisting inmates from the local insane asylum to cast ballots for Northen. When the polls closed, 1,157 people had voted, although only 1,025 had earlier paid the poll tax. In Wilkinson County the Democrats purged the election books just before the October contest, eliminating 116 names, 90 percent of which were Populists. On a technicality, managers at the polls in Wilkes County threw out every precinct that had voted for the People's candidate for the legislature; yet when a Democratic precinct made the same error, its returns were counted. In

28. Augusta *Chronicle*, November 8, 1892; Woodward, *Tom Watson*, 240–41; William W. Brewton, *The Life of Thomas E. Watson* (Atlanta, 1926), 251.

29. Atlanta *Constitution*, October 7, 1892. The county-by-county returns for the Georgia gubernatorial and congressional elections of 1892 can be found in Georgia, Comptroller-General, *Report of the Comptroller-General of the State of Georgia for the Year Ending September 30, 1893* (Atlanta, 1893), 168–79. For the county-by-county returns of the presidential election of 1892 in Georgia, see *World Almanac and Encyclopaedia, 1894* (New York, 1894), 382–84.

Augusta, the bribery and repeating during the November election were spectacular, the Democrats even importing blacks from South Carolina to fatten their count. But like Democrats elsewhere, their zeal seemed to outmatch their good sense, for Augusta reported twice as many votes as it had voters. By losing Augusta, Watson lost Richmond County and thus the election. It was for this reason that he contested Major Black's victory.[30]

Yet the Populists used the same methods as their opponents, if not with the same aplomb. In the gubernatorial election five Populist counties produced more votes than voters. Oconee County had 209 extra votes, and Washington created a surplus of 604. Columbia County Populists apparently employed the same technique used by Augusta Democrats—the importation of South Carolina blacks—to manufacture an excess of 400 ballots. Nor were the third-party men any more principled in the congressional contests. Although Tom Watson venomously condemned the Augusta frauds, he was reluctant to discuss his own tally, for half the counties he carried had reported more votes than they had voters. In particular, Watson's home county, McDuffie, was an embarrassment, having conjured up 267 excess ballots. Suspecting that the third party had counted the votes of poll-tax defaulters, local Democrats demanded to see the tax books. The tax collector, who was a Populist, then announced that all the records going back to 1877—the year the poll tax was instituted—were missing.[31]

But these swindles failed to bring the Populists victory at the polls. Everywhere party members were bedeviled by the same question: What went wrong? Only a few admitted that much of the blame lay in their own camp. Nevertheless, a lack of literature, organization, good speakers, and money had harried them from the start. Even more disabling was the party's lack of talent. Only a few leaders such as Watson, Branch, and Post were exceptional men, and Post did not remain with the party for long. The Populists could boast of only one outstanding campaigner— Thomas E. Watson—whereas the Democrats possessed at least a half

30. Atlanta *Constitution*, October 7, 1892. The number of citizens who had paid the poll tax in each county can be found in *Report of the Comptroller-General, 1893*, pp. 95–102. See also *People's Party Paper*, October 14, 1892; Woodward, *Tom Watson*, 208.

31. *Report of the Comptroller-General, 1893*, pp. 95–102; U.S. Congress, House, *Watson vs. Black*, 641.

dozen. At the same time the Populists had their share of opportunists eager for a quick ride to power and prominence. Although these men seldom remained with the party for long, their brief infatuation with Populism was occasionally ruinous. In two districts the party nominated congressional candidates who campaigned briefly, became discouraged, and eventually withdrew. In the Fifth and Ninth districts, internecine fights shattered Populist chances even before the campaign had begun. But there were other reasons for the Populist defeat that went beyond third-party control. The wool-hat boys were struggling against a machine that had an abundance of experience, organization, and money. Its command of patronage alone gave it great strength. Geography was also a factor. Although the Populists had built their organization upon the structure of the already existing Alliances and suballiances, they soon discovered that creating a new political party from the Appalachians to the sea was a monumental endeavor, especially when much of the electorate lived in isolated farmsteads. Obviously, Populist leaders had underestimated the difficulty of this task.

Nevertheless, many third-party men refused to believe that the Populist campaign or Populism itself was responsible for the debacle. Angry and suspicious, they looked everywhere for an explanation. Many pointed to Democratic frauds, others to a poor turnout of third-party voters. But for some, including William L. Peek, none of these explanations was acceptable. Populists had assumed that blacks would throng to the new party; yet from all over the state reports came of blacks at the polls, bribed and drunk, voting again and again for the Democrats. Peek believed this was the reason for his disastrous showing. "Them doggoned democrats outcounted us," he said the day after his defeat. "They juggled with the negroes yesterday and the day before, and they just outcounted us."[32] Many Populists bitterly agreed: the black man was to blame.

32. Atlanta *Constitution*, October 7, 1892.

The Populists After Dark

The notion that the black man had somehow betrayed Populism would constantly haunt the Georgia People's party. From the very beginning Populists had realized the political importance of blacks. Of the state's forty thousand Republican voters, a considerable majority were former bondsmen. If the white vote were to split, they might decide the outcome of any state election. But therein lay a predicament. How were Populists to court the black vote without losing the white? How were they to keep whites from thinking of them as the "nigger party," the party willing to truckle to the former slaves? Clearly, however, an attempt had to be made to win over blacks. It was a dangerous scheme, but it contained a degree of precedent in state politics. In the 1870s and 1880s, Democrats and independents had sometimes used the same device when the white vote split. In those days many whites were willing to allow the black man the ballot, especially when it could be sometimes bought for as little as a dime or a mouthful of whiskey.[1]

But to lure the Republican vote the Populists refused either to give up leadership of their party or to advocate the social equality of the races. The first was a question of power, the second of prejudice. On the issue of social equality, William L. Peek declared: "Us white men will not tolerate it, and the negroes don't want it." Time and again, Populists stressed this point. "Miscegenation," wrote Tom Watson, "is further off (thank God) than ever."[2]

---

1. *Report of the Comptroller-General, 1892–93*, p. 102; C. Vann Woodward, *The Strange Career of Jim Crow* (2nd ed., rev.; London, 1966), 53–60; George L. Jones, "William H. Felton and the Independent Democratic Movement in Georgia, 1870–1890" (Ph.D. dissertation, University of Georgia, 1971), 314.
2. Atlanta *Constitution*, August 23, 1892; Thomas E. Watson, "The Negro Question in the South," *Arena*, XXXV (1892), 540–50.

On other issues the Populists were willing to compromise. Their demand for an end to convict lease was enthusiastically supported by blacks. After the Civil War, Georgia had little money to spend on prisons, and so it leased its convicts to mining companies owned by Joseph E. Brown, John B. Gordon, and others. Deep beneath the earth, the prisoners lived in a world of dimly lit shafts, savage guards, and crushing toil. Cave-ins and gas took their toll, and many convicts never lived to see freedom. The shabbiest corruption preyed upon this form of legalized slavery. To maintain their labor supply, mine owners encouraged judges to pump as many men as possible into the system. Some citizens believed that a congressional seat was Judge John W. Maddox's reward for sending hundreds of convicts to the mines. Judge Charles L. Bartlett was celebrated for his lengthy sentences to blacks. Bartlett gave one man a sentence of fifteen years for the theft of some milk; a twelve-year-old boy received twelve years for stealing a horse he wanted to ride. Bartlett became a congressman in 1892. Like blacks, many white people also hated convict lease. Humanitarians pointed out that the work required of prisoners was brutal and dangerous. Farmers argued that prisoners should labor on Georgia's rut-filled roads, which so often broke axles and wrecked farm wagons. Others disliked the idea of black criminals taking the jobs of white miners.[3]

Besides their position on convict lease, the Populists were willing to make other concessions to blacks. They demanded the secret ballot and honest elections that were free from intimidation and said this could be done by instituting the secret ballot. They reminded blacks that the predicament of farmers was the same regardless of race; therefore, Populist reforms would help them all. Finally, the third party added one more spice to the brew it offered the black man—representation in Populist councils. Out of about 150 delegates at the 1892 state convention, 2 were black. In the First District, the Populist nominating convention likewise

3. For a discussion of the convict-lease system in Georgia, see Alton DuMar Jones, "Progressivism in Georgia, 1898–1918" (Ph.D. dissertation, Emory University, 1963), 12–40; Clarence A. Bacote, "Negro Proscriptions, Protests, and Proposed Solutions in Georgia, 1886–1908," *Journal of Southern History*, XXV (1959), 483–86; Robert Derrill, "Joseph E. Brown and the Convict Lease System," *Georgia Historical Quarterly*, XLIV (1960), 399–410. Derrill maintains that Joseph E. Brown's treatment of prisoners was for the most part humane.

included a black delegate, who was later appointed to the campaign committee.[4] Although hardly monumental concessions, these acts gave credence to the notion that the Populists were interested in the problems and opinions of former slaves.

On the local level, some Populists also offered enticements. Occasionally black orators were invited to speak from the same platform with whites. One district convention unanimously passed a resolution condemning lynch law. In a few places third-party members promised that if victorious they would put blacks on juries, an alluring prospect because of the salary of two dollars a day. Some third-party men seemed especially sensitive to the feelings of blacks. "The *Chronicle* said I shook hands with negro men, women, and children at Sparta," Tom Watson declared. "I say yes I did it, and have no apologies to make."[5] And sometimes Populist editorials must have astounded blacks with their perceptive and unvarnished view of southern life:

> The argument against the independent
> political movement in the South may be boiled
> down into one word—NIGGER!
> Fatal word!
> Why, for thirty years before our war,
> did the North and South hate each other?
> NIGGER.
> What brought disunion and war?
> NIGGER.
> With what did Abraham Lincoln break
> the backbone of the Confederacy?
> NIGGER.
> What impeded reconstruction?
> NIGGER.
> How did the Republicans rule the South
> for years after Appomattox?
> NIGGER.
> What has kept the South in a cast iron
> straight jacket?
> NIGGER.
> What will be the slogan of our old politicians
> until Gabriel calls them home?
> NIGGER.

4. Woodward, *Tom Watson*, 220; Atlanta *Constitution*, August 11, 1892.
5. Atlanta *Constitution*, August 11, 1892; Macon *Telegraph*, September 21, 27, 1892; Augusta *Chronicle*, October 2, 1892.

> Pious Southern people never dreaded death
> so much as they do now. They fear that when
> they knock at the pearly gates of the New Jerusalem
> St. Peter will peep through the key-hole and say:
> "You can't come in."
> "Why?"
> "NIGGER!"[6]

Yet some blacks remained unimpressed with third-party promises. They remembered that many Populists were poor whites, their traditional enemy since slavery. They were likewise suspicious of the People's party support of the honest ballot. A resolution attached to the Populist national platform condemned federal supervision of elections, one of the few devices that had given the black man political power in the South. Instead, third-party members called for the secret ballot. But most Georgia blacks were illiterate and thus could not read the ballot, let alone fill it out. When Populists answered that they would pass laws allowing officials at the polls to help illiterates vote, blacks became even more wary. Georgia election officials were notoriously corrupt, were largely white, and were the last people they wanted help from when voting. Nevertheless, the majority of Republican leaders, white and black, favored some form of assistance to the Populists. It came on August 11, 1892, when their state convention decided not to nominate a state ticket. Instead, the convention advised party members to vote for the Republican presidential candidate, Benjamin Harrison, and to follow their consciences in the gubernatorial contest. With one exception the Republican congressional nominating conventions did the same. Later Alfred Buck, the most influential white Republican in the state, endorsed William L. Peek.[7]

Democrats constantly asserted that a formal union existed between the Republicans and the Populists. They made the farfetched charge that the national Republican party was sending the People's party vast sums of money to defeat the Democrats in one of their strongholds. The Populist campaign was such a threadbare effort—donations were usually in small

---

6. *People's Party Paper*, August 26, 1892.
7. Hicks, *Populist Revolt*, 443; Atlanta *Constitution*, August 12, 1892; Olive Hall Shadgett, *The Republican Party in Georgia from Reconstruction through 1900* (Athens, 1964), 71; Diamond (ed.), *Guide to U.S. Elections*, 667; Atlanta *Journal*, September 27, 1892.

change—that it was unlikely to have obtained much Republican aid. In October, however, a schoolgirl in Thomson noticed Tom Watson tear up a letter and throw it into the street. She retrieved the scraps, pieced them together, and showed the results to her father, who was a Democrat. When published, the letter caused a sensation. The sender was D. N. Sanders, the secretary of the *People's Party Paper*. Sanders reported to Watson that the newspaper had been short of funds and that he had paid a freight bill with cash borrowed from Alfred Buck. Although the letter made it clear that Watson knew nothing about the deal, the damage had been done.[8] Gleefully, the Democratic press proclaimed that Republican money was indeed helping the Populists. This letter, however, was the only evidence of aid they ever produced.

The Democrats also realized the importance of the former slaves and were quietly at work trying to entice them to their party. They, not the third-party men, first employed black speakers in Tom Watson's district.[9] But the Democrats found other ways to show their regard for blacks. During his first administration, William J. Northen used his influence to increase appropriations for black schools. More important, he seemed to have an honest hatred of lynchings, doing everything he could to prevent them (a risky policy in Georgia, which in 1892 had more lynchings than any other state in the nation). On one occasion he used his personal funds to have a black man, who was accused of rape, rushed out of the hands of a mob to the relative safety of Atlanta. In May, 1892, a triple lynching in Clarksville again brought forth his wrath. "The outrage committed upon the lives of these defenseless men is absolutely without excuse or palliation," he said publicly, and he offered a $200 reward for the arrest of the culprits. A few months later, when masked riders murdered a black man in Dalton, an angry Northen went before the legislature demanding that any sheriff who failed to protect his prisoners be expelled from office, fined, and imprisoned. He also proposed that prisoners or their relatives have the right to sue their county if they suffered damages at the hands of mobs. Finally, Northen warned that if necessary he would order out the militia to disperse mobs. Although

8. Augusta *Chronicle*, October 1, 1892, quoted in Sparta *Ishmaelite*, October 7, 1892; Atlanta *Constitution*, February 3, October 17, 1892; Scrapbook 2, p. 169, Northen Papers.
9. *Tom Watson's Magazine*, September 1906, p. 344.

there were limits to his tolerance (as governor, he had favored a bill making it illegal to chain a white convict to a black convict), many Georgia Republicans planned to reward him with their votes. Among them was Bishop Henry M. Turner, the most respected black clergyman in the state.[10]

Blacks had other reasons for objecting to the third party. William L. Peek seemed to possess little friendship for them, and few could forget his slave bill. James Barrett, the People's candidate for commissioner of agriculture, had earlier declared that the more education the former slaves received, the more dangerous they became. Barrett had advised that, if it was necessary to instruct them, the teachers should be white "in order to protect white society." Tom Watson's record also left unanswered questions. While a member of the legislature he had worked to reduce funds for black schools, and on a technicality he had opposed a black man's obtaining a contested seat, even though the black had received more votes than his white opponent. Finally, in 1883, Watson voted for the Tutt bill, an early version of the Peek slave bill.[11] But blacks feared not only Populist leaders. Many had a visceral dread of poor whites —the people whom they believed were most responsible for lynchings in the South. W. A. Pledger, a prominent black Republican, stoutly objected to a union between his people and the Populists: "The men who have lynched the colored people in the past; the men who have shot and robbed the colored people; the men who precipitated the 'Camilla riot' years ago and who marshalled the red shirter and night riders are now the followers and shouters of Peek and his crowd." Pledger pleaded with blacks to vote for Northen, the man who had "done all in his official power to keep these Third partyites from lynching my people."[12]

10. For Northen's record on race relations, see Bonner, "Gubernatorial Career of W. J. Northen"; Woodward, *Tom Watson*, 221; Sparta *Ishmaelite*, May 27, 1892; Atlanta *Constitution*, May 22, 1892; Atlanta *Journal*, October 27, 1892; Scrapbook 2, p. 205, Northen Papers.

11. Clarence Albert Bacote, "The Negro in Georgia Politics, 1880–1908" (Ph.D. dissertation, University of Chicago, 1955), 162; Woodward, *Tom Watson*, 204; Atlanta *Journal*, August 18, 30, 1892; Atlanta *Constitution*, August 30, 1892; see also Lawrence J. Friedman, *The White Savage: Racial Fantasies in the Postbellum South* (Englewood Cliffs, 1970); Charles Crowe, "Tom Watson, Populists, and Blacks Reconsidered," *Journal of Negro History*, LX (1970), 99–116; Bruce Palmer, *"Man Over Money": The Southern Populist Critique of American Capitalism* (Chapel Hill, 1980), 56–57, 60.

12. Sparta *Ishmaelite*, September 9, 1892. During the state election of 1868, about three

On the local level blacks were also suspicious. The white citizens of Tom Watson's McDuffie County had always been hostile to the former slaves. Intimidation was so great that blacks could never hold a political meeting or cast a ballot for any local candidate who was not a Democrat. The Ku Klux Klan was active as late as 1884.[13] When the Populists came to power, all this changed. Abruptly, the former slaves were allowed to vote, a demonstration, the wool-hat boys argued, of their respect for the black man and his rights. They neglected to point out that some of the men who disfranchised McDuffie blacks in the 1870s and 1880s became Populists in the 1890s.[14] It was unlikely that these public officials suddenly became more tolerant of black voters. Instead, they were faced with the classic Populist dilemma: because the third party would split the white vote, they were forced to appeal to blacks.

White Populists insisted that the blacks' fears were groundless, that they bore them no malice. As election day approached, however, the cheerful grin of the wool-hat boy occasionally changed, and a darker, sometimes even ghastly, visage appeared. What were blacks to make of one Populist's stand against lynch mobs that appeared in the Carnesville *Enterprise*: "Now as to lynching I am opposed to it except in extreme cases. I never was in but one. . . ."?[15]

Many blacks believed the Populists exposed their true racial feelings on October 23, 1892. Late that evening 150 riders, all wearing masks, galloped into Dalton, Georgia. Quietly they turned out the street lamps as they passed through the darkened streets. After finding the marshal, they put a gun to his head and ordered him to take them to the home of a black man named Tom Harlan. There, by the light of flaring torches, they dragged Harlan and his wife from bed and ferociously beat them until they were nearly dead. Then the men rode to the house of Jack Wil-

---

hundred black Republicans attended a political rally in Camilla, Georgia. A race riot erupted in which at least nine blacks were killed and twenty-five wounded (Alan Conway, *The Reconstruction of Georgia* [Minneapolis, 1966], 168–71).

13. See U.S. Congress, House, *Watson vs. Black*, 707, 683, 696.

14. The McDuffie Populists won the election of 1893 and filled all county offices. Most of these officials had served in the same positions for at least a decade. See W. C. McCommons and Clara Stovall, "History of McDuffie County, 1870–1933," 81, typescript in Georgia Department of Archives and History, Atlanta.

15. Carnesville *Enterprise*, September 30, 1892.

son, another black. When they broke down his door, Wilson resisted and was shot through the head and heart. He died instantly. More homes of black people were visited, but their inhabitants heard the riders coming and fled. Having finished their work, the masked men galloped into the night, firing their pistols and waving torches.

No one ever discovered who the riders were or the reason for their crimes. But Dalton Democrats believed they knew and raised a $1,000 reward. Both Wilson and Harlan had voted Democratic in the October election.[16]

No one was able to prove unequivocally that Populists had murdered Jack Wilson and beaten Tom Harlan and his wife. But there were circumstantial reasons to think that they had. In other parts of the state Populists had employed similar methods. The sworn testimony of William Oxford of Jefferson County at the contested election hearings between Watson and Black in 1896 shed light on the matter.

Q. What is your politics?
A. I am nothing.
Q. Did you not formerly belong to the People's Party?
A. Yes sir.
Q. How long did you belong to the People's Party?
A. Since it started in 1892.
Q. For whom did you vote for Congress in 1892, 1894, and 1895?
A. I voted for Watson.
Q. What time did you quit the People's Party?
A. Last fall [1895].
Q. State what incidents of attempted and actual intimidation by the Populists you know of that occurred in any of the elections, both State and Federal, in 1892, and what since then up to the present time.
A. From that time up to now I have been in a good many meetings with the Populists, and the most they did was to try to keep negroes from coming to Louisville [Jefferson County] to vote. They tried to do this by threatening to whip them and do a heap of things to them if they didn't vote for Watson.
Q. Do you know anything about Calvin Joiner [a black man who had supported the Democrats] being whipped by the Populists to keep him away from the polls unless he would go and vote their way?
A. Yes, sir.

16. Atlanta *Journal*, October 24, 1892; Macon *Telegraph*, October 26, 1892; Dawson *News*, November 2, 1892.

Q. Who whipped Calvin Joiner?
A. I did.
Q. Do you know of any other acts of violence the Populists did to scare the
    negroes and keep them away from the polls?
A. They organized and rode everywhere in the county at night in order to
    scare them and keep them away.
Q. How did they arrange these squads to ride over the county?
A. There were men appointed in each district to select a squad of men to
    ride around at night and to scare the negroes either into voting for Wat-
    son or staying away from the polls altogether.
Q. These riders who went around among the negroes—didn't they threaten
    the negroes with what they might do unless they voted for Watson or did
    not vote at all?
A. They would go to the head or leading Democratic negroes in the districts
    and threaten to kill them if they didn't vote for Watson or stay away from
    the polls, and they threatened to whip all the negroes if they didn't vote
    for Watson or stay away from the polls. That was the rule of the club that
    I was a member of, and I suppose the other clubs did the same.
Q. Did you ever whip any negro before you did Calvin?
A. Yes, sir; I have whipped a heap of them. I whipped them before I became
    a Populist and since, too.
Q. Did you ever kill a negro?
A. Yes, sir; about twenty years ago. It was in self-defense.
Q. Haven't you killed more than one negro?
A. I decline to answer.[17]

Oxford explained not only the methods but also the motive of Populist
terrorism. In many places Populists wanted blacks to vote only if they
intended to support the third party. Yet Oxford's testimony did not describe how far Populists would go to intimidate the black man. M. G.
Gamble, a Democrat from Jefferson County, swore under oath that when
he rode to the polls on election day, the Populists there were carrying
sticks and wearing red caps—the symbol of the old Ku Klux Klan of
Reconstruction.[18] Another Democrat from the same county said that the
night before the October contest, third-party men had ridden about the
countryside dressed in "red shirts and red caps." Stopping at one planta-

17. U.S. Congress, House, *Watson vs. Black*, 285–87. In the interest of clarity, the order in which the questions were asked has been somewhat rearranged.
18. For the activities of the Ku Klux Klan in the Augusta region during Reconstruction, see Alfred B. Williams, *Hampton and His Red Shirts: South Carolina's Deliverance in
1876* (Charleston, 1935), 105, 133; Allen W. Trelease, *White Terror: The Ku Klux Klan Conspiracy and Southern Reconstruction* (New York, 1971), 34; Francis Butler Simkins, *Pitchfork
Ben Tillman, South Carolinian* (Baton Rouge, 1944), 64–65.

tion, they fired pistols and threatened black tenants with murder if they voted against Watson. The previous night, a black man from the same plantation was supposedly shot at by Populists wearing red caps. Pleasant Stovall, the Democratic editor of the Savannah *Press*, toured the Tenth District shortly before the congressional election and reported that in places third-party threats were forcing blacks to vote for the Populist party. Stovall asked Judge William Gibson of Warrenton what was afoot. The judge declared that it was a "union between the blacks and the kuklux; and that the lawless element is holding the negro in line at the muzzle of a gun." [19]

Similar coercion broke out in Screven County. A black man who had helped in the Democratic campaign received a letter from the "Unknown Club," cautioning him not to take bribes from "lawyers or merchants with Wall Street money." The letter warned that if he ever again aided the Democrats, he would have his "Goddamned brains shot out." In Briar Creek, C. N. Robinson, a black teacher who had given speeches endorsing Governor Northen, bitterly wrote that Populist threats had compelled him to leave his position and flee for his life. [20]

There can be no doubt that Georgia Populists used terror and intimidation to influence state elections. The cry for an honest ballot was sincere up to a point—as long as the black man voted for the third party, white Populists demanded that his ballot be counted. Otherwise, they did not, and in many places they tried to keep him from the polls—sometimes by means of the Ku Klux Klan. This was especially true in the "terrible" Tenth. There black people realized the consequences of voting or even speaking against the Populists. During the Watson-Black contested election hearing, one black refused to answer a question about a third-party man. When asked the reason, he said that he feared the Populists "after dark." [21]

It was not altogether surprising that some Populists resorted to the regalia and methods of the Ku Klux Klan. The old Klan of Reconstruction had been strong in northwestern Georgia and the area that later became

19. Augusta *Chronicle*, October 22, 1892; U.S. Congress, House, *Watson vs. Black*, 283–85; Sparta *Ishmaelite*, October 21, 1892.

20. Augusta *Chronicle*, October 29, 1892; Sparta *Ishmaelite*, September 16, 1892.

21. U.S. Congress, House, *Watson vs. Black*, 282.

the Tenth Congressional District. The crimes in the latter region were especially heinous. Among other horrors, the Invisible Empire was guilty of murder, rape, bludgeoning, ear cropping, and castration. Warren County led the state in atrocities; on one occasion, local Klansmen killed a black man by whipping him nine hundred times with saddle stirrups. The county became so lawless that in May, 1869, the military commander of Georgia, General Alfred H. Terry, dispatched four companies of troops to Warrenton. Lacking enough men to patrol the entire state, Terry usually ordered soldiers only to those places where the Klan was most active. Eventually, he declared Warren, Columbia, Lincoln, Wilkes, Taliaferro, Glascock, and Oglethorpe counties military subdistricts and occupied them with federal troops. With the exception of Oglethorpe, these counties represented the heartland of latter-day Populism. The other center of Klan power, northwestern Georgia, was also a center of Populist strength, especially during the elections of 1894 and 1896.[22]

The Klan died quickly once the Democrats had regained control of the legislature in 1870.[23] Nevertheless, its memory remained, and it is not difficult to understand why Populists in Jefferson County, and perhaps those around Dalton, revived the old brotherhood, making it an arm of their local organizations. These appear to have been the only places where Populists employed the Klan. But it was not, as in the case of Screven County, the only place where they employed terror, which usually came without the formality of masks, red shirts, and red caps.

Finally, what of that famous day in Thomson, when Tom Watson protected the black minister, Seb Doyle, and hundreds of poor whites galloped to the rescue? How can that response be reconciled with the Populists who, in the same locale, rode the countryside at night terrorizing black people? The answer is fairly simple. The farmers rushed to Thomson to save Watson, not Doyle. The word that went out into the country was that Watson had been murdered, or at least was in danger. It is cer-

22. Trelease, *White Terror*, 226–42, 318–35; U.S. Congress, House, *Testimony Taken by the Joint Select Committee to Inquire into the Condition of Affairs in the late Insurrectionary States: Georgia*, 42nd Cong., 2nd Sess., 1871–72.
23. Trelease, *White Terror*, 242. For an account of Ku Klux Klan activities outside the Tenth District, see Conway, *Reconstruction of Georgia*, 171–81.

tain that some farmers did not know of Doyle's involvement until after they reached Thomson. The Democratic editor of the Lincolnton *News*, when describing the moment word reached his town, said only that Watson was supposedly in danger and made no mention of Doyle. Only when the Lincolnton Populists returned did the press mention the black minister. But the clearest reason for the incident came during the contested election hearings. "The rumor was that they went to Thomson . . . to protect the negro Doyle, was it not?" Watson's lawyer asked a witness from Lincolnton. "No sir; the rumor was that the [Democratic] mob was trying to mob Mr. Watson." And Watson's answers during the same hearings show that other towns besides Lincolnton had received this report. "They came over to Thomson . . . greatly excited," Watson testified, "because news had reached Lincolnton that I had been killed. Numbers of men came in from Columbia, Warren, and perhaps other counties on account of the same rumor." [24]

White Populists did indeed feel sympathy for Doyle. For weeks he had campaigned for the third party at considerable personal risk. Once the farmers were in Thomson, they were willing to protect him as well as Watson. It is doubtful, however, that they would have ridden to save only the black minister. About a week before the Thomson incident, a white man nearly killed Doyle in Sparta. And on that day, no one rode to the rescue. [25]

Whatever the case, the Thomson affair demonstrated that in the Populist mind there were two kinds of blacks: those who supported the third party and those who did not. But only the former—the "good" blacks—deserved protection and free and unintimidated access to the ballot. Besides an end to the convict-lease system and token representation at a few Populist meetings, this was the only concession the Georgia People's party offered the former slaves in 1892. For the black man at least, this was the meaning of the third-party motto, "Equal rights for all, special privileges for none."

Thus William L. Peek's charge that blacks did not fully support the

24. U.S. Congress, House, *Watson vs. Black*, 589–90, 681; Dawson *News*, November 2, 1892.

25. Macon *Telegraph*, October 23–26, 1892; *People's Party Paper*, October 28, 1892: Atlanta *Journal*, August 4, 1906; U.S. Congress, House, *Watson vs. Black*, *passim*.

Populist Party was true. Peek assumed that most of the forty-eight thousand Republicans who voted for Harrison in the presidential election should have favored him in the gubernatorial contest.[26] He lost the support of twenty-three thousand of these voters. Because Northen gained only six or seven thousand, roughly fifteen thousand blacks refused to vote for either candidate—an extraordinary demonstration of their distrust of both parties.

Peek believed that at most twenty-five thousand blacks (or roughly 50 percent of those who voted) supported him. In reality the figure was probably lower—perhaps as little as ten thousand. One historian has recently estimated that Peek received only about 20 percent.[27] Those blacks who favored the Populists did so for a number of reasons. Government ownership of the railroads, the subtreasury plan, and inflation were issues that were color-blind. The Populists, moreover, advocated an end to the convict-lease system and had permitted two blacks to attend their state convention—both unheard-of in Georgia except within the Republican party. Still, most blacks must have supported Populism with trepidation, realizing that they were engaging in a risky union. Just a few months earlier, many of those with whom they were allying had been their mortal enemies—the men who had made Georgia the lynching capital of the nation. It was a strange alliance, and it would bear strange fruit.

26. For a comparison of the results of the presidential and gubernatorial elections, see Diamond (ed.), *Guide to U.S. Elections*, 279; for the results of the gubernatorial contest, see *Georgia House Journal*, October 27, 1892, p. 5.

27. J. Morgan Kousser, *The Shaping of Southern Politics: Suffrage Restriction and the Establishment of the One-Party South, 1880–1910* (New Haven, 1974), 215; see also, Gerald H. Gaither, *Blacks and the Populist Revolt: Ballots and Bigotry in the "New South"* (University, Ala., 1977).

VI

Warriors of the Watson War

In the years that followed, Democrats sometimes referred to the election of 1892 as the "Watson War." Although they had won the conflict with ease, many had been troubled by their opponents. Who were these mutinous farmers? Where did they come from? What did they want? Indeed, what was the nature of this strange uprising? They noticed that Populism seemed to have a hard inner strength, and once a man embraced the cause his enthusiasm frequently spilled onto his wife, his children, and his neighbors. A nearly evangelical passion stirred Populist rallies. "A dose of people's party . . . [is] about as good as to get religion," one man exulted. Third-party meetings opened with a prayer and closed with a doxology. Populists referred to each other as "Brother" and "Sister." Audiences answered speeches with "Amens." Sometimes a camp-meeting atmosphere took hold of their gatherings. Many members believed their cause and that of the Almighty were the same. The Carnesville *Enterprise* challenged anybody to show "an item in . . . the third party declaration of purposes that is not founded upon the teachings of Holy Writ."[1]

Such fervor illustrated the desperation of farmers. Populism offered them a way to economic salvation. It would right old political wrongs, defend the godly against the corrupt. Because most ministers apparently remained Democrats, some wool-hat boys believed their preachers had become stooges of the enemy. Thus alienated from formal religion, they perhaps found spiritual solace in their party. One item that appeared in a Populist newspaper must have struck Democrats as sheer blasphemy:

1. U.S. Congress, House, *Watson vs. Black*, 584; Atlanta *Constitution*, July 19, 1892; Carnesville *Enterprise*, December 11, 1891.

```
                 W
To this     F I E L D      still
  cross        A            we
               V          cling²
               E
               R
```

But the religious zeal that apparently inspired Populism did not go to extremes. Indeed, third-party gatherings were occasionally rather formal affairs. The men would hire a hall, distribute flyers, and build a platform. Their wives would prepare a supper and decorate the podium with flowers. Women, children, and blacks were always welcome at such gatherings, although the former slaves were required to sit in their own section during the speaking and dinner. Almost invariably, newspapers remarked about the dignity and cheerfulness of such occasions. Most third-party rallies, however, were less formal, with perhaps the neighborhood school serving as the meeting place. If there was not enough money to hire a band, a local fiddler might play. The *Alliance and Labor Songster* provided many of the third-party numbers. The most popular were "Dixie" and "Good-bye, Old Party, Good-bye." The latter became the Populist "Marseillaise," and one Georgian observed that when sung it set "the woods on fire and you [could] . . . almost see Populism dropping off the trees and smell it in the air."[3] One stanza in particular captured the anger and pathos of the wool-hat boys:

> I was raised up in the kind of school,
>   Good-bye, old party, good-bye.
> That taught to bow to money rule,
>   Good-bye, old party, good-bye.
> And it made of me a "Georgia fool,"
>   Good-bye, old party, good-bye.
> When they found I was a willing tool,
>   Good-bye, old party, good-bye.[4]

A few third-party rallies turned into political camp meetings. The largest was held at Alpharetta. From fifty miles around thousands came,

2. Carnesville *Enterprise*, October 21, 1892.
3. *People's Party Paper*, June 19, 1896.
4. "Good-bye, Old Party, Good-bye," was written by C. S. White and sung to the tune of "Good-bye, My Love, Good-bye." As originally composed, the song spoke of a "Kansas

turning the town into a "gigantic gypsy camp." Horses, mules, oxen, dogs, wagons, carts, and people overran the camp grounds. Beneath the searing August sun orators preached the gospel of Populism, while their listeners drank apple cider and ate fried chicken and ice cream. There was a sideshow where people might have their pictures taken or watch a man swallow needles. A dubious-looking fellow, who carried his instruments in his pockets, was ready to extract teeth painlessly.[5]

But not all Populist meetings were such merry events. The farmer had to spend his days in the field, so it was frequently necessary to hold outdoor rallies at night. Because these affairs sometimes turned ugly, women were almost never invited. The danger was often so great that a prudent man generally slipped his pistol into his pocket before attending. Without the presence of ladies, the speeches were likely to become incensed and profane. Drunks or Democrats might interrupt the speakers, and many an evening ended with shootings and fisticuffs. A black man described one such rally in Jefferson County: "They whooped and hallooed until what few Populists were there about scared out. . . . There was a great deal of shooting going on part of the time. . . . I stayed close to my buggy; my horse was scary. . . . [One man] . . . seemed under the influence of a good deal of liquor and staggered around there inquiring for me. . . . [He] had a little old pistol in his hand. . . . Finally he throwed up his right hand and come near shooting me and my horse, too, and me talking to him, trying to quiet him, begging him not to do that way."[6]

Election day was almost always dangerous. Coercion was sometimes overt—a man might be beaten if he voted the wrong way. But sometimes it was more subtle. Third-party men complained that Democrats often compelled black tenants to vote for the Democratic ticket, a practice called "voting my boys." Thus a man with twenty tenants could cast twenty-one votes for the candidate of his choice. But many Populist landlords were also guilty of such chicanery. The evening before the election, they assembled their hands and treated them to cigars, cheap whiskey,

---

fool." Georgians, however, were quick to change the words to fit their own situation. See Leopold Vincent (ed.), *The Alliance and Labor Songster* (1891; rpr. New York, 1975), 60.

5. Atlanta *Journal*, August 13, 1896.
6. U.S. Congress, House, *Watson vs. Black*, 750.

and a barbecue. Soon everyone was roaring drunk, and by morning few were in any condition to cause trouble. They climbed or were loaded into wagons that took them to the polls. The landlord then kept watch to make certain that all his ballots were counted. Afterward his voters staggered back to the wagons and were driven to another polling place.

Since the Democrats were equally guilty, few third-party planters felt embarrassed by such activities. "Yes, sir I carried them off to have them vote my way," a Douglas County Populist said of his tenants after one election. "I wanted them to vote my ticket. I did not know but what they might vote the other ticket." Thus he compelled his renters to cast ballots for G. W. Burnett, the third-party candidate for the legislature. During the same contest, other Populists were working for Burnett, including one Bob Brown. As the Lithia Springs marshal later testified:

> The night before the election I was at the Chestnut and Chappell Hill Districts. I saw men taking negro voters into their wagons that night. I met them just below Chappell Hill going South. I guess there was five or six wagons and about 15 buggies. They were full of negroes. They all seemed like they were pretty full, talking loud, singing, hollering and whooping. . . . I heard some one of them holler, come on boys let's take them away from here and get them away from them Democrats. They come running down the road hollering and whooping and yelling at the top of their voices and my horse got frightened at the fuss and I drove him out to one side to let them pass. One wagon passed by and I saw [that] . . . Bob Brown . . . had a pistol in his hands waving it around and [he] said to the negroes, holler for Burnett you sons of bitches you.[7]

But Populism was more than a political movement. It also possessed a social life, which often influenced day-to-day events. In Augusta one could patronize the People's Restaurant, the People's Drug Store, and the Tom Watson Photograph Gallery, cheer for the Wool Hats, a local baseball team, or bet on Lucy, "a little Third-party mare," when she raced a "thoroughbred Democrat" from Henry County. The memberships of some churches were almost exclusively Populist.[8] The move-

---

7. "G. W. Burnett vs. Columbus Blair, T. R. Whitley vs. Bion Williams, Contested Election Cases, [Douglas County], 1894," 45, 170–71, typescript in Georgia Department of Archives and History, Atlanta.
    8. Gracewood *Wool Hat*, June 27, November 18, 1893; McDonough *Henry County Weekly*, May 12, 1893.

ment even inspired some hard-bitten farmers to try their hands at verse. If not always elegant, their poems suggested some of the passion and hero worship common to the third-party cause. As one backwoods bard sang:

> Georgia is coming hear her speak,
> For her Watson, and her Peek;
> One in Congress, one in State,
> Our enemies will be too late.
>
> . . . .
>
> We're coming coming, with our host
> Ellington and, Branch and Post;
> With Mrs. Post, our brilliant sister;
> And Bro. Walker, the wiper-twister.[9]

And a poem entitled "Raven Revisited" suggested that the farmer could also poke fun at himself and his troubles:

> Then I met an aged granger
> Smelling of the farm and manger,
> And I said "your vote, o stranger!"
> Quoth the farmer "'never more'!"[10]

Populism even influenced the lives of youngsters. One third-party newspaper included a children's page and received letters from "Tom Watson Country Boy" and "Two Wool Hat Boys and One Wool Hat Girl." "A Strong Tom Watson Girl" wrote that her one-year-old brother raced around the house shouting, "Hurrah for Tom Watson!"[11]

As these children demonstrated, Populism was more than a political movement. Often it determined what a family read, where it did business, who its friends were, where it worshiped, and even the songs it sang. One historian has argued that Populism created a "movement culture" that helped sustain the party in its darkest hours.[12] Such a culture was vital after the crushing defeat of 1892. Third-party newspapers,

9. Carnesville *Enterprise*, July 29, 1892. "Bro. Walker" was S. A. Walker, a well-known Alliance lecturer, Populist, and legislator.
10. Gracewood *Wool Hat*, December 10, 1892.
11. *Ibid.*, August 26, September 23, 1893.
12. Goodwyn, *Democratic Promise*, 47–51, 58–60, 71–82, 85–86, 91–94, 117–20, and *passim*.

gatherings, and tunes created confidence in the midst of calamity. Perhaps more than anything, this spirit kept the party alive for its next struggle two years later.

The election of 1892 had been a disaster for Georgia Populism. For the first time, however, party leaders possessed some fairly reliable information about their followers and opponents. They probably found it easier to say who had failed to become Populists. Counties in which the third party was strongest rarely had an earlier tradition of electing independents. Nor were Populists those who were especially cowed by the fear of black rule. Although one historian has asserted that the Georgia third party prospered where there were few blacks (and consequently less dread of a black threat in the balance of power), the evidence fails to bear out this assertion.[13] Of the nineteen counties that the third party usually captured in 1892 and afterward, ten had more black residents than white.[14] And in the heartland of Georgia Populism, the Tenth Congressional District, only one Populist county out of nine had a white majority (see map on page xii). The argument that the Farmers' Alliance was the forerunner of Populism was undoubtedly true. But as we have seen, the influence of the order can be overstated. The Alliance had its main strength in the upper Piedmont, along the Chattahoochee River south of Columbus, and in the wiregrass country. With few exceptions, Populism fared poorly in these regions. Of the nine counties with more than a thousand Alliance members in 1890, only three gave consistent support to the third party.[15]

But population statistics and Alliance background failed to answer the question: Who were the Populists? Although the Tenth District was the center of third-party strength, there were other pockets of support. At-

13. Arnett, *Populist Movement in Georgia*, 33, and the unnumbered page facing page 184.

14. For the black-white population figures for these counties, see U.S. Department of Interior, *Compendium of the Eleventh Census, 1890*. For a more detailed discussion of black-white population ratios of the Populist party, see Barton C. Shaw, "The Wool-Hat Boys: A History of the Populist Party in Georgia, 1892 to 1910" (Ph.D. dissertation, Emory University, 1979), 127, n.20.

15. McMath, "Mobilizing Agrarian Discontent"; Atlanta *Constitution*, August 19, 1890.

lanta was nearly ringed by counties that voted at least once for important third-party candidates. There was also some Populist strength close to Columbus. Yet the wool-hat boys were unable to recruit much support in the cities, suggesting a possible town-country antagonism.

Fruit growers, both in and out of the Tenth District, were also drawn to Populism and provided the movement with some of its most able leaders, including Mell Branch, Clarence Ellington, and Tom Watson. In addition, James L. Sibley, John A. Sibley, John D. Cunningham, and John P. Fort were engaged in horticulture. The last two were especially successful. Cunningham owned six farms and 110,000 fruit trees and would shortly be elected president of the American Fruit Growers Association. Fort, who was one of Georgia's most innovative growers, had orchards across the state and employed about 150 tenants.[16] These men were attracted to Populism by its railroad plank. Because their product was perishable, they were at the mercy of the railroads, which often increased freight rates just as the fruit crop was being harvested. Unfortunately for the Populists, horticulture was still in its infancy in Georgia and thus failed to provide them with a large block of voters. Some white Republicans also became Populists. Although their number was not great, like the fruit growers they supplied the movement with some leaders. Charles Post, John D. Cunningham, Thaddeus Pickett, Yancey Carter, and Carey Thornton had earlier been members of the Grand Old Party.

County and local election returns helped Populists learn more about their rank and file. Third-party men seldom resided in towns and cities. Instead, they lived in the countryside, frequently near the edge of a county and usually miles from the county seat. Most were too far removed to become involved in local affairs but not too far to escape the influence of the town lawyer or the crossroads merchant. In such districts old fears and resentments sometimes lingered from earlier political strug-

16. John D. Cunningham to William H. Felton, November 8, 1894, Box 1, in Rebecca Latimer Felton Papers, Manuscripts Division, University of Georgia Library, Athens; Range, *Century of Georgia Agriculture*, 83, 111, 112. For additional information about Fort and his family, see Box 2, Tomlinson Fort Papers, Special Collections, Emory University Library.

gles. In the 1870s and 1880s county politics pitted the big farmer against the little farmer, the townsman against the countryman. Issues concerning fences, game, dogs, town courts, jury selection, and alcohol created sharp political battles.[17] The small farmer often lost these fights, and many believed they had been closed out of politics. In the Tenth District farmers groused about the "Augusta ring"; in Washington County they cursed the "Sandersville clique." Such locales were frequently ripe for Populism.

What had been the lot of rank-and-file Populists in the 1880s? The third party apparently kept no official membership rolls. In a few instances, however, unofficial but accurate records have survived. In 1892 a local newspaper printed the names of twenty-two Populists living in Crawford County; in the same year, another newspaper listed 113 Washington County Populists. It is likely that most of these men were farmers or townsmen with agricultural interests, such as landowning lawyers or physicians. Therefore, they would have been surveyed by the *Georgia State Gazetteer, Business and Planters Directory*, which in 1886 used the tax digests to classify the wealth of farmers having property valued at more than $500. This source provides a rough measure of the worth and status of these men. In 1880, 55.1 percent of Georgia's farmers worked their own land; this figure dropped to 47.2 percent in Crawford County and to 37.1 percent in Washington. Nevertheless, scores of well-to-do growers resided in both areas. Yet the Crawford list included just twelve men (54.5 percent) worth more than $500. None were planters, and only two were worth from $3,000 to $5,000. The Washington list contains the names of eighteen farmers (15.9 percent) who were worth more than $500. Of these, two were planters valued at from $10,000 to $20,000 and eight fell into the $2,000 to $5,000 range. In both counties, most of those worth more than $500 were probably yeomen. The rest (45.4 percent in

17. For examples of the rural strength and urban weakness of the third party on the local level, see the results of various militia district elections in the following counties: Decatur (Bainbridge *Democrat*, November 19, 1892; November 8, 1894), Henry (McDonough *Henry County Weekly*, October 7, 1892), Gordon (Calhoun *Times*, January 12, 1893), and Coffee (Douglas *Breeze*, October 2, 9, 1896). Militia district maps for these counties can be found in the Office of the Surveyor-General, Department of Archives and History, Atlanta. On local issues see Flynn, "White Land, Black Labor," Chapter V; Hahn, "Roots of Southern Populism," 355–77; Jim Alan Furgeson, "Power Politics and Populism: Jackson County, Georgia, as a Case Study" (M.A. thesis, University of Georgia, 1975).

Crawford and 84.0 percent in Washington) were worth less than $500.[18] Some were undoubtedly yeomen, but most were probably tenants. Such information must be used with caution. The sample is small, it includes no blacks, and there exist no corresponding lists of Democrats. It is also possible that a few of these farmers were not living in their respective counties in the 1880s. Still, these findings agree with the usual portrait of third-party men: those who had to struggle to survive in the 1880s frequently became Populists in the 1890s. But such a conclusion is too simple. Many distressed farmers failed to join the Populist crusade. This seems especially true in Crawford County, where the Democrats enjoyed great strength before and during the third-party period.

But what of the rank-and-file Populists of the 1890s? Mell Branch described those living in Lincoln County as "land owners and property owners. They are not what you would call men of large means, but they are home owners, and those who haven't homes are working for that object." But this was only Branch's impression, and he perhaps was putting the best face on a more dreary situation. Fortunately, in 1893 the *People's Party Paper* published a list of 179 Worth County Populists. Of these, 131 were white and 48 were black. This information and the county tax records provide a biracial view of Populism in one locale.[19]

In Worth County, white third-party men were numerous in two militia districts, both located in the eastern portion of the county: Ty Ty and Poulan-Sumner. The wealth of the average county farmer is unclear, but the average farm size was 194 acres. Populists tended to possess considerably smaller holdings. In the Ty Ty district the average third-party landowner had 136.9 acres and was worth $625.35; in the Poulan-Sumner district he owned a 96.9-acre spread that was valued at $336.40. Walter Hannon was a fairly typical Populist yeoman from Ty Ty. In 1893 he worked a 140-acre farm worth $350. He also owned $23 in tools, $60 in furniture, and $264 in livestock. Charley Pittman was a typical Poulan-Sumner Populist. He farmed seventy acres that were assessed at $121. In addition, he possessed $122 worth of tools, furniture, and livestock.

18. Compare the Knoxville *Crawford County Herald*, May 27, 1892, and the Sandersville *Herald and Georgian*, April 7, 1892, with the *Georgia State Gazetteer, Business and Planters Directory, 1886–87* (Savannah, 1886), 322, 271–74.
19. U.S. Congress, House, *Watson vs. Black*, 691; *People's Party Paper*, October 5, 13, 1893.

Many third-party property holders were less fortunate than these men. J. B. Holland, a Ty Ty sharecropper or tenant, owned only a $15 work animal (probably a mule) and $30 in furniture. Preston Parker of the Poulan-Sumner district claimed $35 in furniture, $15 in animals, and $5 in jewelry. For both Holland and Parker a lifetime of toil had produced nothing except some livestock and a few sticks of furniture. Yet even these men were better off than many Populists. In the Ty Ty district, twenty-two (46.8 percent) out of the forty-seven white Populists listed had no taxable possessions; in the Poulan-Sumner district, only fourteen (29.1 percent) out of forty-eight were property holders. The lot of the forty-eight black Populists was even more dreary. Three (5.1 percent) were worth, respectively, $120, $90, and $5. The rest owned nothing that could be levied against. Many of these men, both black and white, were too impoverished to pay the poll tax.[20]

No similar list of Worth County Democrats exists. But the great success of the Democratic party in this county suggests that many renters and yeomen failed to join in the new movement. As we shall see, poverty alone was not always a forerunner of Populism. Still, many hard-pressed farmers did support the People's party, which gladly accepted their aid. Yet in the end, it paid them little heed. Populism reflected the interests of yeomen and small planters—not those of tenants and sharecroppers. The party never objected to the poll tax (which disfranchised thousands of Georgians in 1892); it never tried to reform the lien system; and it nominated for governor the author of the "slave bill."

As time passed, the third party grew even more conservative. In 1893 it quietly dropped the subtreasury demand, and two years later Georgia Populists argued that a national plebiscite should precede government purchase of the railroads. Populists still denounced the exploitation of producers by nonproducers. But their rhetoric notwithstanding, few third-party planters and yeomen could truly believe that all forms of ex-

20. Worth County Tax Records, 1893, Georgia State Department of Archives and History, Atlanta. Overall, 58.2 percent of Worth County farmers were landowners, 29.7 percent were tenants, and 11.9 percent were sharecroppers. In the Ty Ty militia district, the median farm size was 115 acres and the median property value was $483.50; in the Poulan-Sumner district, the median farm size was 70 acres and the median property value was $301.50. See U.S. Department of the Interior, *Report of the Statistics of Agriculture at the Eleventh Census, 1890* (Washington, D.C., 1895), 132–33.

ploitation had to end. Racism and their own stake in tenancy and sharecropping made a broader vision nearly impossible.

The election of 1892 profoundly affected third-party politics. Many
Populists believed their strategy had been amiss. Clearly, they had placed
too much faith in their ability to win over former Alliancemen. Much of
the blame fell on the party chairman, Mark Irwin, and his father-in-law,
William L. Peek. When Peek and Irwin planned the campaign, they in-
correctly assumed most Alliancemen would become Populists. Since the
order claimed about seventy thousand male members of voting age, this
involved a sizable base of support.[21] They also counted on the allegiance
of Georgia's forty thousand Republican voters, as well as thousands of
old independents in the northern part of the state. On paper, at least, this
hope seemed reasonable. In practice it miscarried in almost every respect. Peek received one vote out of every three that were cast. He lost
from 50 to 80 percent of the black vote. His success among former Alliancemen was unknown, but it was obvious that where the Alliance was
strong, the Populists were often weak. Indeed, the center of third-party
strength had been Tom Watson's Tenth Congressional District, where a
clutch of eight counties delivered constant majorities for Populist candidates. Yet the Alliance had only moderate strength in this area.

The election of 1892 did much to discredit Peek and the notion that
the third party should base its strategy on former Alliancemen. Consequently, the Populists faced a dilemma: they could continue their old
ways hoping to get additional Alliance support, or they could try to gain
the loyalty of some other block of voters. Peek favored the first plan and
dreamed of a second gubernatorial race based upon country people and
former Alliancemen. But Watson was growing more and more disen-
chanted with this strategy. He believed the party had to become more
respectable, that it had to make a stronger appeal to the urban middle
class. Such a scheme would mean changes in the Populist platform and
the elimination of party radicals and eccentrics. In the end, Watson
knew, it would also mean the elimination of William L. Peek.

21. Atlanta *Constitution*, August 21, 1889.

◆◎VII◎◆

"Oh, for a Cromwell!"
The Georgia Elections of 1894

Christmas 1892 was a dreary holiday for Georgia Populists. With the chaos of the earlier elections over, the crops harvested, and the weather growing cold, third-party men had time to reflect upon their political past and future. Only the most optimistic could see reason for cheer. In a few places they had elected some local officials, and in such strongholds as Warren, McDuffie, Franklin, and Paulding counties they had captured, or would shortly capture, every county office.[1] But the election of an ordinary or a coroner was little reason for celebration. The Georgia Populists had sent a mere sixteen men to the legislature. They had failed to elect a president, a governor, or even a congressman. Few could be proud of such a record. Everywhere Democratic newspapers proclaimed that the People's party was on its deathbed and merrily predicted its demise. Christmas 1892 was indeed a happy season for the enemies of Populism. Yet five thousand miles away forces had already begun that would summon the Georgia third party back from the grave and deal the Democrats their greatest challenge since Reconstruction.

On November 20, 1889, Baring Brothers of London, one of England's largest banks, declared itself insolvent. Fearing a financial crisis, many Europeans began withdrawing their investments from America. Soon $60 million in gold had exited the United States. Few Americans realized how gravely the economy was being harmed, and for a time business was able to withstand the loss. By Christmas 1892 the country was edging toward disaster. Five months later the price of securities on the New York Stock Exchange suddenly began to fall, and on June 27 the market

1. *People's Party Paper*, January 27, 1893.

crashed. President Cleveland quickly ordered Congress into emergency session. Yet nothing seemed to help. As senators debated, the flower of American capitalism appeared to be withering: the Philadelphia and Reading Railroad, the Erie, the Northern Pacific, the Union Pacific, the Atchison and Topeka—all collapsed within a few months. By December five hundred banks and more than fifteen thousand businesses had closed; possibly two million people were out of work.[2]

There were, however, deeper reasons for the Panic of 1893 than the flight of European investments across the Atlantic. A decade before, Americans had consumed almost everything native factories could produce, so business continued to expand, existing on credit and the faith that the public would continue purchasing. By 1890 consumption had dropped. Farmers were creating only 21 percent of the national wealth— a 5 percent decline from 1880. A fundamental reason for the panic, therefore, was that while factories were producing more and more, tillers were consuming less and less. Everywhere people speculated about what was wrong with agriculture. Businessmen charged that the crisis was the fault of the growers, who had foolishly glutted their market by planting too much cotton and wheat, causing the prices of these commodities to fall. Many farmers scoffed at such arguments. They saw the contracting money supply as the real reason for the panic. In 1865 the United States had $2 billion in circulation; yet although the population doubled by 1890, the amount of money actually decreased. Coin more money, fire inflation, drive up prices, and all would be well, farmers insisted.[3]

But all was not well in America, and in Georgia the situation was becoming desperate. Both the new cotton crop and the effects of the panic grew in the late summer of 1893. Textile mills in Atlanta, Columbus, Macon, and Augusta closed or laid off hundreds of workers. When the cotton was at last harvested, the results were ruinous. Although Georgia

2. Harold U. Faulkner, *Politics, Reform, and Expansion, 1890–1900* (New York, 1959), 141–62, contains a lucid introduction to the causes of the Panic of 1893. For more detailed treatments, see Samuel Rezneck, "Unemployment, Unrest, and Relief in the United States During the Depression of 1893–97," *Journal of Political Economy*, LXI (1953), 324–45; Allan Nevins, *Grover Cleveland: A Study in Courage* (New York, 1933), 524–48; Robert Sobel, *Panic on Wall Street: A History of American Financial Disasters* (London, 1969), 230–73; Hicks, *Populist Revolt*, 87–95.
3. Hicks, *Populist Revolt*, 87–95.

produced more of the staple than any state except Texas, it experienced
the worst yield per acre of any state except Florida. And although the
average southern farmer netted $13.41 per acre, Georgia tillers gained a
mere $11.97.[4] In some places the agony of the farmers was becoming un-
bearable. On October 19 terrorists tacked notices to the doors of every
gin in Cobb, Bartow, Paulding, and Cherokee counties ordering the owners to stop operation until the price of cotton had risen to ten cents a
pound. The whitecaps, as the terrorists were called, promised to burn
any business that failed to comply. A week later they threatened the gins
of Carroll and Haralson counties, and at Temple they sent store owners a
similar warning: "To the Merchants—if you push any farmer we will
burn you out in twenty-four hours."[5]

In autumn Governor Northen released the *Report of the Comptroller-
General* and delivered his annual address to the legislature. He announced that the value of taxable property had declined by $12 million;
that the value of the entire state crop had fallen by more than a quarter of
a million dollars; and that the amount of improved land had plunged by
300,000 acres. "There must be in our midst some power, somewhere,
able to paralyze and destroy, at will, the common interest and the common good," he said. Although Northen blamed the panic on the "monster power" of the tariff, it was apparent that he was as dumbfounded by
the crisis as most Georgians. Writing to President Cleveland in mid-
September, the governor confessed that the "conditions in this State are
fearful and threatening." He noted that the Georgia Populists had won
every local contest in the preceding three months. Imploring Cleveland
to expand the money supply, Northen warned that if nothing were done,
"there can be no hope of holding the farmers to the Democratic party in
the next election. But if conditions can be improved and the farmers
receive nine or ten cents for their cotton they will remain Democratic."
To the anger of many Georgia Democrats, Cleveland refused to heed
Northen's advice. When the farmers harvested their cotton in October,
the extent of the debacle was at last known—the average price had risen

4. Woodward, *Origins of the New South*, 265; U.S. Department of Agriculture, *Yearbook
of the United States Department of Agriculture, 1901*, 754.
5. Dallas *Herald*, October 26, November 16, 1893; Atlanta *Constitution*, October 26,
27, 1893.

no higher than five cents a pound. Later, Congressman John W. Maddox of the Seventh District chanced to see Cleveland in Washington. "Well, Maddox," the president said, "how is everything down in old Georgia? I suppose they are all cussing me."[6] Indeed they were.

On July 4, 1893, Tom Watson began a speaking tour that would take him to thirty-five Georgia counties and 150,000 listeners. Almost everywhere the reception was cordial, the crowds eager to hear his plea for free silver and his denunciations of Cleveland. Probably more than anything, this tour convinced Democrats that the Panic of 1893 was resuscitating the third party. While rumors spread that Watson would campaign as the next Populist candidate for governor, the rage of the farmers was growing daily. "If the present administration is a sample of what modern Democracy is, Lord deliver us from any more of it," a Populist from Plains wrote. "Oh, for a Cromwell to disperse our American Congress before the last knot of the bondsman . . . is fastened and the shackles of slavery are fixed forever!"[7] Many saw Tom Watson as their Oliver Cromwell and their choice for governor.

But Watson had other ambitions. Although he apparently considered running for chief executive, he eventually decided that his candidacy would rip open old hatreds and do more harm than good. Instead he hoped the Populist candidate for governor would be a man who would not only appeal to the farmers but to people in the towns and cities. This criterion clearly excluded William L. Peek, who had run for governor claiming to be a "real dirt farmer." Yet it was an open secret that Peek yearned for another gubernatorial race. When Peek and Watson met to discuss the matter, Peek admitted that his friends were working for his nomination.[8] Watson made it plain that he could not support such a candidacy. At once he began preparations for the boldest move yet of his political career: he planned to crush the Peek wing, dictate the party

6. *Georgia House Journal, 1893*, 10, 13, 14; *Report of the Comptroller-General, 1892–1893*, 4, 107, 127; Scrapbook 2, 270–72, Northen Papers; Atlanta *Constitution*, October 16, November 12, 1893; Cooper, *Story of Georgia*, II, 342.
7. Gracewood *Wool Hat*, July 21, 1894; Woodward, *Origins of the New South*, 273; quotation in *People's Party Paper*, May 11, 1894.
8. Atlanta *Constitution*, August 8, 1894.

platform, and select the next Populist candidate for governor—James Kollock Hines.

In 1894 Hines enjoyed as promising a future as any man in Georgia. At forty-two years of age, his life had already been a success. His mother was a member of the Harrison family of Virginia, thus making her son a distant relative of two presidents and the great-great-grandson of Benjamin Harrison, the signer of the Declaration of Independence.[9] On his father's side, Hines was a direct descendant of a signer of North Carolina's Mecklenburg Declaration. After being reared on his father's plantation in Washington County, young James entered Emory College in 1869 and three years later graduated with first honors. He then studied for a year at Harvard University law school, passed the Georgia bar, and in 1877 was appointed solicitor general of the Middle Circuit. There he came to know and eventually adore Herschel V. Johnson, the circuit court judge. Riding from courthouse to courthouse with Johnson, the young man feasted upon stories of the judge's earlier career as governor and as a Confederate and United States senator. "When aroused his oratory flashed like the lightning of the heavens," Hines recalled. "His powers of invective and sarcasm were terrific." The young man seemed especially stirred by tales of Johnson's attempts in 1860 to prevent southern secession. In that year the hatred of the South turned upon him when he ran for vice-president with Stephen Douglas. Although Johnson died in 1880, Hines had learned much about Georgia politics. In 1884 Washington County elected the young man to the state legislature, and two years later he was appointed to Johnson's old spot as judge of the Middle Circuit. Resigning his seat in 1891, he set up a law practice in Atlanta that soon prospered. At about the same time, he was elected chairman of the Board of Trustees of Emory College.[10]

---

9. For biographical information about Hines, see *People's Party Paper*, April 20, June 8, 1894; Atlanta *Constitution*, March 17, May 6, 1894, May 15–17, 1933; John B. Harris (ed.), *A History of the Supreme Court of Georgia* (Macon, 1948), 238–39; Stirling Price Gilbert, *A Georgia Lawyer: His Observations and Public Service* (Athens, 1946), 136–37; Lucian Lamar Knight, *Georgia's Bi-Centennial Memoirs* (3 vols.; n.p., 1932), I, 217–23; Knight, *A Standard History of Georgia and Georgians* (6 vols.; Chicago, 1917), V, 2488–89; Arnett, *Populist Movement in Georgia*, 119–20.

10. James K. Hines, "Herschel V. Johnson," in *Report of the Forty-First Annual Session of the Georgia Bar Association, May 29–31, 1924* (Macon, 1924), 226–27.

Yet for all his success in the Bourbon world of Atlanta, there remained in Hines a streak of the renegade. Possibly it was a family trait; possibly it came from his days with Herschel Johnson. But whatever the cause, Hines periodically dismayed his more conservative friends. In 1890 he was one of the few well-known professional men in Georgia to support the Ocala demands. In the same year, he endorsed the Alliance platform and ran for the United States Senate. Although crushed in the resulting battle between John B. Gordon, Thomas M. Norwood, and Patrick Calhoun, Hines came to the attention of reform-minded yeomen. Therefore, he fit Watson's criterion for a gubernatorial candidate—he was a man respected by businessmen and professionals but also popular with farmers. Sometime during the spring of 1894 Watson secretly convinced Hines to join the third party. And three weeks before the Populist convention was to assemble, the former judge shocked polite society by announcing that he had become a Populist.

As the convention approached, Watson hurried to complete plans for his takeover of the party. A few weeks before the gathering, he sent out word that he would not run for governor and that he was endorsing James K. Hines. Watson explained his decision in the *People's Party Paper*: "At present we have little or no following among the business and professional men. This has been a source of great weakness to us. Why not select our candidates with a view of getting our full share of the vote? Why not select nominees who will reach elements which heretofore we have been utterly unable to reach?" Watson argued that a man's devotion to Populism and his ability to aid the movement were greater considerations than the length of his party membership. Finally, in a slap at Peek and his son-in-law, Watson assured his readers that he was not related "by blood or marriage, to any gentleman whose name will go before the Convention." Unfortunately for Watson, many Populists had already met at county conventions and had instructed their delegates to vote "first, last, and always" for Tom Watson for governor. Watson reasoned, however, that these delegates were not required to vote for him as long as his name was not placed in nomination.[11]

11. *People's Party Paper*, April 20, 27, May 4, 1894.

A few days before the convention, rumors spread that some Populists would attempt to force Watson to accept the gubernatorial nomination. To mollify these disappointed supporters as well as to strengthen his control over the party, Watson agreed to run for party chairman. When the meeting was at last called to order in Atlanta on May 16, 1894, it was apparent that Watson was in control.[12] When a delegate nominated Mark Irwin for chairman, another quickly put Watson's name in nomination. The cheers that rang through the hall convinced Irwin that his cause was hopeless, and he withdrew. The Peek wing was again defeated when the convention selected the platform committee. Not one important Peek supporter was appointed, and the committee was ruled by two of Watson's most loyal lieutenants, Mell Branch and Clarence Ellington.

But the great test of Watson's power was yet to come. When the call went out for nominations for governor, Watson rose and pleaded with the delegates not to introduce his name. He then placed James K. Hines's name in nomination. After the cheering died, Watson's control of the party seemed to slip. Complaining that Hines had not been with the party long enough, a delegate nominated former congressman Thomas E. Winn. As hisses and cheers filled the hall, Winn, who was a Watson supporter, withdrew his name. Realizing that they had been beaten, the Peek delegates remained silent, and the convention nominated Hines by acclamation. Later it nominated James Barrett of Richmond County for commissioner of agriculture; A. L. Nance of Hall County for secretary of state; J. E. H. Ware of Fayette County for treasurer; W. R. Kemp of Emanuel County for comptroller-general; and J. A. B. Mahaffey of Jackson County for attorney-general.

When the members of the platform committee presented their recommendations, it was obvious that they, too, had been dominated by Watson. And as at the 1892 convention, the delegates accepted every plank without floor fights or even discussion. The platform attempted to assuage the alarm of businessmen by showing that Populists were responsible citizens. The subtreasury plan received only cursory attention,

12. For descriptions of this convention, see Atlanta *Constitution*, May 15–18, 1894; Atlanta *Journal*, May 15–17, 1894; *People's Party Paper*, May 25, 1894; Dahlonega *Signal*, May 25, 1894; Augusta *Chronicle*, May 16–18, 1894; Columbus *Enquirer-Sun*, May 15–17, 1894.

whereas whitecapping was vigorously condemned. On other national issues the platform was more forthright. It damned the economic policies
of both the Democrats and the Republicans and called for the free and
unlimited coinage of silver at a ratio of 16 to 1. It also denounced the
"extravagant and useless diplomatic service," the "costly standing army
and navy," and the monetary policies enacted by Congress. Finally, while
demanding the "preservation of the reserved rights of the states," the
platform censured the national banks, condemned the convict-lease system, and called for the state purchase of school books.[13]

It was a curious document. What, for instance, were the "reserved
rights of the states"? And how could these be reconciled with the Omaha
platform's demand for the government ownership of the railroads and
the subtreasury plan? Even more puzzling was the Populists' position on
race: "We believe, as Jefferson did, that all men are created equal, with a
natural right to life, liberty and the pursuit of happiness." Yet the day
before the convention Watson had attacked Grover Cleveland, who,
while governor of New York, had ordered the integration of public
schools in New York City. Watson assured his audience that, unlike the
president, he had "never advocated social equality"; and during the
Populist convention, the dozen or so black delegates who attended were
apparently segregated in the rear of the hall. Nevertheless, the third
party tried to make some concessions to black sensibilities. The most
dramatic point of the meeting came when Watson's closest friend,
Charles E. McGregor, rose and lambasted the Atlanta *Journal* for satiriz-
ing the black delegates. "When it comes that I cannot pay consideration
to one of God's creatures, no matter how low and humble he may be, I do
pray that the same power that gave me life will at the same moment give
me death," McGregor cried. He then nominated Ephraim White, a black
minister, to the party executive committee. Seconding the nomination,
Watson declared: "The day has come for the black man to be meted out
simple justice as a citizen of this country." Amid cheers, the convention
unanimously made the appointment.[14]

It was a daring stroke by the Populists. For the first time in Georgia

13. For the text of the Populist platform, see Atlanta *Constitution*, May 18, 1894.
14. *Ibid.*, May 17, 18, 1894.

history a leading political party, composed mostly of white men, had placed a black on its most important committee. Yet many former slaves questioned the sincerity of Populist leaders. A black Populist delegate named W. A. Colby wrote later that the show of amity had been a charade. Colby revealed that during the convention he had nominated a white man for state treasurer but was unable to get another delegate to second the nomination. Leaving his seat, he started toward the front of the hall to discuss the matter with Tom Watson. When he arrived at the podium, Colby said that Watson ignored him, and McGregor "ordered me . . . back to the rear of the house where the colored delegates were seated." After the meeting, Colby quit the party, promising to work for the Democrats. "I stand as your colored 'used-to-be friend,'" he told Populists.[15]

Meanwhile, the Democrats were also trying to select a gubernatorial candidate. For a time it seemed as if there would be no contest. The old Bourbon leadership and many of the state's newspapers were agreed that General Clement Evans was the best choice. Even the constantly feuding Atlanta *Journal* and Atlanta *Constitution* endorsed the general. During the Civil War Evans had served under John B. Gordon, and his men had made the last rebel charge at Appomattox. Evans's friends never tired of delivering teary-eyed tributes to his valor and to the five wounds he had suffered in defense of the Confederacy. After the war the general was ordained a Methodist minister and served congregations all over Georgia. When the Board of Trustees of Emory College appointed him a member, Evans became a friend of James K. Hines. Although he had little political experience, Evans seemed an ideal candidate for governor. He embraced no unorthodox views, he favored free silver, and he would shroud the campaign in the Stars and Bars and the cloth of the clergy. As one Democrat wrote, "I tell you it is a hard matter to down an old Confederate General in Ga. politics."[16] There was only one drawback: Evans was sixty-eight years old, and some wondered if he could mount a vigorous campaign.

15. Atlanta *Constitution*, May 17, 1894; Atlanta *Journal*, May 17, 1894.
16. Howell, *History of Georgia*, II, 555–58; George Middleton to James Middleton, March 1, 1894, James Middleton Papers, Special Collections, Duke University Library, Durham.

Unfortunately for Evans, Bourbonism was losing strength. Henry
Grady had died in 1889 and Alfred Colquitt in 1894; Joseph E. Brown,
Evan Howell, and John B. Gordon were growing old. Younger Democrats were now ready to challenge the party chiefs. One in particular,
William Y. Atkinson of Coweta County, was a growing threat. He had
successfully managed Northen's campaign for governor two years earlier,
and as a reward the Democrats had elected him Speaker of the Georgia
House of Representatives. In this capacity he had performed countless
favors, helping many of his friends gain appointments as solicitors-
general and judges of the circuit courts. Such men eagerly endorsed
Atkinson's candidacy, and he also had support in Atlanta's traditional
rivals, Augusta, Macon, and Columbus.[17]

Reared in what he described as a poor family, Atkinson had labored
diligently to improve himself. As a youth he worked as a teamster—an
experience that would later win him the appellation "the Wagon Boy of
Coweta." After graduating from the University of Georgia in 1877, he
took up law. Physically Atkinson was small and frail; his curly, raven
hair, dense mustache, and dark complexion gave him an almost Latin
appearance. Yet behind this unintimidating façade lurked a daring politician who was willing to use all the machine methods the Bourbons had
earlier perfected. During the campaign against Evans, newspapers obtained a private letter in which Atkinson told friends that his nomination
was assured because it had been decided by the "men who control."[18]

Since there were few political differences between the two candidates—both endorsed free silver—the campaign rapidly sank to name-
calling and surly accusations. Old Confederates grumbled that Atkinson
and his young minions represented a thankless generation that did not
appreciate the sacrifices made at Manassas and Gettysburg. Atkinson's
followers answered that Evans, who lived in Atlanta, was a city slicker
who failed to understand the problems of farmers; that at sixty-eight
years of age, he was on the brink of senility.[19]

17. Dawson *News*, April 18, 1894; Werner, "Hegemony and Conflict." For another discussion of the Atkinson-Evans campaign, see Bascom Osborne Quillian, Jr., "The Populist
Challenge in Georgia in the Year 1894" (M.A. thesis, University of Georgia, 1948).

18. Howell, *History of Georgia*, IV, 226–27; *People's Party Paper*, May–July 1894.

19. Atlanta *Constitution*, May 19, 25, 31, August 2, 1894; *People's Party Paper*, March
30, 1894.

Evans took the lead from the beginning. Yet as the contest raged into midsummer, Atkinson mysteriously pulled ahead. The hopes of the Bourbons rallied when word came from Washington that Senator Gordon was rushing to the state to campaign for his former lieutenant. "I am heart and soul for Evans," the senator declared as he made plans to speak in Macon and other towns. A few days later Atkinson allegedly sent Gordon a telegram saying that he had been the foremost supporter of Gordon's candidacy for the United States Senate in 1890: "If you are ungrateful enough to try to beat me I put you on notice you shall hear from me. If you keep your engagement at Macon I shall be there to meet you, from the stage if you will, from the audience if I must." Later Gordon said he had received no such message. But about that time he discovered that Senate business made it impossible for him to canvass the state.[20]

Thus Evans's campaign collapsed, and in late June he withdrew from the contest. Atkinson had scored an extraordinary victory—a coup d'etat that deposed the old leaders and allowed younger Democrats to take control of the party. But the triumph had been costly. Many Democrats believed that Clement Evans had been swindled out of the nomination by a sinister legislative ring, by the "men who control." Atkinson seemed sly, ruthless, and corrupt—a "bombastic upstart," the Atlanta *Constitution* put it. Others noted that every candidate on the state ticket was from Atkinson's region, northwestern Georgia.[21] The fortunes of Atkinson's closest supporters also appeared to be improving. The state Democratic convention appointed Alexander Stephens Clay as the chairman of the party, and soon Clay announced his candidacy for the United States Senate. Two other friends of Atkinson, George R. Gober and George Brown, announced their candidacies for judgeships on the state supreme court and the Blue Ridge circuit court. Many believed that Clay, Gober, and Brown were grossly venal. Former Confederates were furious about Evans's defeat. "[It means] old veterans need not apply," the Milledgeville *Union-Recorder* fumed, and many former rebels swore they would not vote in the October elections.[22]

20. Atlanta *Constitution*, May 26, June 13, 15, 1894.
21. Atlanta *Constitution*, n.d., quoted in *People's Party Paper*, August 10, 1894; Augusta *Chronicle*, September 14, 1894.
22. Conyers *Hales's Weekly*, August 11, 1894; Dawson *News*, September 12, 1894; *Peo-*

If these were not worries enough for Atkinson, he faced other, more serious problems. The Panic of 1893, now a year old, was growing worse. The October cotton prices promised to be the lowest in American history, receivers controlled two-thirds of Georgia railroad property, and in August only thirteen counties reported an increase in tax values.[23] And with Grover Cleveland in the White House and majorities in both the House and Senate, for once Democrats could not blame the opposition for preventing recovery. A scapegoat was needed, and Democratic silverites quickly turned on Cleveland. When the panic had begun, the president reasoned that confidence would be restored if the United States adopted a total gold standard, which he hoped would also end the alarming flow of gold out of the federal treasury. Accordingly, he called Congress into emergency session on August 7, 1893, and demanded the repeal of the Sherman Silver Purchase Act of 1890. This was eventually done, but it did no good. The panic continued, as did the run on government gold. By April, 1893, the reserves had sunk below $100 million—the level most economists believed was the safe point. By the end of the year, $80 million remained. Desperately, Cleveland ordered a series of bond issues, and in January and November, 1894, the treasury issued a total of $100 million in government securities. This expedient momentarily stabilized the situation, but ultimately it was of little aid. By 1894 only $40 million in bullion remained in federal vaults.[24]

To add to the crisis, Georgia Democrats were compelled to explain their party's inept attempts at tariff reform. Both Cleveland and the national platform had condemned the McKinley tariff of 1890, which contained the highest rates in American history. With majorities in the House and Senate, it appeared that Democrats would have an easy time repealing the old tariff and instituting a new one. But this was not to be. Democratic congressmen and senators who supported high rates worked

ple's Party Paper, August 24, 1894; Milledgeville Union-Recorder, n.d., quoted in Savannah Press, June 27, 1894; Dahlonega Signal, July 13, 1894.

23. Appleton's Annual Cyclopaedia and Register of Important Events, n.s., XVIII, 339; Atlanta Constitution, August 22, 1894.

24. Faulkner, Politics, Reform, and Expansion, 141–62; Sobel, Panic on Wall Street, 230–72.

with Republicans to prevent any tangible reduction. When Congress eventually passed the Wilson-Gorman Bill (its so-called reform legislation), it was so similar to the McKinley tariff that a disgusted Cleveland allowed it to become law without his signature.[25]

Thus national events, like those in Georgia, conspired to make Atkinson's election difficult, as the "Wagon Boy of Coweta" may have realized when he spoke to a gathering at Reidsville. Apparently thinking the Populists would admit they had once been loyal Democrats, Atkinson challenged third-party men to tell him what they had been in the 1880s. Instantly, an answer hurled from the crowd: "We were damned fools."[26]

The Populists were not without their own problems. By placing a black man on their executive committee, they were forced to clarify their views on race, if only to stop the whisperings that they were little more than a party of former slaves ruled by a few unscrupulous white men. Watson made his position clear to black people: "If you think the People's Party is going to give you social equality, don't you come to us." Hines agreed: "The color line cannot be broken down. God, in his inscrutable wisdom, made the color line for wise purposes. It cannot be broken down. We do not advocate social equality." When Democrats suggested that the third party wanted blacks to hold public office, Populists roared with indignation. "No such bid for votes has ever been made by the Populists nor any of their candidates," the *People's Party Paper* thundered. In the Tenth District this was plainly the case, for in none of the counties controlled by the People's party had one black been offered a job or placed on a jury. When Democrats charged that not a "single miserable little office" had gone to a black man, the Populists answered by accusing the Democrats of promiscuously distributing jobs to blacks. In a speech, Hines condemned Cleveland for appointing a black man, C. H. J. Taylor, as minister to Bolivia—"a country of white people," Hines reminded his listeners. And although Cleveland later withdrew the appointment, Hines noted that he then named Taylor registrar of deeds for Washington, D.C. The *People's Party Paper* disclosed that state Democrats had hired a New York black to help them recruit Republican

25. Nevins, *Cleveland*, 563–88; Faulkner, *Politics, Reform, and Expansion*, 157–62.
26. Swainsboro *Herald*, n.d., quoted in the Dahlonega *Signal*, July 6, 1894.

votes and that in Richmond County, they had appointed former slaves to juries. Because many of these revelations appeared toward the end of the campaign, some Republicans probably regretted that their party had earlier decided not to run a state ticket.[27]

As election day approached, Populists were confident that Hines would win. They feared, however, that the Democrats might employ some of their old swindles. Thus Hines and Watson demanded that each party have managers at all polling places to make sure no ballots were lost or tampered with. Their demand put the Democrats in a quandary. To deny the Populist request would give the impression they were planning fraud; to accept would ruin the plans of at least some Democrats—which was fraud. In early September the state executive committee met and decided against the third-party request. After the meeting one of its members resigned, telling reporters that he was the only committeeman who had favored having managers from both parties at the polls. Again it seemed as if the Democrats were plotting to steal the election. Two days later, and with only two weeks left in the campaign, Atkinson challenged Hines to a series of debates. Hines retorted that he would debate only if Atkinson agreed to a division of managers at the voting places.[28]

On election day the returns came into Atlanta slowly; yet almost at once the Democrats proclaimed a great victory. But hour by hour Atkinson's lead shrank. By morning jubilant Populists declared that Hines was just a few thousand votes behind his opponent. It was certain, however, that the third party had elected forty-eight members of the legislature—three times their number in 1892. But within a few days, enough counties had reported for newspapers to announce with confidence that Atkinson had won by about twenty-five thousand votes. Populists howled that the "men who control" had robbed them of victory. From all over the state came reports of gross frauds. Most serious was the third-party charge that upon receiving the returns, Democrats in the secretary of state's office had doctored the ballots, thus making certain that Atkinson

27. *People's Party Paper*, June 8, August 24, November 2, 1894; Dahlonega *Signal*, June 22, 1894; Atlanta *Constitution*, August 11, 1894; Shadgett, *Republican Party in Georgia*, 112–15.
28. Atlanta *Constitution*, September 12, 13, 14, 1894.

would win. As one Populist sneered, "Hines was elected and Atkinson was counted in." [29]

Even accepting the official results, it had been a humiliating victory for the Democrats, especially when compared with Northen's triumph of two years before. Hines had received 96,819 votes, or 44.4 percent of the ballots cast; Atkinson had captured 121,625 votes, or 55.6 percent. Hines had beaten Atkinson in the Tenth District and had nearly defeated him in the Seventh and the Ninth. Most surprising was the third-party tally in the Fourth, where Hines trailed Atkinson by only 448 votes. Democrats explained their puny success by claiming apathy among their own party members. But when all the ballots were counted, Secretary of State Allen Candler announced that the election had attracted more voters than any other in Georgia history. [30]

Hines's excellent showing in the Fourth, Seventh, Ninth, and Tenth districts made the congressional contests especially important. The third-party candidate in the Tenth was, of course, Tom Watson. In the Seventh the Populists nominated William H. Felton. Feeble, wizened, and sickly, Felton was nevertheless respected as the personification of the old independency movement. From 1874 to 1880 he had represented the Seventh District in Congress as an independent; then, from 1884 to 1890, he had served in the state legislature. Although he had had some early reservations about Populism, by 1894 Felton was ready to join the cause. In the Ninth District the Populists nominated Newton Twitty, a former legislator known for his sympathies toward farmers; in the Fourth they selected Carey Thornton, a lawyer and former solicitor-general of the circuit court. But third-party men seemed even more excited about their candidate in the Eleventh, Dr. W. S. Johnson. Possibly because Johnson was a professional man, Populists were delighted with his candidacy. The *People's Party Paper* proudly published his picture and the story of his life. The paper also noted that while a member of the legislature, Johnson had proposed a bill that segregated the black and

29. Marginal note written by Rebecca Latimer Felton, Scrapbook 5 (no pagination), Felton Papers; *People's Party Paper*, October 12, 19, 1894.
30. Diamond (ed.), *Guide to U.S. Elections*, 404; *Report of the Comptroller-General, 1895*, 194j, 194g, 194i, 194d; Augusta *Chronicle*, October 13, 1894.

white races on railroad cars. It was the first Jim Crow law in the history of Georgia.[31]

The congressional and legislative elections were similar to the gubernatorial, with the usual fist fights, coercion, and election larcenies. The results were similar, too: in every congressional race the Populists lost. And again the cry went out that the Democrats had stolen the election, that they had swindled their way to victory. In fact, both sides were guilty of frauds. In Gwinnett County the Populists distributed a phony letter purportedly issued by the state Democratic headquarters: "Remember if we can beat the Populists this time we will never allow the 'niggers' to vote again, and in a few years we can make better slaves of them than they were before the war." The letter ended with the words, "No more nigger after this election."[32] Gwinnett blacks voted Populist, and the third party carried the county. But the Democrats were just as unprincipled. In Cartersville they used extraordinary deceit to defeat Felton—a bribed tax assessor and a corrupt county commissioner disqualified three hundred voters. In Rome they trooped inmates from the local poorhouse to the polls. One witness wrote that the paupers "had never paid [the poll tax] or had brains enough to register."[33] Three mentally retarded men appeared at the same polling place. When asked if they were tax defaulters, two said yes and the third could not seem to understand the question. The election officials were gratified to learn, however, that they all wished to vote Democratic.[34] Their ballots were counted. Felton announced that he would contest the election.

But when the frauds against Felton were compared with those perpe-

31. John E. Talmadge, *Rebecca Latimer Felton: Nine Stormy Decades* (Athens, 1960), *passim*; Augusta *Chronicle*, August 17, 1894; *People's Party Paper*, September 28, 1894. For a list of the Populist candidates for Congress and their opponents, see Diamond (ed.), *Guide to U.S. Elections*, 672.

32. *People's Party Paper*, September 28, 1894; "L. F. McDonald and W. P. Cosby vs. Henry L. Peeples and J. F. Espy, Contested Election Case, Gwinnett County, 1894," 9–10, typescript, Georgia Department of Archives and History, Atlanta; see also, "A. O. Blalock vs. W. M. Cook, Contested Election, Fayette County, 1894," 6, 7, 45, 49, typescript, *ibid.*; "G. W. Burnett vs. Columbus Blair, T. R. Whitney vs. Bion Williams," 3–4.

33. Felton, "Memoirs," 654–63.

34. U.S. Congress, House, *Contested Election Case of William H. Felton vs. John W. Maddox from the Sixth Congressional District of the State of Georgia* (Washington, 1895), 4, 153; *House Reports*, 54th Cong., 1st Sess., No. 1743, 1–6.

trated against Watson, they appeared tame. Democrats had openly bull-
ied voters, occasionally with policemen looking on. To assure victory in
Richmond County, they had passed money to hundreds of blacks to vote
again and again for Watson's opponent; thus in a county where only
11,240 people had paid the poll tax, 13,750 ballots had been cast for Major James C. C. Black. One Democratic newspaper called the results a
"damnable steal," and even Major Black admitted that his election was
"shrouded in doubt." [35] At length Black agreed with Watson that a second contest would be necessary.

The election of 1894 differed in many ways from the Peek-Northen
contest. Despite Hines's defeat, the third party emerged from the struggle robust and confident. Its candidate for governor had given the movement a new respectability in the eyes of the middle class, and across the
country people now considered Georgia a fortress of Populism. Many believed that Watson would receive the third party's next presidential nomination. Nor had great bloodshed accompanied Populist gains. Although
violence occurred—the contest was marked by brawls, night riding, and
several killings—it was nothing like the slaughter of 1892. And unlike
the election of 1892, the Populists had done well, in part because of the
panic, in part the feud within the Democratic party. Atkinson's coup
d'etat had left Bourbons and old Confederates sullen and resentful. Allen
Candler, Atkinson's secretary of state, later said that "the Wagon Boy of
Coweta" had raped the party to gain the gubernatorial nomination. [36]

But there remained at least one important reason why Hines was not
more successful; indeed, it was a reason that helps explain not only
Hines's failure but the ultimate failure of Populism in Georgia. Despite
third-party claims to the contrary, there were in fact few differences between Georgia Democrats and Populists. Democrats had hedged on ending convict lease, and their platform of 1894 mentioned nothing about
the state purchase of school books. Nevertheless, they continued to ad-
here to the Ocala demands. "Believing in the doctrine of equal rights to

    35. Woodward, *Tom Watson*, 269–71; Atlanta *Commercial*, n.d., quoted in Dallas *Her-
ald*, October 18, 1894; *House Reports*, 53rd Cong., 2nd Sess., No. 1147, 1–6.
    36. Augusta *Chronicle*, October 26, 1894; Atlanta *Constitution*, October 26, 1894; J. M.
Barnes to Thomas E. Watson, October 30, 1894, Box 2, folder 13, Watson Papers, UNC;
U.S. Congress, House, *Watson vs. Black*, 266, 285–86; Felton, "*Memoirs*," 679.

all and special privileges to none," the state Democratic platform of 1894 called for a lower tariff, a graduated income tax, and laws against "dealing in futures of all agricultural and mechanical production." On the money question it demanded that the "amount of circulating medium be speedily increased" by the free and unlimited coinage of "both silver and gold on a parity with each other."[37] Indeed, many Georgia Democrats gladly embraced the 16 to 1 plan, and of the state's congressmen only three opposed the silver standard. Although there was some quibbling among the remaining eight over the exact ratio—16 to 1, 17 to 1, 18 to 1, or 20 to 1—this failed to represent a significant difference from the Populists. Among these eight congressmen, five endorsed the 16 to 1 ratio.[38]

On the race question the two parties were also similar. A resolution attached to the Populist platform of 1894 denounced "the evil practice of lawless persons taking the law into their own hands, familiarly known as white capping." In the same year the Democratic platform condemned "every form and species of mob violence and lynch law." But unlike the Populist proposal, this demand was a plank rather than a resolution. Moreover, Democrats in the state legislature had earlier passed an antilynching bill. It is also possible that the Populists were not thinking about lynching when they condemned whitecaps. Georgians seemed to have drawn a distinction between the two forms of terror, considering whitecapping a crime against property and lynching a crime against life. As the Atlanta *Constitution* wrote in 1893, shortly before whitecapping erupted in Georgia, "The white cap business in Alabama, Mississippi, Louisiana, Indiana and Illinois is very different from lynch law. The men engaged in it are not as a rule, bent on avenging some great wrong. They burn cotton gins because planters market their cotton before it reaches 10 cents, whip men because they are unpopular, and they have even been known to whip a woman." During the same year Democratic legislators introduced two bills to suppress mob violence in Georgia, one specifically prohibiting whitecapping, the other specifically condemning lynching.[39]

Ultimately, both parties took a weak stand on lynching, whitecapping,

37. Atlanta *Constitution*, May 18, August 3, 1894.
38. See Sparta *Ishmaelite*, September 1, 1893; Atlanta *Constitution*, August 27–29, 1893.
39. Atlanta *Constitution*, May 18, August 3, 1894, October 1, December 3, 1893.

black voting, and black officeholding. The Populists had invited blacks to their conventions, had placed a black man on their executive committee, had condemned the convict-lease system, and had encouraged blacks to vote as long as they intended to cast ballots for the People's party. At the same time, their thugs continued to intimidate black voters, they opposed black officeholding, and they had run the father of Georgia's Jim Crow laws for Congress. Similarly, the Democrats had intimidated black voters, had engaged in night riding, and had failed to welcome blacks to their conventions. Yet their stand on lynching was far stronger than that of the Populists. In Watson's district they were the first to encourage blacks to speak from a platform with whites. And in that same district, where scores of former slaves had been beaten or killed for supporting the third party, the Populists had never given them a job. In Richmond County, which was controlled by the Democrats, blacks sat on juries even in cases involving white people.

In April, 1895, a congressional committee heard William Felton's claims to the Seventh District congressional seat and unanimously ruled in favor of his opponent. Felton's wife described the preceding investigation as a "reign of terror—where political judges and solicitors went in, from stem to stern, to browbeat and cower our witnesses." Undoubtedly, there was truth in her words. A Democrat had earlier threatened a Felton witness with a knife, and a fist fight had broken out during one of the hearings.[40] In the Tenth District, Tom Watson and Major Black had already fought their third battle for Congress. As agreed, Black resigned his congressional seat on March 4, 1895, but the election was not held until seven months later. Democrats claimed this lengthy period was needed to allow passions to subside; in reality they were waiting for the legislature to change the election laws. In December, 1894, the General Assembly passed a bill establishing a three-member registration committee in each county of the Tenth District. These committees would rule on the eligibility of voters. Two Democrats and one Populist were appointed to each committee.[41]

40. Felton, "*Memoirs*," 668; *House Reports*, 54th Cong., 2nd Sess., No. 1743, 1–6.
41. Woodward, *Tom Watson*, 273–75; James C. C. Black to Thomas E. Watson, March 27, 1895, Box 2, folder 11, Watson Papers, UNC.

During this period, Watson created a new strategy to defeat Black. The citizens of Augusta had given him little support in the campaigns of 1892 and 1894. Watson blamed his failures there on the "Augusta Ring," a coalition of businessmen and Irish-born mill workers. In return for allying with business leaders, the Irish were given most city jobs and political positions. Even so, the ring did not have the support of the majority of Augustans. But any time the mill workers nominated their own candidates, their enemies bribed enough voters to give themselves a majority. Thus many poor whites in Augusta grew to resent the Irish. For some this enmity turned into a hatred of Catholicism. About 1894 these white Protestants affiliated themselves with an anti-Catholic order called the American Protective Association (APA), which by 1896 claimed 2.5 million members. A number of Augusta APA leaders were Populists, and to some extent their prejudice influenced the local third party. Shortly after the election of 1895, the People's party executive committee from Watson's district condemned three election officials, saying: "It has come to a nice state in public affairs when the suffrage of Southern men is to be passed upon by an Irishman, a Scotchman, and a Yankee Republican." A week later, the Lincolnton *Home Journal* claimed that Populism would continue even if Watson should die. Possibly believing Protestantism and Christianity were synonymous, the *Journal* asserted: "Go ask the catholic world when they persecuted and tortured at the stake, if they succeeded in killing the Christian reformation." [42]

Up to this point Tom Watson had expressed no anti-Catholic opinions, and on one occasion he had observed that some of the best members of his party were Roman Catholics. Yet after an APA editor sent him a questionnaire about his political views, many APA leaders suddenly endorsed him. Although Watson's response was never published, one man said, "[His] answers are satisfactory to me as an A. P. A." A prominent Populist also believed Watson's views amounted to an endorsement of the anti-Catholic organization. At the same time, the *People's Party Paper* began

42. William B. Hamilton, "Political Control in a Southern City" (Honors paper, Harvard University, 1972), *passim*; Donald L. Kinzer, *An Episode in Anti-Catholicism: The American Protective Association* (Seattle, 1964), 177; U.S. Congress, House, *Watson vs. Black*, 362; Lincolnton *Home Journal*, n.d., quoted in *People's Party Paper*, October 18, 1895.

to publish items about Catholicism and the APA. In one issue it reprinted an article from the Boston *Standard*. After describing a riot supposedly caused by Irishmen who attacked an APA parade, the piece remarked: "The mask has fallen from the face of Rome. The devilish
features which struck terror into the souls of thousands in the days of the
Inquisition now grin in hellish defiance to a free people." Usually, however, coverage was only mildly anti-Catholic. When a Methodist minister
from Augusta condemned election frauds, the *People's Party Paper*
claimed that local Catholics considered the clergyman a heretic. A week
later the newspaper noted that Major Black was a Protestant who favored
the state support of a "sectarian school." It was also noted that Black
had been sympathetic to the Augusta saloon interests with their large
Irish clientele, whereas Watson had supported Georgia's local option bill
of 1882.[43]

This episode was probably the genesis of Watson's later ravings against
Catholicism. Twice he believed his district had elected him to Congress,
and twice the Augusta ring, composed mostly of Irishmen, had stolen
these victories from him. Certainly the members of the APA believed
Watson was an anti-Catholic, and two years later one of their editors in
Washington, D.C., argued that he would make an ideal vice-presidential
candidate.[44] Yet it would take a decade for Watson's prejudice to tran-
scend a simple contempt for the Augusta Irish. By then his suspicions
and fears had swept far beyond the boundaries of his little district, and
Rome, not Augusta, was the seat of corruption, tyranny, and fraud.

On October 2, 1895, the third Watson-Black election was held, and
again Black was victorious. Once more word went out that Augusta
Democrats had employed all manner of swindles to win. As in 1892,
Watson announced he would contest the election. Although he claimed
to be undaunted by the results, it is impossible to think he was not dis-
heartened. Three times he had run for Congress, and three times his enemies had apparently stolen victory from him. He had devoted so much of

43. U.S. Congress, House, *Watson vs. Black*, 89, 113, 362; Gracewood *Wool Hat*, July
28, 1894; *People's Party Paper*, July 12, September 6, 13, 1895.
44. Kinzer, *Episode in Anti-Catholicism*, 233.

his time to Populism that his law practice was disintegrating. His temper, which was volcanic under the best of circumstances, frequently burst forth in venomous sarcasm, often aimed at close friends.[45]

Still Watson had reason for pride. Through an act of political wizardry he had taken control of his state party and was now being discussed as a possible candidate for president of the United States. The risks he had taken, his defeats, his speeches, his stirring editorials, had made him an idol. To the plain folk of backwoods Georgia he was a godlike hero who could put their rage into words. Time and again his speeches were interrupted by shouts from the crowd: "That's it!" "Lay into 'em!" "You tell 'em, Tom!" For some he was a Cromwell, who could do battle with the Bourbons and the rings. For others he was a kind of cracker Christ—"my Jesus," one man called him.[46] For still others he was as dear as a member of the family, grizzled farmers often referring to him as "our Tom" and "Uncle Tommie." No man expressed this feeling better than the delegate who seconded Watson's nomination for Congress in 1894: "I tried to sit still but I cannot. I love the Bible. I love Jesus Christ. I love the People's party, and I love Tommie Watson."[47]

45. *House Reports*, 54th Cong., 3rd Sess., No. 2892, 1–14; Lulu M. Pearce to Thomas E. Watson, June 1, 1895, Box 2, folder 13, Watson Papers, UNC; W. J. Henning to Thomas E. Watson, October 14, 1895, Box 2, folder 15, *ibid.*; Jackson *Herald*, August 24, 1895.

46. U.S. Congress, House, *Watson vs. Black*, 670, 713. For other religious references to Watson, see Woodward, *Tom Watson*, 240; Augusta *Chronicle*, August 22, 1894; Jackson *Herald*, August 24, 1894; Carroll *Free Press*, September 14, 1894.

47. Augusta *Chronicle*, August 22, 1895.

◆◑◒VIII◓◐◆

"The Men Who Control"
The Georgia General Assembly, 1892 to 1897

Shortly after the Georgia legislature of 1897 adjourned, a Chicago news-paper described its performance as the most "glaring instance of legisla-tive incompetence on record." "Mulish inefficiency" and "stubborn defiance of popular will" were some of this journal's observations about the late General Assembly. Although most Georgia legislatures failed to attract such attention, many were little better. While on his deathbed in 1885, Robert Toombs was told that the General Assembly was in session. "Lord, send for Cromwell," the dying man exclaimed. And Woodrow Wilson wrote, after witnessing the proceedings of the senate of 1881, that one could learn "in this provincial town of Atlanta enough of a certain sort of human nature to stock two or three immortal comedies."[1]

There was much truth in Wilson's claim and much justice in Toombs's call for the lord protector. Often the atmosphere in the state's governing body was akin to that of a country hoedown. To demonstrate approval, legislators frequently pounded their desks and stamped their feet. On one occasion they executed the buck dance and the chicken wing at the close of a session. Lobbyists thought nothing about walking onto the floor to solicit support for legislation. During the 1890s bills were intro-duced to prohibit the playing of football, the sale of cigarettes, and the performance of "coochee coochee dances." One representative called for the legalization of bullfighting. Sometimes it was difficult to maintain a quorum. In 1897 a frustrated Speaker of the House ordered the doors locked and sent the sergeant at arms out to arrest the absent members. This tactic failed to prevent the escape of two solons who, according to a

---

1. Chicago *Herald*, n.d., quoted in Atlanta *Constitution*, December 16, 1897; Phillips, *Life of Toombs*, 273; Arthur S. Link (ed.), *The Papers of Woodrow Wilson* (23 vols.; Prince-ton, 1967), II, 355.

reporter, charged the doorkeeper "like [a] center rushes in . . . football." A few days later the president of the senate found that he had no quorum. To keep those present from escaping, he locked the windows and armed the doorkeepers with clubs. Thus confined, the senators merrily ate sweet potatoes and possum while waiting for their tardy colleagues.[2]

But there was more to Georgia statecraft than the buffoonery of the legislature. Much of the business of government was carried on at the Kimball House, the Markham, and other Atlanta hotels. When the General Assembly was in session, hotel lobbies were thick with politicians, officeseekers, and those wanting advice or favors. Upstairs in private rooms, politicos made deals and discussed delicate matters. Indeed, in these rooms the judiciary of Georgia was bought and sold every few years. Because the legislature appointed state judges, those who seriously aspired to the superior court bench or to a solicitor-generalship usually rented suites, hired waiters, bought cases of whiskey, and invited legislators up for refreshment and conversation. With forty-six judgeships and solicitor-generalships to be had, and more than two hundred legislators to be influenced, the convening of the General Assembly frequently resembled a drunken auction. But for those whom the legislature appointed, the trouble and expense were worthwhile. Solicitors were partly paid in fees, and citizens who could pay the highest price often found the state's charges against them dropped or at least reduced. Judges not only received handsome salaries but were in excellent positions for advancement. The convict leaseholders always smiled upon those who helped keep up the supply of prisoners. With such support, many judges soon found themselves holding seats in Congress.[3]

Thus it was understandable why thousands of Georgians believed their state was ruled by a "ring." Rather than the product of neurosis or paranoia, this belief indicated political sophistication. There was in fact a ring or, more accurately, several rings in Georgia. William Y. Atkinson founded his "dynasty" while serving as Speaker of the House. By helping to make his friends solicitors and judges of the superior courts and by

2. Atlanta *Constitution*, November 13, 1894, December 1, 15, 20, 1896, October 29, November 16, 26, December 5, 16, 1897.
3. Atlanta *Journal*, October 25, 1892; Atlanta *Constitution*, November 12, December 17, 1896; *People's Party Paper*, November 9, 23, 1894; Bacote, "Negro Proscriptions," 486.

granting favors for legislators with influence in their counties, he was able to depose the old Bourbon ring perfected by Henry Grady and the Triumvirate. When Atkinson wrote in 1894 that the "men who control" had assured his election, he was referring to his allies in the legislature, the judiciary, and the courthouses of Georgia.

Atkinson failed to understand the growing contempt many Georgians held for such unruly politics. The bartering of judgeships and elections, the loutish antics of the General Assembly, and a system of government that returned little to the people did nothing to encourage a respect for law in Georgia.[4] As one editor lamented, "The politician is my shepherd, I shall not want. He leadeth me into the saloon for my vote's sake. He filleth my pockets with five-cent cigars and my beer glass runneth over. He inquireth concerning the health of my family even to the fourth generation. Yea, though I walk thro the mud and rain to vote for him, and shout myself hoarse, when he is elected he straightway forgetteth me. Yea, though I meet him in his own office he knoweth me not. Surely the wool has been pulled over my eyes all the days of my life."[5]

The time was right for the arrival of the Populists. Between 1892 and 1897, the People's party held ninety-nine seats in the Georgia General Assembly. At no time did it have a majority in either chamber, and at the height of its strength in 1894, the party claimed only 21 percent of the house and senate membership.[6] Consequently, it could influence legislation only when the majority divided—something Democratic leaders strove to prevent. To add to their difficulties, Populist legislators were confused about how their doctrine was to influence state government. The People's party had been founded as an answer to national and inter-

---

4. For a detailed description of how one election was bought, see Savannah *Press*, October 10, 1896.

5. Dahlonega *Signal*, July 29, 1892.

6. Populists in the Georgia House and Senate (total membership in each chamber in parentheses):

	House	Senate
1892	15 (175)	1 (45)
1894	41 (176)	6 (45)
1896	30 (176)	6 (44)

The membership of each General Assembly usually included two or three Republicans and occasionally an independent. In all, seventy-seven Populists held the ninety-nine third-party seats between 1892 and 1897.

national problems, and the St. Louis and Omaha platforms addressed themselves only to these issues. Both documents were silent about the role of Populist legislators. The Georgia General Assembly could do little to bring about federal ownership of the railroads, the subtreasury plan, the free and unlimited coinage of silver, or an end to the national banks of issue. Thus the question remained: What did Populism mean on the state level?

At first the Georgia People's party seemed baffled by the problem, its platform of 1892 containing only two vague demands: an end to convict lease (without saying what was to replace it) and, when feasible, lower taxes. But by 1894 the party seemed to be attaining an identity. Its new platform supported the secret ballot, the election of all government officials, and the monthly payment of schoolteachers. In an attack on Georgia's notorious fee system, it also demanded that whenever possible public servants receive salaries. The platform ended with a plank calling for the state control of prisoners and a resolution denouncing the whitecaps. The proposals of 1896 were similar to those of 1894, except that the Populists replaced the whitecap resolution with an antilynching plank. In addition, they called for the construction of a state reform school. Only two of their demands during this period went beyond a desire for honest government and less mob rule. In 1894 the platform argued that the state, rather than the parents, should pay for primary school textbooks, and two years later it came out in favor of prohibition.[7]

Democrats constantly charged that Georgia Populism and socialism were synonymous. But a careful reading of the third-party's state platforms would have caused little alarm. Most surprising was the absence of any challenge to the economic order in Georgia. As much as farmers strained under the lien system and the South's seemingly feudal notions of land tenure, there was no demand for reform. Whatever the real nature of Georgia Populism, it was not the bomb-throwing radicalism that so many Democrats feared.

Indeed, in 1892 the danger of Populism appeared slight. "The Third party organization will not last in Georgia. In fact it is practically dead

7. Atlanta *Journal*, July 21, 1892; Atlanta *Constitution*, May 18, 1894, August 8, 1896. The Populist stand on prohibition is discussed in Chapter IX.

already," wrote the Atlanta *Journal* two days before the first Populists took their legislative seats. In the house there were fifteen third-party men out of a membership of 175; in the senate, one out of 45. It looked, indeed, as if the *Journal*'s prediction would come true. But two years later, with the near victory of James K. Hines in the gubernatorial election, Populist membership swelled to 43 members in the house and 7 in the senate.[8]

As usual Tom Watson's influence was evident. His *People's Party Paper* printed numerous suggestions to legislators, and two of his lieutenants ruled the Populists in each chamber. In the house, Mell Branch's cheerful disposition made it difficult to believe that this watermelon farmer was known as "hell-raising" Mell and that he had once chaired the committee that had written the Omaha platform of 1892. Branch's knowledge of parliamentary procedure, his understanding of national and state politics, and his ability to remain on pleasant terms with Democrats made him an able minority leader. In the senate the Populist chief was Major Charles E. McGregor, the man who had both defended and angered black delegates at the third-party convention of 1894 and had gruffly rebuked a black man for trying to speak to Tom Watson. McGregor was well known in Georgia. A veteran of the Civil War, he lived and practiced law in Warrenton, owned a two-thousand-acre plantation, and was worth more than $13,000. In 1882 McGregor had been elected to the legislature, but it was not until 1888 that he became famous. In that year he murdered Warrenton's most prosperous merchant. "I have killed Jim Cody. Come instantly," McGregor's telegram to his lawyer read, thus beginning one of the celebrated trials of the day.[9]

The episode stretched back to the evening of December 23, 1887.[10] McGregor was entering his yard when a figure stepped out of the darkness and fired a bullet into his stomach. It took six months for McGregor to recover, and during that time he became haunted by the fear that his

8. Atlanta *Journal*, October 24, 1892; *Georgia State Gazetteer and Business Directory for 1896* (Atlanta, 1896), 68–72.

9. Knight (ed.), *Standard History of Georgia*, VI, 3113; *Georgia State Gazetteer, 1886–87*, 271; Tax Records, Warren County, 1892, Georgia Department of Archives and History, Atlanta; Brewton, *Watson*, 203.

10. For details about the trial, see Brewton, *Watson*, 204–12; Woodward, *Tom Watson*, 150–53; Georgia Watson Lee, "The McGregor Case," *Watsonian*, II (January, 1928), 404–11; Atlanta *Constitution*, December 10–11, 1896.

assailant would return. A friend told him his attacker had been Jim Cody, who thought McGregor had insulted one of his relatives. On October 12, 1888, McGregor chanced to see his enemy on the street in Warrenton. Quietly walking up to him, the major drew his pistol. Without warning, he fired three bullets into Cody's head, neck, and chest.

McGregor was charged with murder, and the Cody family employed some of the finest lawyers in the state to make certain he should hang. McGregor's attorney had only his client's testimony on which to build a defense, but he fought tenaciously. Evidently realizing that an appeal to reason would only send McGregor to the gallows, the lawyer decided that an appeal to emotion was the wiser course. During the trial he stripped off his client's shirt, pointing to the scars that disfigured McGregor's stomach. As he gave his impassioned summation, he instructed the major's disconsolate wife and children to enter the courtroom. He asked the jurymen to envision what a guilty verdict would mean: their neighbor, "poor Charlie McGregor [with] a hempen rope around his neck . . . his body idly swaying back and forth . . . that awful black cap hiding his distorted features." The attorney asked the jury to envision the effect of a verdict of guilty with a recommendation of mercy: "Charley McGregor, clad in a striped suit, chained to a negro, working out his life beneath the earth amid the humid horrors of a Georgia coal mine." As evening fell and the candles were lit in the darkening courtroom, the lawyer continued his defense. For three hours he pleaded for his client, reminding the jurymen that they, too, would one day stand before the Almighty, longing for the same judgment as McGregor. Then, like a merciful Lord of Hosts, the attorney pointed to each juror, called out his name, and passed judgment: "Not guilty . . . not guilty . . . not guilty." For five days the jurors considered the evidence. Finally, they returned to the courtroom, and the foreman pronounced McGregor innocent. To the day of his death, there burned in McGregor an almost slavish devotion to his lawyer, Tom Watson.[11]

So when Charles McGregor joined the senate in 1894, he came with a reputation. All during the dangerous campaign of 1892 he had dogged Watson's steps, helping to edit the *People's Party Paper* and aiding in the

11. Brewton, *Watson*, 209–10.

defense of Watson's home against the men who threatened Seb Doyle. Democrats realized McGregor was Watson's closest friend and was in the best position to know the thinking of the Populist chief. Remembering the Cody shooting, they also realized McGregor was not a man to be provoked. In many respects, he was the second most important Populist in Georgia.

But Major McGregor was only one of seventy-seven third-party men who served in the General Assembly between 1892 and 1898. As a group they possessed less wealth, less status, less education, less political experience, and more limited prospects than their Democratic colleagues. Although information about their schooling is sketchy, it is possible that only two received any formal education beyond the common school level. Nevertheless, their ranks included two lawyers (who apparently read law as young men), a director of a cotton mill, a physician, and a minister. But most were engaged in agriculture. In the 1880s fifty-three were farmers or, in a few cases, men who combined farming with some other business. It is likely that most continued in this field in the 1890s. Besides McGregor, none was a large or even a medium-sized planter; indeed, in 1886 only ten (18.8 percent) were small planters—that is, men who employed tenants and who were worth between $5,000 and $10,000. The remaining forty-two held property valued at less than $5,000, and of these, twenty-two (41.5 percent) fell into the $1,000 to $2,000 range. A few were men of modest means, five being worth only $500 to $1,000. It is not known how these men fared in the early 1890s, but it is unlikely that many prospered. None, however, was a tenant, a sharecropper, or a black. Only nine (11.6 percent) had previously served in the legislature.[12]

By almost every index the Populists differed from Democratic legislators. At forty-two years of age, the average Democrat was almost five years younger than the average Populist. He was also better educated—

12. Information about the seventy-seven Populist members of the General Assemblies of 1892 to 1898 was obtained from a collective biography based on each man's age (32), occupation (56), formal education (10), previous legislative experience (58), later political experience (58), and the highest office he held over the course of his life (58). (The figures in parentheses represent the number of men in each category about whom data were found.) Information on these Populists came from the *Georgia State Gazetteer, 1886–87*, 65–284, from the biographical sources and county histories listed in the Bibliography, and from the Biographical Data File at the Georgia Department of Archives and History, Atlanta. Nothing could be found on nineteen (24.6 percent) of these men.

65.4 percent having attended college, law school, or some other institution of higher education. Two-thirds were professionals, of which 56.0 percent were lawyers and 10.6 percent were physicians. In the 1880s only one in five was engaged in agriculture, and of these 45.4 percent were planters. Nearly a third (29.2 percent) had previously sat in the legislature. Many were up-and-coming young men who would one day rule the state. Indeed, a random sample of just a fourth of their number turned up a future governor, United States senator, congressman, state commissioner of agriculture, public service commissioner, judge of the federal court of appeals, and seven future judges of the superior court. Among all the Populists, there were only a future state pension commissioner (Charles McGregor, who served from 1923 until his death in 1924) and a superior court judge.[13]

Despite their inexperience, Populist legislators labored diligently to master the workings of the General Assembly. At first, the demand for honest elections was a secondary concern. But after the questionable defeats of Watson, Hines, and Felton, election reform became a passion with them. Soon they were submitting bills favoring the Australian ballot, the initiative, the referendum, and the election of all public officials.[14] Most of these proposals died in committee. One exception was the Populist demand for the election of superior court judges and solicitors-general. Countless Georgians had been disgusted by the tawdry auctions that preceded appointments to the superior court bench. Even Democrats in the legislature were beginning to grouse about the cost of these affairs. Other politicos, and especially the supporters of Clement Evans, complained that the judiciary had fallen into the hands of their enemies. Thus by 1897 numerous legislators favored the measure. With Populist

13. Information about the Democratic legislators who served between 1892 and 1898 was obtained from a random sample of one-fourth of their membership, which produced 130 names. A collective biography was then assembled to find each man's age (86), occupation (74), formal education (55), previous legislative experience (111), later political experience (111), and the highest office he held over the course of his life (111). (The figures in parentheses represent the number of men in each category about whom data were found.) Information on these Democrats came from the *Georgia State Gazetteer, 1886–87*, 65–284, from the biographical sources and county histories listed in the Bibliography, and from the Biographical Data File at the Georgia Department of Archives and History, Atlanta. Nothing could be found on nineteen (14.6 percent) of these men.

14. Atlanta *Constitution*, May 18, 1894; *Georgia House Journal*, 1893, pp. 869–70; 1894, pp. 136, 279; *People's Party Paper*, November 23, 1894.

support, it easily passed through both chambers and was signed by the governor.[15] Although Democrats proudly claimed the bill as their own, the third party had been crusading for it since 1894. This was the only important election reform bill that was enacted during these years.

But Populists had other legislative interests. In particular, they seemed driven by a desire to reduce waste. In the house they tried to reduce the salaries of the governor, the members of the legislature, and all state judges; in the senate they attempted to lower the salaries of almost every other state employee. A few Populists even objected to paving the street in front of the governor's mansion, and some grumbled when the lower chamber hired an extra page. W. F. Goldin, a third-party senator from the Thirty-Eighth District, was especially famous as a legislative miser. "He watches the expenditure of every dollar with the scrutiny [of] . . . a hawk eye[ing] a chicken with which it has prospective business," wrote the Atlanta *Constitution*.[16]

The Populists especially enjoyed attacking appropriations for the state militia.[17] Not only did they view this organization as a "sinful extravagance" lavished upon city dudes, but they feared that someday the troops might be turned on the third party. During the election of 1892, Governor William J. Northen had ordered companies from Atlanta and Augusta to be ready to move into the Populist counties at a moment's notice. And in July, 1893—after frightened citizens in Washington, Georgia, wired Northen that armed Populists were about to seize the town—the governor had again alerted the militia. "Reports are current tonight that rioting is greatly feared," Northen informed the commander of the Augusta companies. In Washington the local militia took up positions in the town armory, while a hundred Democrats patrolled the streets. Judge William M. Reese, who helped prepare the town for the Populist attack, later reported: "If the Third Partyites had started a row that day there would have been a great massacre of them, for we were

15. *Georgia Laws: Acts and Resolutions of the General Assembly of Georgia*, 1897, pp. 16–18.

16. Atlanta *Constitution*, October 25, 1894, November 25, December 17, 19, 1896; *Georgia House Journal*, 1892, pp. 592–93; *Georgia Laws*, 1892, pp. 20–21.

17. *Georgia House Journal*, 1894, pp. 758–60; *People's Party Paper*, December 23, 1892, December 7, 1894.

ready." [18] When the Populists entered Washington, they were alarmed to see a large number of coffins stacked on the railroad station platform. No riot occurred; the third-party people had merely come to town to hear Tom Watson deliver a speech.

When explaining their tightfistedness, Populists made it plain that they took seriously the conventional wisdom of the day: in times of depression the government, like the citizen, should reduce expenses. Yet on some matters, People's party legislators were not entirely frugal. They usually favored adequate appropriations for the common school fund, but they objected to professionals or a select group of citizens controlling educational institutions. Instead, they called for the election of all school commissioners and boards of education. They were sometimes less than generous in making appropriations to Georgia's state university and colleges. Most probably agreed with the *People's Party Paper* when it condemned as "useless" a $25,000 grant to the Georgia Normal and Industrial College at Milledgeville. [19]

Following the dictates of their party platforms of 1894 and 1896, Populists favored an end to convict lease and urged the building of a state prison and reform school. They also demanded that less dangerous prisoners repair Georgia's rut-filled roads, a scheme they knew would win black votes. Some were sincerely anguished by the brutality of the lease system. But this sentiment was not shared by most third-party legislators, who voted against a bill for the "better care and humane treatment of misdemeanor convicts." Nor was the Populist remedy for convict lease especially humane. They suggested that the state provide prison wagons for the convicts working on the roads. Opponents argued that it would be criminal to lock men in such unsanitary "cages." Populist opposition to convict lease left many other unanswered questions. Because the state placed the money accrued from the leasing of prisoners in the Georgia school fund, the abolition of convict lease would cripple the state educational system. Nor did the Populists explain where Georgia was to obtain

18. Atlanta *Constitution*, July 20, 21, 1893; Atlanta *Journal*, July 21, 1893; U.S. Congress, House, *Watson vs. Black*, 715.
19. *People's Party Paper*, August 26, December 23, 1892, November 9, December 7, 1894.

the money to build a prison and a reform school. Presumably, a consider-able tax increase would be necessary, but the third-party platform of 1898 demanded lower taxes, an end to convict lease, and no reduction in the common school fund.[20]

One final expense Populists were willing to accept was the state pur-chase of common school textbooks. As early as 1892, J. H. Boyd of McDuffie County introduced such a measure in the house, and two years later it became part of the party's platform. "The [textbook] bill is social-istic," the Atlanta *Constitution* grimly warned.[21] Yet this was the closest that Democrats came to proving that Georgia Populists were wild-eyed extremists. Nor did third-party reasons for the bill help the Democrats' argument. Rather than advocating Marxism, the Populists were simply angered by the high cost of books and the infuriating habit of many school districts of constantly changing the texts.

Besides the schoolbook bill, People's party legislators proposed noth-ing that suggested they were edging toward government paternalism. In-deed, much of the evidence suggested the opposite. When a group of citi-zens in Atlanta built an old soldiers' home and offered it to the state, Populists vigorously opposed the gift. The aging veterans should stay at home, they argued, and not be taken to the Atlanta "poor house" to be-come wards of the state. Populists made few attempts to regulate the marketplace except for resolutions by Mell Branch demanding that the governor enforce the laws against railroad monopolies.[22] Populist leg-islators also voted for a weak antitrust bill and for an investigation of pools.[23] Beyond this they did little to try to control large business combinations.

How were Democratic proposals similar to and different from those of the Populists? The Alliance legislature of 1890 and the rise of the Atkin-

20. Atlanta *Constitution*, November 29, December 7, 8, 1897; *People's Party Paper*, De-cember 21, 1894; *Georgia House Journal*, 1893, p. 860. For the votes of third-party legisla-tors on the convict question, see Atlanta *Constitution*, December 7, 10, 1897. On the reform school issue, see *Georgia House Journal*, 1893, pp. 16–18, 639–40; Atlanta *Constitution*, August 8, 1896; December 10, 1897. On the 1898 platform, see *ibid.*, March 17, 1898.

21. *Georgia House Journal*, 1892, p. 245; Atlanta *Constitution*, May 18, 1894. Seven Populists voted for this proposal; three were opposed (*Georgia House Journal*, 1892, pp. 250–51; *People's Party Paper*, December 23, 1892).

22. *Georgia House Journal*, 1892, pp. 220, 580–82; 1893, pp. 264–65; 1895, p. 407; Atlanta *Constitution*, November 19, 1896.

23. *Georgia House Journal*, 1893, pp. 345–46; Atlanta *Constitution*, November 18, 1893.

son "dynasty" had forced many old Bourbons from the halls of the capitol. Younger men had taken their places, and some had come into office demanding change. Certainly many were as reform-minded as their Populist opponents and on some issues even more so. They called for prohibition, a reform school, an end to convict lease, a longer school term, a graduated income tax, a stronger railroad commission, the election of circuit court judges and solicitors-general, and the creation of a state board of medical examiners. They also championed a number of antitrust and antilynching laws.[24] Although many of these proposals died in committee, the introduction of such bills showed that Democratic legislators were not a monolithic group and that some were eager for reform. In addition, they demonstrate that the roots of Georgia progressivism stretch back into the nineteenth century.

Generally, these proponents of change were young, middle-class legislators, who did not revere the old Bourbon tradition with the passion of their elders. Many came from Georgia's towns and cities and thus possessed a first-hand knowledge of urban life. In this respect they differed from Populist reformers, who were more interested in the problems of the countryside. When, in 1897, the reform Democrats in the house introduced a bill to prohibit factories from hiring children younger than thirteen years of age, the Populists took little part in the debate. They listened as their opponents slashed at each other over the merits of child labor. "The employment of these small children," one Democrat said, "may make smoke curl high over the cities of Griffin and LaGrange, but I had rather see the fires all banked and the furnaces cold in my town than to see the smoke curling from the slavery of these little children! I had rather see no factories at all than to have the children shut out from God's own sunlight in a big, dusty and unhealthy factory! If we have to have a Lowell down south, let the manufacturers hire children over twelve years of age." When it was argued that mill owners sincerely cared about the boys and girls they employed, a Democrat angrily snapped: "These factories are not working for the poor children. Did you ever hear of a corporation working in the interests of the people?" Nearly one-

---

24. Atlanta *Constitution*, November 8, 18, December 3, 1893, November 9, 23, 1894, November 1, 5, December 8, 1895, December 2, 16, 1896.

half of the People's party members were unmoved by such pleas, and they voted with the majority in defeating the bill.[25] Again demonstrating their town and middle-class upbringing, in 1893 the reform Democrats proposed legislation calling for a state board of medical examiners to license physicians. The reformers, often coming from places where doctors were plentiful, could afford to scrutinize a healer's credentials. The enemies of the bill, including almost all the Populists, opposed any law that might lessen the number of doctors practicing in the countryside. They also feared that such a board would drive out popular but unorthodox fields of medicine such as homeopathy.[26]

But Democratic reformers were not always townsmen, and many were deeply concerned about farm problems. In 1894, C. W. Gray, a Democrat from Catoosa County, proposed a bill that would aid tenant farmers who disputed the amount of cotton due their landlords at harvest. Under Georgia law a tenant could bring his landlord to court only after supplying a bond worth twice the value of the disputed property. The Gray bill allowed the tenant to sue without furnishing bond, as long as the sheriff retained possession of the cotton. Both Democrats and Populists gave the measure enthusiastic support, and it passed through the General Assembly without a dissenting vote. Three years later, Democrats proposed bills that would allow the poor to obtain a writ of *certiorari* and to appeal a case to a superior court without posting bond. With the aid of the third party, this legislation also became law.[27]

On other issues, however, the Democrats differed from the Populists. Both parties in the legislature voted for antilynching laws, but Democrats led the way. From 1892 to 1897 they proposed every antilynching bill to appear before the General Assembly. In late 1894 and early 1895, Georgia was alive with mobs. In Brooks County a "race war" erupted, killing four people and forcing Governor Atkinson to order the militia to the scene. During the same period a mob of possibly a thousand attacked

25. Atlanta *Constitution*, November 10, 1897. Eleven Populists supported the bill, ten were opposed, and eight failed to vote (*Georgia House Journal*, 1897, pp. 330–32). For a discussion of the crusade against child labor in Georgia, see Jones, "Progressivism in Georgia," 41–82.

26. *Georgia House Journal*, 1893, pp. 734–35; Atlanta *Constitution*, November 3, 1893.

27. *Georgia House Journal*, 1894, pp. 348, 703; *Georgia Senate Journal*, 1894, pp. 483, 578; *Georgia Laws*, 1894, pp. 51–52; 1897, pp. 32, 33–34.

the jail in Augusta bent on a lynching. After a hundred shots were fired and one person was killed, the crowd dispersed.[28]

Governor Atkinson seemed even more hostile to lynching than was his predecessor, William J. Northen. In his first address to the General Assembly in 1895, Atkinson deplored the five lynchings that had occurred in the early months of his administration. Confessing that the rewards he had offered had failed to bring the culprits to justice, the governor asked for the authority to dismiss any sheriff who surrendered his prisoner to a mob. He also recommended that relatives of lynching victims have the right to sue the county where the crime had occurred for the "full value of . . . the victim's life." A year later Atkinson again condemned lynching before the General Assembly, pointing out that a crowd had recently taken a prisoner from a courtroom and hanged him on a public street. The governor argued that faster trials, public executions, and the death sentence for attempted rape might reduce the reason for mob justice. Some time before, Atkinson had written to the legislature about four "unjustifiable, disgraceful, and shocking" lynchings. In one case the sheriff had been unable to arrest the culprits because he could not organize a posse. Atkinson advised that the General Assembly make it illegal for an able-bodied man to refuse to join a posse when called. The governor's last address to the legislature was filled with frustration. He reported that during his years in office twenty-two lynchings had occurred in Georgia, and in a number of cases he was certain the victims had been innocent. Accordingly, Atkinson made a remarkable proposal by the standards of his day: all sheriffs should be expected to defend prisoners with their own lives. If the sheriff could not or would not do this, he should be required to unshackle and arm the prisoner and allow him to defend himself. Finally, Atkinson suggested that the state investigate every lynching to make certain the authorities had done their duty. Reminding Democratic legislators that their party had promised laws against lynching, he challenged them either to enact strong legislation or to tell the people they had lied about the issue.[29]

28. *Annual Cyclopaedia*, 1895, s.v. "Georgia"; Atlanta *Constitution*, December 24, 25, 1894.
29. *Georgia Senate Journal*, 1895, pp. 35–37; *Annual Cyclopaedia*, 1895, s.v. "Georgia"; *Georgia Senate Journal*, 1897, pp. 27–40.

In response, Democrats proposed several reforms. They introduced and passed a bill making clear the penalties for lynching: those guilty of "mobbing or lynching any citizen of this State" would be sentenced to from one to twenty years; and if the incident resulted in death, they would be tried for murder. This law also granted the sheriff the authority to use any reasonable means, including shooting into a mob, to protect a prisoner. An able-bodied man who refused to join a posse when called would be guilty of a misdemeanor. To control the whitecaps who had threatened Georgia gins in 1893, the legislature made it illegal to post a notice threatening to burn a gin, barn, house, or other building. (Arson was already a capital crime.) Finally, during the legislature of 1895, J. H. Pitman, a Democrat from Troup County, sponsored a measure making it illegal to interfere with a law officer who was carrying out court orders after a trial. An unusual incident had prompted Pitman's bill. The year before, a mob had overpowered a sheriff and lynched his prisoner just after that man had been tried and sentenced to death.[30]

A casual reading of these laws might have given the impression that Democrats despised lynching and were eager to suppress it. This was not the case. They had designed the whitecap law to discourage violence against property. And although the penalties for lynching were strong, they were based on the questionable assumption that a white jury would pass harsh judgment against a white man. In many cases, the only way a conscientious sheriff could abort a lynching was to organize a posse, but the citizen who failed to answer the call was guilty only of a misdemeanor.

Even so, blacks were delighted with the new laws. They applauded Atkinson for his courageous stand against lynching and praised Democrats for passing legislation against mob murder. Although Populists supported these laws, too, most blacks realized they had been originated by Democrats. That there was little real difference in the racial attitudes of Democrats and Populists in the General Assembly became evident in 1892, when W. H. Styles, a black Republican from Liberty County, attempted to repeal the law requiring the separation of the races on Geor-

30. *Georgia Laws*, 1893, pp. 128–30; 1895, pp. 69–70; Atlanta *Constitution*, November 4, December 3, 1893, December 8, 1895; *Georgia House Journal*, 1893, pp. 142, 290, 319, 562; 1895, pp. 688–90; *Georgia Code*, 1882, p. 1150.

gia's trains. The Speaker sent the Styles bill to the railroad committee, which included five Populists. At length the committee unanimously reported against the measure.[31] More than anything, this vote indicated the sentiments of both Populists and the Democrats on the race issue.

Thinking back over their years in the General Assembly, former third-party legislators probably remembered their Democratic colleagues with some fondness. On most bills there had existed surprising unanimity. When dispute flared, as in the case of the election of superior court judges, a considerable number of Democrats had voted with the Populists. The third-party demand for free textbooks, the Democrats' intransigence on election reform, and the battle over convict lease produced the appearance of great struggle. But for the most part, this was an illusion. Indeed, one is struck by the similarity rather than dissimilarity of the views of these men.

With such harmony, some citizens wondered why the Populist party ever appeared in Georgia. They forgot that Populism had been founded as an answer to national issues. The People's party needed an organization in the state only to turn out the vote in federal races and to elect legislators who in turn would appoint United States senators. On many state questions there was little reason for the party's existence. Democratic reformers already sat in the legislature, and because the Farmers' Alliance had elected some of these Democrats to office in 1890, many possessed ideas similar to those of the Populists. They differed from third-party legislators only in that they had failed to renounce the Democratic party and could not accept every provision of the Omaha platform. Indeed, the real legislative battles of these years were usually between reformers and Bourbons rather than Democrats and Populists. Such battles foretold the struggles of the progressive era.

31. *Georgia House Journal*, 1892, pp. 245, 320. For the law Styles was trying to repeal, see *Georgia Laws*, 1890–91, pp. 157–58.

IX

"No Watson, No Bryan"
The Campaigns of 1896

"You have now the opportunity of your life," read the note from Clark Howell, editor of the Atlanta *Constitution*. Gazing at the message, its recipient quickly scribbled in the words, "You will not be disappointed."[1] He then prepared for the opportunity of a lifetime. When his name was called, he rushed from his chair, striding to the rostrum amid thunderous applause. He was a young man, thin yet strong, with a massive jaw and forehead, dressed in a black alpaca suit.

Slowly, the crowd grew still, eager to hear the beginning of his speech. "I come to speak to you in defense of a cause as holy as the cause of liberty—the cause of humanity," he said. "The individual is but an atom; he is born, he acts, he dies; but principles are eternal; and this has been a contest over principles." The young man's words were distinct and melodious; they could be heard in the farthest reaches of the auditorium. As his sentences poured forth, the words were hypnotic and beguiling. Soon almost everyone was cheering, the sound crashing through the hall like the roar of artillery. Hundreds of men and women climbed upon their chairs, many with tears in their eyes, shouting their approval. Above the din, the magical words continued: "We have petitioned, and our petitions have been scorned; we have entreated, and our entreaties have been disregarded; we have begged, and they have mocked when our calamity came. We beg no longer; we entreat no more; we petition no more. We defy them." The crowd grew more and more impassioned, answering each sentence with cheers that exploded in every corner of the auditorium. "You come to us and tell us that the great cities are in favor of the gold standard," the young man cried; "we reply that the great cities

---

1. Atlanta *Constitution*, July 11, 1896.

rest upon our broad and fertile prairies. Burn down your cities and leave our farms, and your cities will spring up again as if by magic; but destroy our farms and the grass will grow in the streets of every city in the country." The words seemed electric, thrilling, holy. Soon, however, the speech was rushing toward its conclusion, stirring the crowd to the edge of hysteria: "If they dare to come out in the open field and defend the gold standard as a good thing, we will fight them to the uttermost. Having behind us the producing masses of this nation and the world, supported by the commercial interests, the laboring interests, and the toilers everywhere, we will answer their demand for a gold standard by saying to them: You shall not press down upon the brow of labor this crown of thorns, you shall not crucify mankind upon a cross of gold."[2]

In an instant the hall was still. The speaker stood before them, his arms extended, his head flung back—the very image of the crucified Christ. For five seconds there was a silence. Then rebel yells pealed from the Georgia delegation. The spell was broken. The roar of twenty thousand voices thundered through the hall. It sounded the beginning of a great presidential campaign. It sounded the doom of the Populist party.[3]

The next day, July 10, 1896, the Democratic national convention nominated William Jennings Bryan of Nebraska as its candidate for president of the United States. Although his Cross of Gold speech had not convinced the delegates to endorse bimetalism—by the time Bryan spoke, the silverites already had control of the meeting—it did assure that a relatively obscure Nebraskan would receive their nomination. To balance the ticket, the convention selected an easterner, Arthur Sewall of Maine, as the vice-presidential candidate. A banker, shipbuilder, railroad executive, and president of a trust, Sewall seemed an unlikely running mate for Bryan. But he advocated free silver and would, it was hoped, give the ticket strength in the East.[4]

Most Democrats were delighted by Bryan's nomination, but third-

2. William Jennings Bryan, *The First Battle: A Story of the Campaign of 1896* (Chicago, 1896), 199–206.

3. For descriptions of Bryan and his delivery of the Cross of Gold speech, see Paolo E. Coletta, *William Jennings Bryan* (3 vols.; Lincoln, 1964–69), I, 137–42; Louis W. Koenig, *Bryan: A Political Biography of William Jennings Bryan* (New York, 1971), 194–99; Paul W. Glad, *McKinley, Bryan, and the People* (Philadelphia, 1964), 136–39.

4. Glad, *McKinley, Bryan, and the People*, 140–41.

party men were profoundly troubled. Few had believed their opponents would repudiate Grover Cleveland by nominating a silverite. Instead, the Populist national committeemen had assumed that both old parties would select goldbugs. Thus they scheduled their convention in St. Louis to follow those of the Republicans and Democrats. They were half correct; on June 18 the Republicans nominated William McKinley, a former governor of Ohio popular with monometalists. But Bryan's candidacy now threatened the existence of the People's party. "You struck us a fearful blow when you nominated Bryan," one Georgia Populist told a Democrat. "Our people think so much of him that I fear many will be led off."[5] This danger was especially to be feared in the West. Realizing that a third-party ticket would split the silver vote and assure the election of McKinley, westerners argued that they were compelled to put principle above party and also nominate Bryan. Soon almost every well-known Populist on the plains had embraced the idea, including James B. Weaver, Jerry Simpson, and Mary Elizabeth Lease.

But southern party members refused to agree and sneeringly referred to the Democratic candidates as "Bryan and Swill." Calling themselves "middle-of-the-roaders" because they claimed to stand in the center of the Populist highway, they argued that fusion would murder the People's party. Southerners pointed out that free silver was just one of many Populist beliefs. They were also reluctant to believe that the Democrats intended to carry out reform, especially because they had nominated Arthur Sewall as their vice-presidential candidate. Similar duplicity had been used to destroy the Alliance, the *People's Party Paper* argued: "The Alliance lamb agreed to lie down with the Democratic lion. Result: lamb soon dissolved in the gastric juices of said lion."[6]

Georgians were determined that their party would not suffer that fate. To stress their dedication to the midroad philosophy, they had met in Atlanta six months before the national party convention and formulated instructions for their delegation. The Georgia platform endorsed all the doctrines of pure Populism: free silver at a ratio of 16 to 1, government ownership of the railroads, the direct election of United States senators,

    5. Hicks, *Populist Revolt*, 350–51; Atlanta *Constitution*, July 21, 1896.
    6. For a discussion of the debate between the fusionists and middle-of-the-roaders, see Hicks, *Populist Revolt*, 340–59; *People's Party Paper*, July 26, 1895.

and an end to banks of issue. In addition, the platform proposed that before the government buy the railroads it hold a plebiscite to obtain the approval of the people—an obvious weakening of party doctrine, which called for federal ownership of the railroads with no mention of a popular vote. The platform also insisted that "Church and State be forever kept separate." Thus the growing fear of Catholicism had become an official principle of the state party.[7]

When it came time to choose delegates to attend the national convention in St. Louis, Georgia Populists were again ruled by their midroad thinking. Out of a delegation of sixty-two members, only two were fusionists. Among the middle-of-the-roaders selected were Tom Watson, James K. Hines, William L. Peek, Clarence H. Ellington, Mell Branch, and Charles McGregor. "If the Savior of mankind himself was nominated by the Democratic party on a platform of the 10 commandments, I would vote against him," one delegate declared. "That is how I feel about the Democratic party." Rather than accept the nomination of Bryan, the Georgians planned to support Tom Watson for president or vice-president. Yet just before they left for St. Louis, Watson declined to attend the convention, telling his supporters that "under no circumstances" would he accept a nomination.[8]

When the Georgia Populists reached their destination, they quickly joined forces with the huge Texas delegation to work for a middle-of-the-road ticket. But the preconvention meetings were chaotic. With Watson refusing to run, they could agree upon only two weak candidates: S. F. Norton of Illinois for president and Frank Burkitt of Mississippi for vice-president. Meanwhile, the city was filling with fusion delegations from the plains. Unlike the southerners, they were ably led by Weaver, Simpson, and Lease. Most alarming was their great number. Every hotel was crowded with confident men, speaking in western accents about the nomination of William Jennings Bryan. The Georgians had never suspected Bryan would command such strong support. To complicate mat-

---

7. *People's Party Paper*, December 27, 1895. See also, Charles McGregor to Thomas E. Watson, October 28, 1895, Box 2, folder 15, Watson Papers, UNC.

8. Atlanta *Constitution*, July 24, 1896; Atlanta *Journal*, July 23, 24, 1896; Savannah *Press*, July 25, 1896; *People's Party Paper*, July 17, 1896. For the middle-of-the-road sentiment of the rank and file, see Dallas *Herald*, July 16, 1896; Atlanta *Constitution*, July 19, 1896.

ters, a third faction, which in the end proved to have a majority, hoped to find some way to nominate Bryan without nominating Sewall. They spoke of replacing him with a southern midroader. This proposal might preserve the party while preventing a split in the national silver vote.[9]

On the first day of the convention, the Georgians were not interested in such a scheme. During a meeting of the national executive committee, the compromisers nominated for temporary chairman Senator Marion Butler, a fusionist from North Carolina. Mell Branch countered by nominating the midroader Ignatius Donnelly of Minnesota. Although the committee eventually selected the North Carolinian, the Georgians were undaunted. When Butler gave his opening address to the convention, at least one member of the delegation loudly hissed him. After the speech, and just as the convention was adjourning, a Georgian named Yancey Carter rose and shouted for the midroad delegates to stay. That evening, Carter bellowed, the middle-of-the-roaders planned a rally before the nominations for permanent chairman. Midroad delegates followed Carter's instructions and arrived at the auditorium early. To their dismay, they found the lights were out. In the darkness they tried to begin a demonstration, but it failed as curses and shouts filled the hall. Many were convinced the fusionists had tampered with the electricity to prevent them from seizing control of the meeting.[10]

The convention had to wait until the next day to select a permanent chairman. As the time neared for nominations, the hall grew fiercely hot, and everywhere palm leaf fans flickered about perspiring faces. It was a critical moment for the midroaders. Their delegates seemed despondent over the failure of their earlier rally; yet all were agreed that the vote for permanent chairman would decide which faction would rule the convention. Suddenly, Mell Branch burst through the main door of the hall, carrying a huge banner inscribed with the words:

MIDDLE OF THE ROAD
STRAIGHT TICKET

9. See Robert F. Durden, *The Climax of Populism: The Election of 1896* (Lexington, 1965), 23–44; Atlanta *Constitution*, July 22, 23, 1896; St. Louis *Globe-Democrat*, July 23, 1896; Atlanta *Constitution*, July 24, 1896; Savannah *Press*, July 25, 1896.

10. Atlanta *Journal*, July 23, 1896; St. Louis *Globe-Democrat*, July 24, 1896; Atlanta *Constitution*, July 24, 1896; Savannah *Press*, July 25, 1896; Durden, *Climax of Populism*, 33–34.

The showdown had come. The Georgia, Texas, Mississippi, Missouri, and Maine delegations clamored from their seats, following Branch up and down the hall. Green tickets tumbled from the balcony proclaiming the virtues of pure Populism. But most of the other delegations remained seated, impassive and unmoved. William V. Allen, a fusionist from Nebraska, received 758 votes for permanent chairman. His opponent, an obscure midroader named James E. Campion, obtained only 564. Bryan's nomination was virtually assured. The losers were furious, claiming their opponents had employed all manner of tricks to defeat them. In the Texas and Georgia delegations, men openly talked of a bolt. "We will have an independent ticket if we have to nominate it ourselves," warned John Sibley of Georgia.[11]

But most middle-of-the-roaders were reluctant to walk out of the convention, not wanting to bear responsibility for dismembering the party. Moreover, they had a plan that might yet save the cause. Their leaders sent word throughout the hall urging the delegates to support the selection of the vice-presidential candidate first. Since a majority of delegates wanted to prevent a bolt and had little love for the Democratic vice-presidential nominee, they would almost certainly vote against Sewall's nomination. Midroaders also hoped Bryan might refuse to run on a Populist ticket without his Democratic running mate. Despite opposition from the fusionists, the convention accepted the proposal.[12]

The Georgia delegation was under immense pressure. Although considering themselves middle-of-the-roaders, its members had been sobered by the success of the fusionists. As each hour passed, more and more of them searched for a compromise. There was still talk of a bolt but only if both Bryan and Sewall were nominated. During a speech, Hines had earlier told the midroaders: "They cannot press down upon our brows a crown of Democratic thorns; they cannot crucify us upon a cross of silver." But shortly afterward, he informed a reporter that the Georgia delegates "would probably be willing to cut off the head of their ticket if the Democrats would be willing to cut off the tail of theirs."[13]

11. Atlanta *Journal*, July 23, 1896.
12. Hicks, *Populist Revolt*, 363–64; Goodwyn, *Democratic Promise*, 482–83; Durden, *Climax of Populism*, 34–35.
13. Atlanta *Journal*, July 23, 24, 1896.

Other delegations were demanding Watson's nomination. At first, the Georgians refused. But it became apparent that Watson's candidacy might prevent a bolt by the extreme midroaders. Also, men close to James K. Jones, chairman of the Democratic National Committee, had quietly told them that the Democrats would withdraw Arthur Sewall if Watson were nominated. Not completely convinced, the delegation wired William Jennings Bryan, asking if he would accept the Populist nomination. They received no reply. With time running out, a Georgia delegate named J. L. Cartledge wired Watson that his candidacy could prevent a bolt and that the Democrats had promised to withdraw Sewall. Would he accept the nomination? The next day, hours before the contest for vice-president, the delegation received a wire from Thomson, Georgia. It read: "Yes, if it will harmonize all factions." [14]

That evening the hall again sweltered, and hundreds of delegates flailed the stuffy air with palmetto fans. Finally, Arthur Sewall and Tom Watson were nominated for vice-president. But the extreme midroaders, puzzled that Watson would run with Bryan, nominated Frank Burkitt. The Texas delegation was especially wary. When Amzon A. Murphy of Georgia was seconding Watson's nomination, a Texan interrupted, demanding to know if Watson would stay on the ticket to the end of the campaign. Murphy's answer came like a shot: "Yes, sir. Yes sir. Until hell freezes over." [15]

The voting began late in the evening, and soon it was past midnight. After the first ballot Watson was far in the lead, but he remained short of a majority. Abruptly, the Texas delegation announced that it was switching its 105 votes from Burkitt to Watson. Then the Tennessee delegation was recognized; it, too, was changing its votes to Watson. North Carolina delegates demanded to be heard, but before they could switch their votes, the chairman announced that Thomas E. Watson was nominated. Instantly, the lights flickered out. As curses and shouts filled the hall, reporters lit candles that dimly illuminated the growing pandemonium. Gesticulating men howled that the fusionists were again sabotaging the convention. Yet somehow a voice was heard above the din, shouting the

14. Brewton, *Watson*, 268; Durden, *Climax of Populism*, 41n.; Atlanta *Journal*, July 25, August 1, 7, 1896.
15. St. Louis *Globe-Democrat*, July 25, 1896; Hicks, *Populist Revolt*, 365.

news: Watson had been nominated at exactly sixteen minutes before one o'clock. The extraordinary words passed from lip to lip. And suddenly from across the darkened hall rolled forth the cheer: "Sixteen to one! Sixteen to one!"[16]

The next day the Populist convention selected William Jennings Bryan as its candidate for president of the United States. His nomination did not come easily. Extreme midroaders, still supporting S. F. Norton, engaged in a terrific struggle to prevent the Nebraskan's nomination. But when the balloting, the fist fights, and the chaos of the last session were over, Bryan had defeated Norton by 1,042 votes to 321. The Georgia Populists, who at the start of the convention were considered among the strongest of midroaders, gave Norton only five votes. The remaining fifty-seven delegates supported Bryan, and James K. Hines seconded his nomination.[17]

For the Georgians it had been a strange finish to a strange convention. During the train ride back to Atlanta they must have wondered about the wisdom of their actions. Had they erred in giving up their midroad philosophy, in allowing the nomination of Watson, in expecting the Democrats to withdraw Sewall? Certainly by the time they left St. Louis they had heard Chairman Jones's announcement that he had made no deals with the Populists and that the Democrats would not withdraw Sewall. The Georgians had been duped.[18]

Twenty-five years later, William L. Peek still maintained that Jones had personally assured the delegation that Sewall would be eliminated. But by that time Peek was eighty-five years old, and his memory was not as clear as it once had been. Just after the convention he had written a letter to the Atlanta *Journal* explaining what had happened in St. Louis. The letter merely said "it was understood with the Democrats" that Sewall would be withdrawn. Yet there had still been an agreement. John D. Cunningham, the new chairman of the Georgia Populist party, later admitted that Jones's lieutenants, but not Jones himself, had given

16. St. Louis *Globe-Democrat*, July 25, 1896; Atlanta *Constitution*, July 25, 1896.
17. For vivid descriptions of the last day of the convention, see St. Louis *Globe-Democrat*, July 26, 1896; Atlanta *Journal*, July 25, 27, 1896; Goodwyn, *Democratic Promise*, 485–92; Hicks, *Populist Revolt*, 366–67; Durden, *Climax of Populism*, 41–44.
18. Durden, *Climax of Populism*, 39.

them assurances that Sewall would be eliminated. How the Georgia delegation, which had had considerable experience with Democratic duplicity in the past, could have been taken in by such a ruse was difficult to
explain.[19]

Watson's role in the deal also left unanswered questions. Some believed that he really desired a presidential or a vice-presidential nomination and that his failure to attend the convention was a way of promoting
his own candidacy. Although Watson believed he could easily have had
either nomination, it seems more likely that he did not want the honor.
By July 20 he had virtually decided on another race for Congress and let
it be known that he would not attend the St. Louis convention. The reason for this last-minute decision probably had nothing to do with what
might have occurred in St. Louis. Instead, four days earlier, Watson's
nemesis, Major James C. C. Black had announced that he desired "not
to be considered" a candidate for the Democratic nomination in the
Tenth District.[20] With Black out of the contest, Watson's chances for victory were bright. Why, Watson may have reasoned, should he give up a
seat in Congress for the empty honor of running for the presidency or
vice-presidency in a race he would probably lose?

The question also remained why Watson, who was an implacable opponent of fusion before the convention, eventually agreed to run on a
fusionist ticket. The Georgia delegation had informed him that his candidacy might prevent a bolt and that the Democrats had agreed to withdraw Sewall. By oversight or design, the delegation had neglected to tell
Watson that a midroader was already running for the vice-presidential
nomination. Watson later said that had he known of Burkitt's candidacy
he would not have allowed his own nomination.[21]

Whatever the motives of the delegates, they now faced serious problems. But despite Jones's assertion that the Democratic vice-presidential
candidate would not be withdrawn, the Georgians still believed Sewall
could be driven from the ticket. They made it plain that if the Democrats

19. Arnett, *Populist Movement in Georgia*, 199n.; Atlanta *Journal*, August 1, 3, 1896;
Brewton, *Watson*, 267–68; New York *World*, August 4, 1896. Brewton (p. 270) suggests that the Georgia delegation was carried away in its effort to gain Watson the vice-
presidential nomination.
20. Atlanta *Journal*, July 16, 20, 1896.
21. Brewton, *Watson*, 268–70.

would not support Watson, the southern Populists would not support Bryan—hence their new slogan was "No Watson, No Bryan." This plan might save Populism, eliminate Sewall, and elect Watson. But it might destroy Populism, defeat Watson, and elect McKinley.

Returning to Atlanta in the last week of July, Georgia delegates found they had much explaining to do to their middle-of-the-road constituents. They also hastened to complete preparations for a convention to be held in Atlanta in early August. The Watson wing already possessed a scheme for winning the state election. In 1892 the party had selected "dirt-farmer" William L. Peek and had been severely beaten. Two years later they had nominated a "respectable" candidate, James K. Hines, and had nearly won. In 1896 the Watsonites claimed that a new ingredient would bring them victory: prohibition. Populist legislators had generally supported antisaloon bills, and it was believed that twenty-five thousand tee-totalers lived in Georgia. To tap this vote, the Populists had merely to endorse prohibition and find a respectable prohibitionist to run for governor. Undoubtedly, they would have selected Hines, who had favored temperance since his youth, but he refused to run. Finally, the Watson wing settled on James Bruton Gambrell. The president of Mercer University from 1893 to 1896, a prominent Baptist minister, and a leader of the Georgia Prohibition party, Gambrell appeared to be an ideal contender for governor. But when word spread of Gambrell's candidacy, many Populists were dismayed. Gambrell had never been a party member, and they feared that a strong stand on prohibition might lose votes among blacks. Thus this faction began to organize, hoping to convince Hines to run against Gambrell. If this failed, they planned to support Peek, who was eager for another gubernatorial race.[22]

When the convention met on August 6, 1896, there seemed little doubt that Gambrell would be nominated. Yet by the afternoon, his movement had been crushed. At the last moment, members of the Peek faction discovered that Gambrell was ineligible to become governor. Gleefully, they pointed out that to serve as governor, state law required a man to have

22. Atlanta *Journal*, July 31, August 1, 1896; Blakely *Early County News*, August 30, 1894; Spright Dowell, *A History of Mercer University, 1833–1953* (Macon, 1958), 205–17; Atlanta *Constitution*, August 6, 7, 1896; Augusta *Chronicle*, August 7, 1896; Dallas *Herald*, July 16, 1896.

been a citizen of Georgia for six years. Gambrell had lived in the state for only three years. Still the Watsonites were determined to withhold the nomination from the Peek wing. Quickly wiring Seaborn Wright, a Floyd County lawyer, they requested that he hurry to Atlanta. There they convinced him to run for the gubernatorial nomination. The next day the Peek forces were still outnumbered, and they reluctantly offered no opposition to the new candidate.[23]

At thirty-eight years of age, Seaborn Wright was as "handsome as Apollo," with long raven hair and fine, almost ascetic features. He easily fit the Populist formula for victory: he was a prohibitionist who was the soul of respectability. His father, a former United States and Confederate States congressman, had left his son a comfortable inheritance. Seaborn then married the daughter of a wealthy Atlantan and later built one of the finest houses in Rome. Although his property was assessed at less than $19,000, rumor had it that he was rich. Nevertheless, few questioned Wright's loyalty to the reform movement in Georgia. Except for his service as a Democrat in the legislature of 1881, he had mostly remained an independent. His idol was William H. Felton, and Wright publicly denounced Democratic swindles that occurred during Felton's race for Congress in 1894.[24] At the congressional hearings that followed, Wright and a Democratic lawyer engaged in a heated exchange.

"You, Seaborn Wright, came here today to consume our time and interrupt our proceedings," the lawyer declared.

"I pronounce that statement false," Wright replied.

"I pronounce you a liar, Seaborn Wright," cried the Democrat, who abruptly rushed across the courtroom screaming, "I'll slap your face." Wright ended the discussion by punching the lawyer in the jaw.[25]

But some party members doubted the wisdom of Wright's nomination, complaining that he was too much of a dandy; he wore fine linen suits, immaculate shirts, and the latest straw hats. Others wondered how loyal

23. Columbus *Enquirer-Sun*, August 7, 1896; Atlanta *Constitution*, August 7, 1896; see also Georgia Constitution (1877), art. V, sec. I, par. VII. On Wright, see Augusta *Chronicle*, August 7, 1896; Douglas *Breeze*, August 14, 1896.

24. Augusta *Chronicle*, August 8, 1896; Savannah *Press*, August 8, 11, 1896; Atlanta *Constitution*, August 8, 1896; Seaborn Wright, Biographical Data File, Georgia Department of Archives and History, Atlanta.

25. Felton, "*Memoirs*," 667.

he would be to the state platform. Despite his sympathy for Populism, Wright was not a party member and had a history of nonconformity. In addition, he frequently sounded self-righteous, lecturing his audiences on their need for integrity and reminding them that Seaborn Wright had never compromised his principles. For a third-party politician in particular this was a dangerous quality.

Wright attempted to change his habits. He gave up his smart summer suits and fastidious ways. "Yesterday Mr. Wright appeared in funeral black," one witness wrote upon seeing the candidate at the Populist headquarters. "A slight [stubble] . . . of uncut hirsutes fringed his lower jaw. His tie was massed in a knotty heap, and his hat was pulled down over one eye with a careless jerk. There was a good coating of Lawrence-ville dust on his shoes and the trousers bagged about the knees. He threw himself loosely about and now and then dropped into an indolent drawl strongly suggestive of the mountaineer brogue." But Lawrenceville dust and the want of a shave could not hide the fact that Wright was a city slicker who was thought to be worth hundreds of thousands of dollars. His brilliant tongue rather than his backwoods garb won farmers to the cause of Populism. Crossing the state, he gave a series of stirring addresses, and soon many communities were demanding visits by the third-party candidate. Even the opposition was eager to hear him. When word came that the candidate was to speak in Brunswick, the Democratic *Evening Advertiser* exclaimed: "He is coming, Seab the speaker, Seab the man of many creeds; Seab the lightning changer, keen-eyed, quick to see the people's needs. Pop and prohi, platform-mixer, fusion artist unexcelled. Watson's darling, Gambrell's gosling, centuries of gloom dispelled. Hamlet-featured, silver tongued, he, from the seven hills of Floyd." [26]

In their search for respectability, Georgia Populists did not stop with Seaborn Wright. Their candidate for state treasurer was William Crapon Sibley, the owner of the Sibley Manufacturing Company. In 1895 Sibley's Augusta mill had boasted of 40,256 spindles, 1,109 looms, and capitalization at $900,000. Sibley was also president of the Warrior Coal & Coke Company, the Round Mountain Coal & Iron Company, and the

26. Atlanta *Constitution*, September 10, 1896; Brunswick *Evening Advertiser*, n.d., quoted in *ibid.*, August 31, 1896.

Coaldale Brick & Tile Company—all located in Alabama—as well as director of the Commercial Bank of Augusta. How could such an individual, seemingly the apotheosis of the New South businessman, have become a Populist? There were evidently two reasons. Just as Tom Watson had hoped, the prohibition plank made Populism more acceptable to the upper and middle classes. Undoubtedly, this was what induced Sibley, whose wife was president of the Georgia Women's Christian Temperance Union, to run for state treasurer. Also, two of his half brothers, John A. and James L. Sibley, were prominent Populists.[27]

Prohibition had indeed made the third party more respectable, although its position on the saloon issue was surprisingly moderate. The state platform observed that "civilization, to say nothing of religion, has entered up judgment of condemnation against barrooms. The public conscience revolts at the license system." To fight the saloon, the platform demanded laws to maintain "local prohibition already obtained, to abolish the beverage sale of intoxicating liquors, and to provide for the sale and for other purposes under public law." Shortly afterward, John D. Cunningham, the party chairman, explained the plank more fully.[28] The Populists opposed all privately operated saloons. Instead, they called for state dispensaries at which liquor might be bought but not drunk. Such dispensaries should be established only where a majority of the local citizens demanded them. Thus the Populists were able to have a prohibition plank without advocating total prohibition. For the teetotalers of Georgia to agree with such a proposal seems odd, but many considered the platform an excellent first step. Others apparently were seduced by the Populists' selection of prohibitionists as their candidates for governor and treasurer.[29] Nevertheless, the strategy of endorsing prohibition was filled with peril. Roman Catholics, who had little love for

27. *National Cyclopaedia of American Biography*, II, 217, *Memoirs of Georgia*, II, 811–12; Georgia Department of Agriculture, *Georgia Historical and Industrial* (Atlanta, 1901), pp. 335–47, 810–11. The other members of the state ticket were not well-known: for attorney general, Donald H. Clark of Chatham County; for commissioner of agriculture, W. E. Smith of Decatur County; for secretary of state, Dr. J. A. Parsons of Milton County; and for comptroller general, Seaborn J. Bell of Burke County. See Atlanta *Constitution*, August 8, 1896. For details about Mrs. Sibley's life, see *National Cyclopaedia of American Biography*, I, 364.

28. Atlanta *Constitution*, August 8, 1896; Atlanta *Journal*, August 14, 1896.

29. Others, including Bishop H. M. Turner, called for total prohibition and refused to endorse either Wright or Atkinson (*People's Party Paper*, September 11, 1896).

Populism anyway, now had another reason to oppose the third party. And although the Catholics were not an important force in state elections, they were critical in Tenth District congressional contests. Even more important than the Catholic vote was that of blacks. Many Populists were apprehensive that prohibition had alienated this large block of voters.

The third-party strategy possessed additional hazards. Workingmen in particular were angered by the new turn of events. Although Populist newspapers usually expressed sympathy for urban laborers, the state Populist platform said almost nothing about their needs. Likewise, the demand for inflation, and therefore an increase in the price of food and clothing, was unwelcome. Laborers were most galled by the candidacy of William C. Sibley. In 1878 Sibley maintained that his employees "cheerfully" worked eleven hours a day. Possibly it was this attitude that prompted the anger of James Barrett, the Populist candidate for commissioner of agriculture in 1892 and 1894. While drunk he had once suggested that the workers blow up the wheel at the Sibley mill in Augusta. Although Sibley's employees ignored Barrett's advice, in 1898 they began a strike that eventually involved four thousand men, women, and children. The difficulty started when the Sibley mill and other Augusta textile factories reduced salaries by 10 percent. The strike was eventually broken.[30]

After the state convention of 1896, William L. Peek could only reflect upon another humiliation at the hands of Tom Watson. But if Watson ruled the party in Georgia, Peek at least ruled the Populists in the Fifth District, and there he was determined to make a race for Congress against Lon Livingston. His candidacy troubled the Watsonites, who knew that "dirt-farmer" Peek would capture few votes in Atlanta, the district's largest metropolis. Without a strong showing in Atlanta, there was little chance he could win the race for Congress. Thus they decided to oppose Peek in his own bailiwick by supporting Thomas R. R. Cobb,

30. John L. Maxwell, *Hand Book of Augusta* (Augusta, 1878), 26. For Barrett's remark about destroying the wheel at the Sibley mill, see U.S. Congress, House, *Watson vs. Black*, 629; for the strike, see Richard H. L. German, "The Augusta Textile Strike of 1898–1899," *Richmond County History*, IV (Winter, 1972), 35–47.

an Atlanta Democrat and lawyer with third-party leanings. Some Populists, however, were beginning to resent the attempts to gain respectability through fusion. The party had picked a Democrat for president,
a prohibitionist for governor, and now seemed set on nominating a lawyer and a city slicker for Congress. Many believed that the wool-hat boys
had been forgotten. Such men turned to Peek for leadership. For them
Peek represented old-fashioned Populism uncorrupted by fusion. "I am
in favor of Peek because he is a wealth producer," a gray-bearded farmer
said at the Fifth District nominating convention. "It is wealth producers
who make this nation. It is time the professional men were downed.
There are too many of them in control. . . . A man is colored by his environment. What does a professional man know about the wants of the
farmer until he associates with the men in the country? I urge you, gentlemen, to stand in the middle of the road. I urge you not to go outside
the party. Keep in the middle of the road." When a Cobb supporter argued that the party had to "broaden out," another Populist snapped, "I'd
rather see the party go down in defeat than see a sickly half-way Populist
take it."[31] Peek was nominated.

Not since 1892 had Watson received such a setback within his party. In
the Tenth District, there was no question that his will was law, but it was
difficult to find a candidate to replace him in the race for Congress. Several important Populists could have campaigned, but for various reasons
all were unavailable. The self-effacing Mell Branch immediately bowed
out. Charles McGregor withdrew his name, saying that he did not have
the money to make the race. Only two other prominent Populists were
left—Clarence Ellington and James Barrett. Although eager to run,
Ellington had had a dispute with Watson over a legal matter, and so Watson opposed his candidacy. As for Barrett, almost everyone in Augusta
had learned about his treatment of northern prisoners during the Civil
War. Moreover, Watson had quarreled with Barrett and probably believed he was mentally ill. In desperation, the Tenth District Populists
searched for another candidate. Finally, Watson's former law partner,
John T. West, reluctantly consented to run.[32] In other districts the story

31. Atlanta *Constitution*, August 21, 27, 28, 1896; Augusta *Chronicle*, August 21, 1896.
32. Augusta *Chronicle*, August 2, 14, 26, 1896; Atlanta *Constitution*, August 26, 1896;
Sparta *Ishmaelite*, August 28, 1896.

was similar: relatively obscure Populists entered the race for Congress. Most prominent were the candidates in the Second and Ninth districts, John A. Sibley and Thomas E. Winn. Both had previously campaigned for Congress, and both had been badly beaten. As was often the case, the prospects in the congressional races were not bright.

The Democrats were also preparing for the contest. Realizing that prohibition would be the main issue, they came out for local option and nominated William Y. Atkinson for another term as governor. His candidacy failed to cause the severe splintering of the party that had occurred two years before. In fact, Atkinson's popularity had grown after he was stricken by appendicitis in the early months of his administration. Although his doctors did not expect him to survive, Atkinson announced that he would get well. He then made a recovery that astounded his physicians and won him the respect of Georgians. He entered the contest physically weak but politically stronger than during the election of 1894.

If there was hope that the campaign would be based on a reasoned discussion of prohibition, it was soon disappointed. Indeed, the contest rapidly turned into a nasty struggle in which issues were forgotten in favor of name-calling and racism. The Democrats outmatched their opponents in character assassination, claiming that John D. Cunningham, the chairman of the Populist party in Georgia, was a gambler and drunkard and had recently stabbed a man in the back during a fight. Although the knifing charge was false and the other accusations exaggerated, the Democrats spread the news across the state. Even more shocking was Atkinson's behavior, when he mocked the physical deformity of one reformer by calling him "Benjamin Hunchback Blackburn." The Populists returned the fire as best they could. William L. Peek accused Lon Livingston of being a mule thief, but for the most part third-party charges were tame. The Populists, however, were more adept at race-baiting. Undoubtedly troubled by Atkinson's immense popularity among blacks, they needed an issue that might discredit him. During the last days of the campaign it was found: they accused Atkinson of encouraging blacks to rape white women.[33]

33. Atlanta *Constitution*, September 23, October 4, 6, 1896; Augusta *Chronicle*, October 4, 1896; *People's Party Paper*, October 2, 1896.

The charge, which became the talk of the state, originated in a Democratic circular entitled "What Governor Atkinson has done for the black
man." Designed to be distributed among Republican voters, the eight-
page leaflet described Atkinson's record in aiding blacks and putting
down lynchings. But only one sentence caused the furor: "He pardoned
Adolphus Duncan, a negro who was twice convicted of rape on a white
woman and was sentenced to be hanged." The Populists did not question
the pardon—they, too, believed Duncan had been innocent. They were
enraged, however, that the document might encourage attacks upon their
wives and daughters. Branding the leaflet the "rape circular," the Populists used it as their main campaign weapon. The executive committee
distributed tens of thousands of copies, and the *People's Party Paper* published two lurid accounts of rapes "to demonstrate the terrible effect" the
circular would have.[34]

White Georgians were stunned, many honestly believing that one ill-
chosen sentence had jeopardized the safety of all white women. "Read it.
Read it, you fathers and brothers and husbands!" wailed one Democrat.
"Does it not make your blood boil to see a man or set of men so low and
depraved?" He pointed out that the circular mentioned nothing about
Duncan's innocence, suggesting the governor would pardon any black
rapist. "See for yourselves what impression it will make on the ignorant
and besotted fiend that roams at will our exposed districts."[35]

The "rape circular" threatened the Democrats with disaster. Alexander Stephens Clay, the state chairman, hastened to say that he was unaware his headquarters had distributed the flyer. And Governor Atkinson
was put in the absurd position of telling the people that he opposed the
rape of white women. But Atkinson refused to back down on the ethics
of his pardon. "I pardoned Adolphus Duncan because he was innocent,"
he said. "If you want a governor to allow an innocent man to be hanged
just because a heinous crime is charged against him, then you should
elect another man. So help me God, I will hold the place with that
understanding."[36]

34. Atlanta *Journal*, September 24, 1896; *People's Party Paper*, September 25, 1896.
35. *People's Party Paper*, October 2, 1896.
36. Atlanta *Constitution*, October 3, 1896.

Such talk did little to endear the governor to whites. On election day thousands either voted for Wright or tore Atkinson's name from the Democratic ballot. Nevertheless, Atkinson was victorious, capturing 123,206 votes to Wright's 85,981. The "rape circular" had lost the governor many white votes, but it had told any wavering blacks how to vote. Even the Populists conceded that the vast majority of blacks had supported Atkinson. As one black editor wrote before the election: "We colored Republicans will not smite the hand that gives us bread. We will not strike down the strong arm of the executive that acts when justice demands. We will never kiss the foot that kicks us. We are citizens. We are free men. We are a grateful people."[37]

The defeat of Seaborn Wright left Populists angry and fearful. Rather than bringing victory and respectability as so many had hoped, prohibition had seemingly eroded support for their party. In 1894 at least 44.4 percent of the electorate had voted for James K. Hines; in 1896 only 41.1 percent had voted for Wright. Just as ominous was the third-party showing in legislative races, in which the Populists captured only thirty-six seats—eleven fewer than in 1894.

To add to these setbacks, Watson's campaign for the vice-presidency had been hobbled from the start. James K. Jones, the national Democratic chairman, continued to insist that Sewall would not be withdrawn and went out of his way to insult the People's party. Southern Populists, Jones predicted, "[will] do all they can to harass the Democracy and create confusion, and in the end they . . . will fuse with the Republicans and vote for McKinley. They will go with the negroes where they belong." At the same time, Watson was feuding with his own party chairman, Marion Butler. Apparently thinking that Bryan might refuse to become the third-party candidate, Butler was slow in sending both Bryan and Watson their official notices of nomination. Watson was put in a humiliating position. Although actively campaigning outside Georgia, he was still not technically his party's nominee. Watson fretted that Butler, who in 1894 had been elected to the United States Senate as a fusionist,

37. Diamond (ed.), *Guide to U.S. Elections*, 404; *People's Party Paper*, October 16, 1896; Atlanta *Constitution*, August 27, 1896.

was trying to drive him from the ticket in favor of Sewall. Finally, he was forced to ask for notice of his nomination. Yet Butler continued to stall and did not send the formal notice until late in the campaign. By that time fusion Populists in many states were withdrawing their Bryan-Watson electors in return for local concessions made by the Democrats— a process that would eventually involve twenty-eight states. As Watson wrote, many Populists were beginning to think that they had been "tricked, sold out, betrayed, misled."[38]

In Georgia this feeling was especially strong. As each day passed the consequences of the "no Bryan, no Watson" strategy became more and more evident. Were the Populists really to support McKinley if they failed to force the Democrats to give up Sewall? Many, and especially the rank-and-file, said yes. "Shall we submit to this dirty scheme to utterly annihilate a party that we old middle of the road Populists have sacrificed home, property, social and business relations?" wrote one. "Never! Some of us will die before we will do it." A man from Munnerlyn swore that he would as soon vote for McKinley as Sewall, "and there are 'train loads of fellows' in these parts like me."[39]

On October 16 the campaign committee gave the Democrats five days to unite with the Georgia People's party or face the consequences. To demonstrate its good intentions, the committee suggested that six Populists and seven Democratic electors join a fused ticket pledged to Bryan and Watson. Rumor had it that if the Democrats failed to concur, the third party would withdraw its electors and join with the Republicans in favor of William McKinley. Georgia Democrats, confident that McKinley could never carry the state, were unintimidated by this ultimatum. But national Democratic leaders were of another mind. As the campaign neared the finish Chairman Jones, who had earlier said that southern Populists would "go with the negroes," suddenly discovered that in Georgia this prophecy might come true. He feared that the treatment

---

38. Jones quote in New York *World*, August 3, 1896, quoted in Woodward, *Tom Watson*, 310. The controversy between Tom Watson and Marion Butler is discussed at length in Durden, *Climax of Populism*. See also, Woodward, *Tom Watson*, 315–18, 325–28, 333. Watson quote in New York *World*, October 5, 1896, quoted in Woodward, *Tom Watson*, 325.
39. *People's Party Paper*, October 23, 1896; Atlanta *Journal*, October 15, 1896.

given Watson had so infuriated many Populists across the country that on election day they might stay at home. He therefore insisted that Georgia Democrats work out a compromise with the third party. If this could not be done, he favored accepting the demands of the Populist campaign committee. During the next five days the Democrats held a series of secret meetings with Tom Watson. Chairman Jones selected Evan Howell, the editor of the Atlanta *Constitution*, as his personal representative, and Howell hastened to Thomson to confer with the Populist leader.[40]

The situation in Georgia was looking increasingly ominous for the Democrats. While the Populist campaign committee was meeting privately with state Republican leaders, rumors spread that McKinley's campaign manager, Mark Hanna, was rushing thousands of dollars to Georgia to promote a Republican-Populist fusion. Many Populist leaders were now openly threatening to support McKinley if the Democrats failed to fuse with the third party. As one member of the campaign committee put it, "We are for fusion or kicking the whole thing overboard." In desperation the Democrats hinted to Watson that if he withdrew, Bryan would appoint him to the cabinet.[41] Watson refused. Thus stymied, the state Democratic executive committee announced that third-party demands were too great and that it could not abandon Sewall. The Populist campaign committee then met and withdrew its electors, making it impossible for Georgia Populists to vote for Tom Watson.[42]

Reading about these machinations, Democrats must have believed the Populists had gone mad. Watson's humiliation at the hands of Democratic and People's party leaders had seemingly deranged the third-party mind. In revenge Populists had made it impossible for their followers to

40. Durden, *Climax of Populism*, 117; Atlanta *Journal*, October 17, 1896; Atlanta *Constitution*, October 17, 1896.

41. Atlanta *Journal*, October 20, 1896; Brewton, *Watson*, 272; Woodward, *Tom Watson*, 325; Durden, *Climax of Populism*, 116–20.

42. Atlanta *Journal*, October 26, 28, 1896; Atlanta *Constitution*, October 25, 1896. C. Vann Woodward calls the withdrawal of the Georgia Populist electors the "crowning affliction that fell upon the head of the Populist Job" (*Tom Watson*, 327). Yet if this was an affliction, it was not a betrayal. Nor is there any reason to think that Watson viewed it as such. Always one to retaliate when he believed he had been ill-treated, Watson apparently never complained about the withdrawal of the Populist electors and even participated in one of the executive committee meetings before the withdrawal. See Atlanta *Constitution*, October 21, 24, 1896; Augusta *Chronicle*, October 21, 1896.

support Watson. Then in the ultimate *reductio ad absurdum*, they promised to vote for William McKinley, the candidate who represented all they despised.

In the last weeks of the campaign the agony of the third party was great. Georgia Populists had originally favored middle-of-the-road candidates for national office; but they had been willing to accept Bryan to preserve the party and elect Watson to the vice-presidency. They had also reasoned that the "no Bryan, no Watson" strategy would eventually drive Sewall from the Democratic ticket. That strategy had failed. But even after the electors had been withdrawn, party leaders were divided about what to do. Hines argued that despite their humiliation, reason required that they vote for Bryan over McKinley, and on election day some undoubtedly did so. Wright asserted that the logical choice was now Joshua Levering, the Prohibitionists' candidate for president. Perhaps as many as four thousand Populists agreed. Another six thousand followed the example of Watson by voting only in the congressional contest.[43] Finally, tens of thousands either failed to vote or followed the lead of William H. Felton and supported McKinley.[44]

For the rank and file, the seemingly suicidal act of voting for McKinley satisfied their desire for revenge and justice. But they had practical reasons. Many members of the campaign committee believed that the inability to fuse with the Democrats had assured a Republican victory. Therefore, whatever they did, the presidential election was lost, and only in the congressional contests was there hope of electing Populist candidates. Unfortunately for the third party, the state Republicans had already divided the anti-Democratic vote by nominating their own candi-

43. Atlanta *Constitution*, October 25, 28, 31, November 4, 5, 1896. The *Constitution* estimated that "several thousand" Populists voted for Bryan. In 1892, 988 Georgians voted for John Bidwell, the Prohibition candidate for president; in 1896, 5,483 voted for Levering. The difference was mostly caused by Populist votes (Diamond [ed.], *Guide to U.S. Elections*, 279, 280; see also, Walter B. Hill to Rebecca Latimer Felton, n.d. [1896], Box 1, Felton Papers). In 1896, 6,786 Georgians voted in the congressional contest but failed to vote in the presidential election. Most of these voters were probably Populists. Compare the total Georgia vote for president (Diamond [ed.], *Guide to U.S. Elections*, 280) with the total congressional vote (Atlanta *Constitution*, November 14, 1896).

44. Compare the number of ballots cast in the state election of 1896 with those cast in the federal election (Atlanta *Constitution*, November 14, 1896; Diamond [ed.], *Guide to U.S. Elections*, 404). There is no way to know exactly how many Populists voted for William McKinley. But he carried most of the third-party counties of the Tenth District. All of these counties also voted for the Populist, John T. West, in the congressional contest.

dates. After a number of meetings with Republican leaders, the campaign committee struck a deal: the Populists would vote for McKinley and withdraw their congressional candidates in two districts; in return, the Republicans would withdraw their candidates in four districts. Both parties would then vote in unison for the remaining candidates. Although not formal fusion, it was nearly so. Indeed, it seemed the only way the Populists could save what remained of their party.[45]

Even this effort failed. Although McKinley won the national election, Georgia voted for Bryan and Sewall. In every congressional district the Democrats were triumphant. Most distressing for the Populists was John T. West's defeat in the Tenth District. Across the nation Tom Watson could find only 217,000 supporters and twenty-seven electoral votes. "Our party, as a party, does not exist anymore," he wrote after the calamity. "The sentiment is still there, the votes are still there, but confidence is gone."[46]

45. In the Third, Sixth, Tenth, and Eleventh districts, the Republican candidates withdrew; in the Fourth and Fifth districts the Populist candidates (William L. Peek and Carey Thornton) retired (Diamond, [ed.], *Guide to U.S. Elections*, 677; Atlanta *Constitution*, November 1, 5, 1896).

46. Diamond (ed.), *Guide to U.S. Elections*, 677; Woodward, *Tom Watson*, 329; *People's Party Paper*, November 13, 1896.

X

The Wool-Hat Boys

The fall of the People's party left some Georgians with a sense of relief, others with a feeling of loss. But in the months and years that followed there was little time to consider the nature of this strange political uprising. It is a question that still bedevils historians. Who were the Populists? Where did they come from? What did they believe in? And, in the end, what was their place in the history of Georgia and American politics?

Especially perplexing are the origins of the movement. Except for Marion and Taylor counties, third-party strength was mainly confined to two areas: the Tenth Congressional District and parts of northern Georgia. Why did the People's party bloom in these places and fail to take root in the coastal counties, the wiregrass country, and the western cotton belt? The classic explanation holds that Populism developed in regions where there were few blacks and thus where whites were less intimidated by the cry "Negro rule."[1] Northern Georgia, with its small black community, is a good example. Yet of the thirty-one counties that made up the congressional districts of northern Georgia, only five consistently supported the third party. The other side of this argument would be that Populism would seldom emerge in places where there were large numbers of blacks. But, as we have seen, this claim is belied by the Tenth District, where blacks outnumbered whites in all third-party counties except one. In Columbia County, for example, there were 8,038 blacks to 3,243 whites; in Greene, 11,719 blacks to 5,332 whites.[2] One would

---

1. Arnett, *Populist Movement in Georgia*, 33 and the maps facing p. 184. Citing Arnett, Woodward gives a similar explanation in *Tom Watson*, 67–69, and *Origins of the New South*, 246.

2. U.S. Department of the Interior, Census Office, *Compendium of the Eleventh Census*, 1890, Part 1, 479–81.

think that these places would have been firmly in the Democratic camp. Clearly, there must have been other reasons for the strength of Populism in this region.

What made the Tenth District different from the rest of Georgia? Were its residents educated in a different way, making them more receptive to mutinous ideas and unorthodox schemes? Again the traditional explanation does not hold: the Grangers, the Greenbackers, and the independents were never strong in the Tenth.[3] The Farmers' Alliance undoubtedly helped prepare the way for Populism, but it was not decisive. As we have seen, almost every region of Georgia had vigorous suballiances, and every region remained Democratic except for the Tenth, parts of northern Georgia, and a few other places. Nor do findings about Populists in other states tell us much about the origins of Georgia Populism. In Alabama, Populism frequently flared in places attractive to new settlers, many of whom felt no allegiance to local customs and behavior. Yet the Tenth District counties averaged only a 28 percent increase in population from 1870 to 1890, while the rest of Georgia saw a 34 percent increase.[4] Nor, as in parts of Tennessee, did Populism grow where new land was being cleared and opened to settlers. With the exception of the coastal counties, the region along the Savannah River was the oldest in the state, Augusta having been founded in 1735.[5]

Perhaps a more obvious but profitable way of finding the seeds of Georgia Populism is to listen to the farmers themselves. In a welter of platforms and resolutions penned between 1892 and 1896, they constantly asserted that many of their problems were economic. During these years the market value of crops in Georgia fell 45.4 percent; in the Tenth it plunged by 63.3 percent. Yet farmers were taxed at roughly the same rate as before the panic. During this period, taxes in the Tenth dropped by only 1.22 percent. Finally, the majority of Tenth District farmers were not landowners; in four of its counties over 70 percent were

3. Woodward, *Tom Watson*, 68–69; Arnett, *Populist Movement in Georgia*, 33, 36.
4. Hackney, *Populism to Progressivism in Alabama*, 4, 26, and *passim*; U.S. Department of the Interior, Census Office, *Compendium of the Eleventh Census*, 1890, Part 1, 12–13.
5. Roger L. Hart, *Redeemers, Bourbons, and Populists: Tennessee, 1870–1896* (Baton Rouge, 1975), 197; Ray Rowland and Helen Callahan, *Yesterday's Augusta* (Miami, 1976), 9; R. P. Brooks, "Race Relations in the Eastern Piedmont Region of Georgia," *Political Science Quarterly*, XXVI (1911), 193–221.

either tenants or sharecroppers. In Washington County only one farmer in four owned his own land.[6]

But the importance of tenancy and falling profits in bringing Populism to Georgia should not be overstated. Putnam County had declines in profits nearly as disastrous as those in the Tenth District; other counties experienced tenancy rates as high or even higher.[7] Yet they remained faithful to the Democratic cause. Economics is only a partial explanation of the nativity of Georgia Populism. Something else, deep in the history of the Tenth District, turned poverty into protest and protest into a political party.

Unlike the western portion of the state, the counties near Augusta were old, their soil weary from scores and scores of plantings. A hundred years before, the land had been some of the richest in the state, ideal for cultivation of tobacco. Like a magnet it drew settlers into the region, who eventually built shabby little farms and settlements on the edge of the frontier. This rude existence ended with Eli Whitney's invention of the cotton gin in 1791. Thousands of additional settlers poured into the region, and in time an aristocracy developed, which busied itself transforming log cabins into respectable frame dwellings. Like many slaveholders with lofty pretensions, the local squires joined the Whig party. From 1836 to 1848 the district consistently voted for Whig presidential candidates and sent to Congress two leading foes of the Democratic party: Robert Toombs of Wilkes County and Alexander H. Stephens of Taliaferro.[8]

Citizens of this area fretted about the North's views on slavery. Nevertheless, they shrank from disunion and longed for a compromise that might protect the planters, the states, and the nation. As late as 1852 both Toombs and Stephens championed the presidential candidacy of

6. Compare Georgia, *Report of the Comptroller-General*, 1892, pp. 123–33, and *ibid.*, 1896, pp. 161–65 (because the information about Lincoln County in this report appears to be in error, I have excluded it when calculating the decline in the market value of the Tenth District crop); U.S. Department of the Interior, Census Office, *Report of the Statistics of Agriculture in the United States at the Eleventh Census, 1890*, 128–32.

7. Compare Georgia, *Report of the Comptroller-General*, 1892, pp. 123–27, and *ibid.*, 1896, pp. 161–65. See also U.S. Department of the Interior, Census Office, *Report of the Statistics of Agriculture in the United States at the Eleventh Census, 1890*, 128–32.

8. James E. Callaway, "The Early Settlement of Georgia" (Senior thesis, Princeton University, 1935), chap. 6, p. 2; Washington *Chronicle*, October 10, 1892; W. Dean Burnham, *Presidential Ballots, 1836–1892* (Baltimore, 1955), 332–62.

Daniel Webster, the unionist senator from Massachusetts. When the Whigs chose Winfield Scott instead, many in this region obstinately refused to concur. On election day thousands voted for Webster—who had died ten days before the balloting. After the demise of the Whig party, the district continued on its independent course. Although Toombs slowly moved into the secessionist camp, other former Whigs joined the nativist American party, or, as it was more commonly called, the Know-Nothing party. Meanwhile, Stephens labored to find some way to preserve the Union without sacrificing the interests of the South. During the presidential election of 1860 he opposed John Breckinridge, the candidate popular with the southern secessionists. The district resolutely followed his lead. Four counties supported John Bell, who represented the Constitutional Union party, and five others astounded Georgia by voting for Stephen Douglas, the nominee of the "northern" Democratic party. Not only did Alexander Stephens support Douglas, but Herschel Johnson of Washington County campaigned as Douglas's running mate.[9]

Despite the labors of Stephens and Johnson, Abraham Lincoln won the election and John Breckinridge captured Georgia. On January 16, 1861, a state convention met to consider secession. There Stephens and Johnson tried to prevent immediate withdrawal by urging Georgia to make one last attempt to save the Union. The delegates from their districts agreed, with only two out of fifteen favoring secession. When the convention rejected this proposal, the dismemberment of the Union was a certainty. Nevertheless, six of these men continued to fight immediate withdrawal until the end of the meeting.[10] But once the ordinance of secession had been signed, the district joined the rebel cause and Alexander Stephens was elected vice-president of the Confederacy. After the defeat of the South, Toombs refused to take the oath of allegiance to the United States. Thus disqualified from holding federal office, he spent the rest of his days railing against Bourbonism and railroad monopolies. The district, however, continued to elect Stephens to Congress. Although

9. Paul Murray, *The Whig Party in Georgia* (Chapel Hill, 1948), 169; Ulrich Bonnell Phillips, *Georgia and States Rights* (Washington, 1902), map facing p. 205; Percy Scott Flippin, *Herschel V. Johnson of Georgia: States Rights Unionist* (Richmond, 1931), 121.

10. Michael P. Johnson, *Toward a Patriarchal Republic: The Secession of Georgia* (Baton Rouge, 1977), 112, 114–16; Ralph Wooster, "The Georgia Secession Convention," *Georgia Historical Quarterly*, XL (1956), 41–52.

now calling himself a Democrat, Stephens often battled the Triumvirate. Indeed, the anti-Bourbonism of Toombs and Stephens made an independent uprising in the Tenth District unnecessary.

So for almost fifty years—from the birth of the Whig party to Toombs's death in 1885—there existed little love for Democrats in the Tenth Congressional District. The Whigs, the "Webster Whigs," the Constitutional Unionists, the Know-Nothings, the "Douglas Democrats," as well as Alexander Stephens, Herschel Johnson, and Robert Toombs, all had worked to make the unorthodox respectable. Dissent was a tradition handed down to the youngsters of the region. Tom Watson grew up listening to Stephens and Toombs tell tales of their early days in politics. Of Robert Toombs, he wrote, "I derived from environment, impressions of his grandeur, before I was old enough to understand what it was all about." Watson described Alexander Stephens as the "holy of holies." James K. Hines venerated Herschel Johnson and delighted in his stories about the election of 1860. Many Populists believed a direct link existed between their movement and the past. "Did not the same men that oppose Watson, oppose Stephens also?" one asked in 1893. "Did the Augusta Ring ever elect Stephens or support him?" With such a political tradition, it was hardly surprising that Populism flourished in this region.[11]

But other parts of Georgia had not been tutored in this Tenth District school. Such Alliance bastions as the wiregrass country and the western cotton belt failed to join the cause. Nor was Populism successful in northern Georgia, once the stronghold of the independents. Out of the thirty-four counties that made up the old independent congressional districts, only six consistently voted for the Populists. Of these, just two were earlier centers of independent strength.[12]

11. Thomas E. Watson, *Sketches: Historical, Literary, Biographical, Economic, etc.* (Thomson, 1912), 4; Hines, "Johnson," 226–27; Gracewood *Wool Hat*, February 4, 1893.
12. U.S. Department of the Interior, Census Office, *Report on the Statistics of Agriculture in the United States at the Eleventh Census, 1890*, 47–49, maps between pp. 42 and 43. Of the nineteen Georgia counties that gave third-party candidates consistent support between 1892 and 1896 only four (Greene, Gordon, Jackson, and Oconee) had an earlier tradition of electing independents to the General Assembly. (For the purposes of this study, I have defined a county with an independent tradition as one that had formerly elected independents three times to the legislature.) See the maps showing independent legislative victories in Jones, "William H. Felton."

The People's party was also unsuccessful in the cities and towns of Georgia. Occasionally, however, it gained some support on the outskirts of such places as Atlanta and Columbus. Clarence Ellington believed that the contests of the 1890s were largely town-farm battles, as they were in his county, where Tom Watson never carried Thomson and never failed to carry the country districts. Railroad discrimination, courthouse rings, and the merchants' control of credit did much to cause this enmity. But there were other reasons. Nothing was more infuriating to the farmer than when a townsman treated him like a lout or hayseed. James Barrett complained about "a lot of city dudes who consider every person born in the country a stupid ass who was created as a beast of burden to support them in their gingerbread life." Watson told party members to do business only with merchants who were sympathetic to Populism so that they would not have to tolerate "many an insolent clerk, who has for months been turning up his nose." [13]

Despite such ill-feeling, Watson was convinced that Populists had to venture out of the countryside and obtain a portion of the urban middle-class vote. In 1894 and afterward, they nominated such respectable gentlemen as James K. Hines of Atlanta, William C. Sibley of Augusta, and Seaborn Wright of Rome. For a time, the party also attempted to win the votes of urban workers. Like Populists everywhere, third-party men in Georgia dreamed of a union between the toilers of the country and city. "The cause of labor is the same everywhere, whether in the fields or factory," Tom Watson said. Augusta, with its thousands of textile workers, seemed especially ready for Populism. In 1884 the Knights of Labor had established a local there, which soon claimed more than two thousand members. Two years later the Augusta workers walked off their jobs, demanding a wage increase. Angry and alarmed, the owners banded together and locked out their employees. The largest strike yet seen in southern history had begun, and for three months the mills were all but idle. As the strike fund evaporated, the mill owners hired scabs, and

13. Atlanta *Journal*, August 17, 1892; *Tom Watson's Magazine*, September, 1906, p. 340; Gracewood *Wool Hat*, April 28, 1894; *People's Party Paper*, n.d., quoted in *ibid.*, November 26, 1892. For other expressions of hard feeling between town and country people, see Macon *Telegraph*, August 6, 1892; Dawson *News*, October 19, 1892; Carnesville *Enterprise*, January 8, 1892; Vol. 3, p. 72, Northen Papers.

rumors spread that poor blacks might be brought in to replace the white workers. The owners then began to evict strikers from company houses. With winter coming on, the starving mill hands gave up and returned to their jobs.[14]

In spite of this defeat, the Populists realized that they might win considerable support in the workers' wards of Augusta. Although most mill hands were afraid to rejoin the Knights, a small local remained active. More important, a Workingman's party had been created to fight the candidates of the mill owners in city elections. After 1891 this organization dissolved, and its members joined the People's party. With such a hopeful beginning, Populists started a campaign to recruit Augusta mill hands. Third-party newspapers published items about the Knights of Labor and other unions, with emphasis on strikes in the North. When in 1894 Andrew Carnegie used Pinkerton detectives to break a strike at his steel mill in Homestead, Pennsylvania, Watson urged that "Remember Homestead" become a motto of the People's party. Watson also applauded Emory Speer, the federal judge of the Southern District of Georgia, who ruled that union membership was insufficient reason to fire a man from his job. In 1894 Georgia Populists again demonstrated sympathy for the workers. In that year Jacob Coxey lead an "army" of five hundred men to Washington, D.C., demanding employment for the poor. While the Democratic press was calling the marchers bums, freeloaders, and anarchists, the third party came to their defense. One Georgia Populist, J. B. Osborne, even traveled to Washington to help make arrangements for the army's encampment.[15]

But in the end, the third party of Georgia failed to win the support of labor. Although its national platform contained a number of planks attractive to workers, most laboring men viewed these concessions as sops. The Populist demand for inflation would drive up the price of food and clothing; the platforms of the Georgia third party almost totally ne-

14. Watson, speech delivered in May, 1891, *People's Party Paper*, September 11, 1896; Melton Alonzo McLaurin, *Paternalism and Protest: Southern Cotton Mill Workers and Organized Labor, 1875–1905* (Westport, 1971), 91–112.

15. Hamilton, "Political Control in a Southern City," 40; Dahlonega *Signal*, 1894; People's Party Paper, January 6, 1893; Conyers *Living Issues*, May 31, 1894; Carnesville *Enterprise*, January 22, 29, 1894; *National Economist*, July 16, 1892; Atlanta *Constitution*, May 10, 1894.

glected their interests. Besides the convict-lease plank, which included a provision that prison labor should not compete with free labor, there was never any mention of the mill workers or their problems.[16]

Even more disturbing was the Populist opposition to strikes. Like the mill owners, white farmers desired an ample supply of servile workers. The landlord needed tenants at planting time, and the yeoman required pickers at harvest. Their position became clear in September, 1891, when the Colored Farmers' Alliance began a cotton-pickers strike in Texas. The white Farmers' Alliance denounced the uprising, and fifteen Texas strikers were killed in shootouts. Georgia farmers ominously warned their pickers not to follow the Texans' lead. Such men had little sympathy for strikes, whether they happened in the country or the city. Many well-known Populists agreed. Charles Post, the first chairman of the Georgia third party, had earlier been a member of the Union-Labor party. The platform of that organization said that "arbitration should take the place of strikes and other injurious methods of settling labor disputes."[17] Silas Reed, the most important Augusta labor leader to support the Populists, also seemed timid about strikes, having lamely advised workmen "to go to the mills in an honorable and pleasant way and ask for what they want." When Tom Watson spoke to the Augusta locomotive engineers in 1891, he offered a number of suggestions about how to promote their interests. Yet nowhere in his speech did he mention the most effective and obvious weapon of labor—the strike. After the election frauds of 1894, some Populists urged farmers to ship their next cotton crop to Charleston rather than Augusta. Such talk left Watson uneasy, and he advised his followers to do nothing rash. When the demand persisted, Watson publicly opposed it. At about the same time, he argued that both sides were wrong during the recent Pullman strike in the Midwest. "God knows I would despise myself to make a poor man hate a rich one," he wrote. Mell Branch and William Henning, the editor of the Wool Hat, also objected to strikes. And when the Dahlonega Signal an-

16. Atlanta Constitution, May 18, 1894.

17. Holmes, "Demise of the Colored Farmers' Alliance," 187–200; Olin Burton Adams, "The Negro and the Agrarian Movement in Georgia, 1874–1908" (Ph.D. dissertation, Florida State University, 1973), 134–36; Goodwyn, Democratic Promise, 291–96; Thomas Hudson McKee, The National Conventions and Platforms of all Political Parties, 1789 to 1905 (n.d.; rpr. St. Claire Shores, Mich., 1970), 250.

nounced that the Homestead strike had been crushed, its headline read "Joyful Tidings."[18] For many workers the last straw must have come in 1896, when the Populists nominated for state treasurer William C. Sibley, one of the men who had broken the Augusta strike of ten years before.

Hard feelings had always existed between country folk and mill hands. Most farmers liked to think of themselves as independent tillers who had not stooped to the level of wage earners. "Factory rats," "cotton-tails," "lintheads," and "cotton mill trash" were some of their nicknames for such people. But there was more to the farmer-labor schism. The Populists had not stupidly repudiated the workers; they had consciously spurned them. This decision had not come overnight or without a certain amount of tension within the organization. After the election of 1892, it became apparent that a party appealing only to former Alliancemen could never capture the state. So in 1894 and 1896 the Watson wing attempted to entice the middle-class vote by promoting the candidacies of Hines, Wright, and Sibley. Sibley's nomination plainly demonstrated that Populist leaders were willing to cast off labor for an alliance with the middle class. Nor was it an unrealistic strategy. Only three thousand cotton-mill workers lived in Augusta, many of whom were nonvoting women and children.[19]

There were, of course, some similarities in the thinking of farmers and factory hands. Just as the Augusta mill workers were developing a sense of class consciousness, so were some farmers. Third-party men frequently argued that only two groups existed in America: the exploiters and the exploited. "The fight is between labor and capital," one Georgia Populist wrote. "Be not deceived, for there is no other issue but the tyranny of capital, or the independence of labor." A few farmers even spoke of revolution. "We intend to assert our rights or put our blood behind the ballot," cried a third-party man at a Jackson County rally. "We have ten

18. Reed quoted in Hamilton, "Political Control in a Southern City," 47. Watson's views appear in *People's Party Paper*, September 11, 1896, November 16, 1894, May 3, August 16, 1895; and Gracewood *Wool Hat*, July 2, 1894. See also *ibid.*, May 13, August 5, 1893; Dahlonega *Signal*, July 13, 1894.

19. McLaurin, *Paternalism and Protest*, 37; U.S. Department of the Interior, Census Office, *Report on Manufacturing Industries in the United States at the Eleventh Census, 1890* (1895), 44; see also Palmer, *"Man Over Money,"* 34–35.

times the occasion for revolution that we had in the contest for Independence." Another Populist said, "[The] world has got to be revolutionized. All must be torn down, and eventually build upon a righteous basis."[20]

But most third-party men rejected such ideas. Although Georgia political campaigns were noted for their riots and murders, such bloodshed was seldom organized and never had a revolutionary purpose. Most talk of violence was simply the bluster of hotheads. Georgia Populists almost never espoused the philosophies associated with revolution—anarchism, socialism, and communism. They were, however, occasionally willing to ally with the socialists if it would serve their own ends. At the national Populist convention of 1896, the Georgia delegation voted to seat socialists from Milwaukee and Chicago, but only because they were middle-of-the-roaders. Among Georgia third-party leaders only one, J. B. Osborne, later became a socialist. Nor did the rank-and-file Populists consider themselves radicals. When Osborne ran for governor in 1906 as a kind of populist-socialist, he received 148 votes.[21]

Almost all third-party leaders deplored radicalism and professed their devotion to honest capitalism. "I am not an anarchist; I am not a communist," Seaborn Wright said while campaigning in Atlanta. Earlier he predicted that if he could get the "ear of the business men of this state I shall be elected governor beyond a doubt." While John T. West was campaigning for Congress the same year, he echoed Wright's sentiments: "I am not a long hair anarchist . . . I am no anarchist, no socialist." Hines made it clear that he, too, objected to radicals.[22]

Only Watson betrayed some sympathy for socialists, and occasionally the *People's Party Paper* included news about their activities. But about 1894, when the party was attempting to become respectable to the urban middle class, his attitude changed. Watson was especially vexed by the Omaha platform's "land plank," which proclaimed that land was the

20. Carnesville *Enterprise*, March 18, 1893; Jackson *Herald*, July 10, 1896; *People's Party Paper*, July 22, 1892; see also Carnesville *Living Issues*, May 31, 1894; *People's Party Paper*, December 19, 1895, January 17, 1896.

21. Griffith and Talmadge, *Georgia Journalism*, 221; Atlanta *Constitution*, July 24, 1896; Coulter, *Georgia*, 377.

22. Atlanta *Constitution*, October 7, 1896; Savannah *Press*, August 31, 1896; Augusta *Chronicle*, September 12, 1896; *People's Party Paper*, June 20, 1894.

"heritage of the people, and should not be monopolized for speculative purposes." Fearing that this statement smacked too much of collectivism, Watson announced that Populists opposed only land monopolies and not the private ownership of the soil. Within a year he was turning much of his editorial fire on socialists in other states. "There isn't a tribe of savages in history which did not practice Socialism—and they never quit being savages until they quit Socialism," he warned. Watson doubted that the Georgia third party would have a "corporal's guard left" if it embraced such a philosophy. In particular, he scorned Jacob Coxey, whom he believed had dallied too closely with radicalism. When Coxey attended the 1895 state convention, Watson took pains to snub him. "We will have nothing to do with any lot of extremists who make war on private property," he explained. Other third-party leaders agreed, and the state executive committee unanimously declared that the land plank should be rewritten "so as to free it from the suspicion of Socialism."[23]

Watson's ideas on capitalism and socialism bear further examination. Although he firmly believed in government ownership of the railroads, other forms of property were inviolable. He believed, for example, that the courts were compelled to deal firmly with the thief—"even if he [has] stolen to satisfy his hunger." As Watson told his audiences: "In the race of life you have the right to accumulate property if you can. It is not only your right . . . [it is] your duty." In his speech to the Augusta locomotive engineers he developed this idea at length. "Don't understand me to be making war upon capital, as such," he said. "I am but denouncing that capital which is used tyrannically." Watson believed that the reasonable profits one man obtained from another man's labor were legitimate and ensured civilization's progress. Indeed, such profits ensured the existence of a "leisure class [that could] devote themselves to science, to music, painting, book-making, law-making, school teaching." Without such a group "there could be nothing but the simplest labor—there could be no manufactures, no railroads, no steamboats, no foundries, no merchants and no bankers." Anticipating that his defense of banking might baffle his listeners, Watson insisted that in the past he had attacked

23. Hicks, *Populist Revolt*, 443; *People's Party Paper*, August 2, 1895, January 17, 1896, November 1, 1895.

only the abuses of this institution—"I do not wage war on banking itself." Watson concluded his speech with a paean as old as the Protestant
ethic and democratic capitalism: "The healthy, happy, prosperous community is not that which consists either of capitalists alone or of laborers
alone. Neither can do without the other. You are a laborer. Remember
that it is possible you may be a capitalist tomorrow."[24]

But Watson was not the only leader of the Georgia Populist movement.
What were his colleagues like, and how did they compare with the chiefs
of the state Democratic party? Before the 1890s, the twenty-five most
important Populists had been men of local prominence and moderate
means.[25] Several, however, had gained statewide recognition. Three—
Thomas E. Watson, Thomas E. Winn, and William H. Felton—had
served as congressman, and James K. Hines had run for the United
States Senate. A few were men of wealth. William C. Sibley was a large
mill owner, and John D. Cunningham owned six farms and 110,000 fruit
trees and was president of the American Fruit Growers Association. The
treasurer of the national party, H. W. Reed, was president of the First
National Bank of Brunswick, Georgia.

Despite the success of some Populist leaders, most had started life
with limited opportunities, had achieved only moderate success, and
would shortly disappear into the obscurity from which they had come.
Their relative lack of prominence is especially evident when they are
compared with the twenty-five most important leaders of the Georgia
Democratic party.[26] Whereas only six Populists were educated beyond
the common school level, twenty-two of the Democrats had attended college, law school, or business school, and nineteen had graduated. Most

24. Raper, *Tenants of the Almighty*, 120; *People's Party Paper*, May 25, 1894, September
11, 1896.
25. I have defined an important party leader as one who held a major office within the
party. Leaders of party factions, legislative chiefs, candidates for high offices, and men who
did especially well in congressional races were also included. These twenty-five men were
Thomas E. Watson, William L. Peek, James K. Hines, Seaborn Wright, James R. Hogan,
Yancey Y. Carter, John D. Cunningham, William H. Felton, Mark Irwin, James Barrett,
Charles E. McGregor, Mell I. Branch, Clarence H. Ellington, Charles C. Post, J. L.
Gilmore, Samuel Small, Thaddeus Pickett, John A. Sibley, Carey Thornton, W. T. Carter,
J. N. Twitty, John T. West, Thomas E. Winn, H. W. Reed, and William C. Sibley. Bio-
graphical information was gathered from such standard sources as Northen, *Men of Mark*,
Ham, *Representative Georgians*, Howell, *History of Georgia*, *Memoirs of Georgia*, and the
Biographical Data File at the Georgia Department of Archives and History, Atlanta.
26. The same criteria for defining an important party leader and the same sources of

were alumni of the University of Georgia, but one was from Yale, one
from Princeton, and two from Georgetown. Very few had been poor
boys, who by luck and pluck had worked their way through college. Indeed, some came from families not only of means but of power. Alfred
Colquitt's father had studied at Princeton before becoming a congressman and a United States senator. His son, who graduated from Princeton
in 1844, was a congressman, a senator, and a governor. Pope Barrow, a
United States senator from 1882 to 1883, was the grandson of Wilson
Lumpkin, another Georgia senator and governor. Hoke Smith's father
had served as president of Catawba College and as a professor at the University of North Carolina. Even William Y. Atkinson, the reputed poor
"Wagon Boy of Coweta," was the son of a planter who was reported to
have owned "many slaves."

Differences between Populist and Democratic leaders became striking
at the point when, early in life, they decided upon a career. Of the twenty
Populists whose occupations can be determined, ten were farmers. Two
of these were also lawyers and one a physician. Among the remaining
third-party leaders, five were lawyers, two were ministers, one was an
editor, one a bank president, and one the owner of a large textile mill.
The occupations of Democratic leaders were less diverse. Out of a sample of twenty-five, eighteen were lawyers, two were editors, and two were
editors as well as lawyers. In addition there was a banker and two farmers. One of these husbandmen was Senator Alfred Colquitt, whose farm
was in reality a plantation. As these figures suggest, most Democratic
leaders had little firsthand knowledge of agriculture, except for the few
who lived on farms when they were boys. On the other hand, they all
seemed to have a solid understanding of law, business, and the require-
ments for political success. By 1892 most were financially successful.
Whereas the median wealth of Populists was $6,275.50, that of Demo-

biographical information used for the Populists were used for the Democrats. At least forty
men fit the definition. The following are representative of the Democratic leadership: Wil-
liam J. Northen, William Y. Atkinson, Augustus O. Bacon, James C. C. Black, Allen D.
Candler, John B. Gordon, Alexander Stephens Clay, Alfred H. Colquitt, Boykin Wright,
Evan Howell, Clark Howell, Patrick Walsh, Clement Evans, Joseph E. Brown, Charles F.
Crisp, William H. Venable, Robert Berner, Charles L. Bartlett, Rufus E. Lester, Elijah B.
Lewis, William H. Fleming, William C. Adamson, Pope Barrow, Hudson A. Jenkins, and
Hoke Smith.

crats was $8,585. One Populist and seven Democrats were worth more than $20,000. The Democrats' prosperity becomes especially evident when mean wealth is calculated. Whereas the average Populist was worth only $8,405.68, the average Democrat could boast of $18,714.22 in real property and other assets.[27]

Among the Populists, only two, Tom Watson and James K. Hines, achieved later political importance. The rest drifted quietly back into obscurity. The Democrats, however, present a different story. By the end of their lives, three had served as governor and four had been members of the United States Senate. Three others had been both governor and senator, and another had been governor, senator, and a member of the United States cabinet. Seven had served in Congress, two of whom had held their seats for twenty years. One had been Speaker of the House. Almost all of these twenty-five Democrats appear to have led comfortable lives and a few, including Alfred Colquitt, Joseph E. Brown, and William H. Venable, died very wealthy.

Many of the leaders of both parties might be consigned to that catchall category called the middle class. Yet in some important ways Populist and Democratic chiefs differed. By 1896 the Democrats led an alliance of railroad men, industrialists, professionals, urban and rural businessmen, planters, blacks, and workers. To control such a melange, Democratic chiefs sorely needed the skills of compromise and consensus. It was fortunate that so many were lawyers. Some honestly sympathized with the plight of farmers and hoped that free silver might bring relief. But unlike the Populist leaders, few possessed an intimate knowledge of agriculture and its rigors. The vision of many was narrowed by their profession and wealth.

But if the Democrat saw the world through a lawyer's lens, the Populist chief also peered through a glass that gave reality its own peculiar cast. Many third-party leaders were from the Tenth District, where such

27. The aggregate wealth (value of land, town property, stocks, and bonds) of each Populist and Democratic leader was obtained by examining the county tax records for 1892, located at the Georgia Department of Archives and History, Atlanta. For those for whom information was available, the median and average wealth of the seventeen Populists was, respectively, $6,340 and $9,258.23; the median and average wealth of the nineteen Democrats was, respectively, $8,585 and $38,018.73.

uncompromising teachers as Alexander Stephens and Robert Toombs had taught the evils of Bourbonism and railroad monopolies. Implicit in their lessons was a Whiggish disdain for the Democratic party. Out of this academy came Tom Watson, Clarence H. Ellington, Charles Mc-Gregor, James Barrett, John T. West, James R. Hogan, and Mell I. Branch. Their schooling sometimes gave them remarkable insights about politics and economics. But it was an education with an ugly side—indeed, the "terrible Tenth" deserved its nickname. The former stronghold of the Ku Klux Klan, it was a place where quarrels, both personal and political, were frequently settled by violence. Three of the star pupils of the Tenth District school had learned these lessons well: McGregor was a murderer, Barrett was a war criminal, and Watson was soon to become a vicious enemy of Catholics, Jews, and blacks.

As we have seen, Populism appealed to many groups. Although women were disqualified from voting, they held an important place in the movement. Many Populists in the states beyond the Mississippi River advocated woman suffrage, and Kansas provided two of the party's most effective agitators, Mary Elizabeth Lease and Annie L. Diggs. Through the efforts of the western Populists a resolution was included in the St. Louis platform calling for woman suffrage.[28] This demand rankled southern Populists, and five months later at the Omaha convention they worked to have it dropped from the list of demands. The resolution too fiercely challenged some southerners' view of a lady's place in society. Others were motivated by practical considerations. To have advocated such a reform in the South would have handed the Democrats a terrible weapon. They pointed out that it was virtually unheard-of for a woman to speak publicly on a political issue, let alone to vote. Others argued that elections in the South were so violent that no lady should be exposed to them.

Despite such intransigence, Populism seems to have softened some men's ideas about women. If a man's wife worked in the fields alongside her husband, it was difficult to argue that she was too delicate for politics. Women were welcome as members of the Farmers' Alliance and

28. Hicks, *Populist Revolt*, 439–44.

possibly made up one-third of the membership in Georgia. Populist leaders also realized that a woman might influence the votes of her husband, son, or brother. Almost invariably the third-party leaders invited women to the rallies. Only if the debate threatened to be heated or if there was a chance of violence did they ask that women not attend. In response, the wives and daughters of Georgia Populists rallied to the cause with as much zeal as their men. A yearly dinner at the Methodist church in Hopewell broke up after a furious wrangle between the wives of Populists and Democrats. Black women seemed equally dedicated to the movement, sometimes being seen at Populist gatherings holding their babies aloft so that they might get a glimpse of Tom Watson. In Sparta a number of black women rushed Watson and breached southern etiquette by shaking his hand. When the third party endorsed prohibition, more women came to support the movement, including such prominent matrons as Mrs. William C. Sibley and Mrs. Walter B. Hill, whose husband later became chancellor of the University of Georgia.[29]

Yet for all this feminine enthusiasm, Populists gave women little responsibility beyond preparing food at picnics. There were, however, exceptions. A Democratic reporter was astounded to discover that the clerk at the state Populist headquarters was female. Another woman, Lulu Pearce, had served as secretary and bookkeeper of the *People's Party Paper*. In Carroll County, Mrs. L. T. Russell edited a local newspaper entitled the *Populist*. Finally, Rebecca Latimer Felton, the wife of William H. Felton, was profoundly respected in third-party circles. It was common knowledge that she directed her husband's campaigns, and party leaders were always eager for her views on politics in northern Georgia.[30]

Still, no native-born Georgia woman felt free enough to deliver a political speech. Northern and western women who chanced to be in the state showed no such hesitation. Georgia was scandalized when Mary Elizabeth Lease campaigned in 1892. Her crusty repartee—"That gentleman who interrupted me . . . is a long-eared animal"—silenced

29. Carnesville *Enterprise*, May 6, 1892; *People's Party Paper*, February 24, 1896.
30. Atlanta *Constitution*, July 31, 1896; Box 2, folder 11, Watson Papers, UNC; Talmadge, *Felton*, 40–42, 46–48, 63–66, 86–89; Savannah *Press*, October 22, 1896.

hecklers and won her the respect even of Democrats. Helen Wilman Post likewise shocked Georgians by giving at least one political speech after William J. Northen accused her of sending money to the Haymarket anarchists. Her talents were lost when she and her husband left, or possibly fled, the state in 1892.[31]

A few Populist men appear to have developed an unusual respect for women. Both the Carnesville *Enterprise* and the Gracewood *Wool Hat* endorsed woman suffrage. J. H. Boyd, Jr., an important Populist legislator, once noted that the franchise for women was not part of the third-party platform, but "if it was, that wouldn't hurt anything." James Barrett attacked Governor Northen for voting "against the railroad commission and the women." And the *People's Party Paper* endorsed a bill allowing females to serve as state librarian. In the end, however, the Populist party of Georgia granted women very little. But when compared to Democrats, who conceded them virtually nothing, the Populists' tolerance was surprising. By allowing a few women to speak on the hustings and to participate in party business, the wool-hat boys demonstrated a reliance upon the opposite sex seldom seen in the late nineteenth-century South.[32]

The Populists were also reasonably tolerant of other groups. With only 240 orthodox Jews and 1,846 reform Jews living in the state, few viewed them as a threat. It is true, Populists sometimes used the words "Shylock" and "Rothschild" when describing their enemies. But they almost never said that Jewish merchants or bankers were engaged in a conspiracy to plunder the United States. The word "Shylock" served for all the amorphous enemies of the people. On one occasion the *People's Party Paper* published an article entitled "Shylock Can't Stand Before Good Government." The piece did not mention Jews but discussed the corrupt Democrats of Paulding County. On at least one occasion the *People's Party Paper* printed a friendly article about a Jewish merchant living in Atlanta. Ultimately, Populist sentiment toward Jews was little different

31. Atlanta *Constitution*, September 22, 1892; Greensboro *Herald-Journal*, May 27, 1892.
32. Carnesville *Enterprise*, May 6, 1892; Gracewood *Wool Hat*, October 1, 1892; Augusta *Chronicle*, July 28, October 21, 1892.

from that of most Georgians and almost identical to that of Democrats. Democratic newspapers employed the term "Shylock" with roughly the same precision as Populists. Shortly after the Atlanta *Constitution* printed an editorial entitled "Shylock on Top Again," it ran an item praising the role of Jewish soldiers in American history. Like the Populists, its anti-Semitism seldom went beyond moderately derogatory catch phrases.[33]

But there were exceptions. Mark Irwin, who was chairman of the state Populist party from 1892 to 1894, lived in a county that had no Jewish residents, yet he was surprisingly anti-Semitic. "Goggle-eyed Jews, European Shylocks and plutocratic American traitors" were plotting to buy all the American mines, Irwin wrote in his newspaper. He also warned that "treasonable agents of Wall Street" and "London and Frankfurt Jews" were purchasing American bonds. One of his reporters described the Atlanta *Journal* as a "filthy goldbug sheet" representing Grover Cleveland and the Rothschilds.[34]

J. A. Bodenhauer, the Populist editor of Paulding County's Dallas *Herald*, was even more anti-Semitic. Like Irwin, Bodenhauer resided in an area that had no Jewish citizens. Still his newspaper insisted upon waging a private war against the "Jew Shylock." A headline blared:

RUSSIA FEARS THE JEWS
Dread of the Hook-Nosed Three
Brass Ball Men

Bodenhauer claimed that Jews already had "America by the throat." "It is not only the Jew, but the Jew instinct, which threatens the existence of our Republic today," he asserted. The Dallas *Herald* included pieces about Congressman Isidor Rayner, "the Jew Democrat from Maryland"; Henry Villard, the financier and "great Jew gold-monger"; and Thomas F. Bayard, the American ambassador to England, who had been "Rewarded by the Shylocks." Another article claimed that the silver debate could be reduced to "England vs. America—The Jew and the Gen-

33. U.S. Department of the Interior, Census Office, *Report on Statistics of Churches in the United States at the Eleventh Census, 1890*, 413–18; *People's Party Paper*, February 1, 1895, November 26, 1897; Atlanta *Constitution*, September 24, 1891. For other examples of articles with anti-Semitic headlines but stories that fail to mention Jews, see Gracewood *Wool Hat*, September 9, 1893, January 13, 1894.
34. Conyers *Living Issues*, May 31, 1894.

tile."[35] Yet for all Bodenhauer's venom, his anti-Semitism had little influence in his county. Like third-party men all over Georgia, the Paulding County Populists apparently never published any resolutions attacking the Jews.

The third-party attitude toward Roman Catholics was more complex. The American party, a nativist and somewhat anti-Catholic organization, had flourished in the Tenth District before the Civil War, and some residue of its philosophy may have lingered. Yet it was not until Watson's congressional campaign in 1895 that anti-Catholic articles began to appear in the Populist press. There seems to have been no previous anti-Catholic feeling among Georgia Populists. Had it existed, it surely would have exploded in 1894, when Governor Northen appointed Patrick Walsh to the United States Senate. Walsh, who was editor of the Augusta *Chronicle*, had been born in Ireland, favored a high tariff, and was a prominent Catholic. Besides serving as a leader of the Augusta ring, he constantly used his newspaper to harass Tom Watson. There were few men whom Watson and the Populists had better reason to despise. From outside the state a number of Baptist clergymen decried the appointment, branding Governor Northen a Protestant Judas. Yet the third-party press of Georgia was oddly silent, neither condemning nor condoning the selection and making no comment about Walsh's theology. Indeed, during the election of 1894, Watson had demonstrated unusual religious tolerance. "Some of the best men of our party are Irishmen," he said during a speech at Grovetown. "Some of the best men are Catholics. . . . Why should we draw a line on them, why should we throw this bone in the people's face. Down with such an idea, let a man's religion be his private affair."[36]

Watson's later ideas about Catholicism were a strange mix of ignorance, traditional Protestant hostility, and a desire for intellectual freedom. He believed that religion had progressed from phallic worship to paganism to Christianity. The next step in the ascent would only come when the "tyranny of the priest" had ended. "When and where has the

35. Dallas *Herald*, June 15, 29, July 27, August 3, 1893.
36. Vol. 3, pp. 183, 188, Northen Papers; Watson quoted in Gracewood *Wool Hat*, July 28, 1894.

Roman catholic church done anything for the masses," Watson demanded in 1897, "when has it ever failed to side with enthroned tyranny?" He noted that in the Philippine Islands priests persecuted the natives; in South America a Catholic newspaper praised the Spanish Inquisition and the "holy work of the rack, the wheel and the stake"; in the United States, Catholics were members of William McKinley's cabinet and conspired against public schools. Above all the *Index Librorum Prohibitorum* sought to control the minds of the Catholic laity. The purpose of this oppression was plain: "The orthodox catholic doctrine is that Protestantism must be uprooted and cast out, as wholly damnable heresy." [37]

Despite Watson's views, most wool-hat boys who lived outside the Tenth District seemed little affected by anti-Catholicism. Within the Tenth, contempt for Catholics sometimes turned into a hatred of foreigners and especially the Irish. Anti-British items occasionally appeared in the third-party editorials and resolutions. [38] Xenophobia among Georgia Populists, however, was mild. Had foreigners made a greater effort to buy land in the state, perhaps this prejudice would have been stronger. As it was, only Populists living near Augusta seemed concerned about the danger of aliens.

The third party's attitudes about Catholics, Jews, laborers, and blacks helped fashion its campaign strategy between 1892 and 1896. The Populists first attempted to forge an alliance with blacks and workers; yet their own racism and exploitation of labor made concessions almost impossible. They then tried to win over the urban middle class. Led by Tom Watson, the party nominated "respectable" candidates, dropped the subtreasury plan, and endorsed prohibition. But by watering down Populist doctrine, they angered middle-of-the-roaders and ruined any hope of further labor or black support. By the end of the decade, the organization was coming to pieces. At the same time, Bourbonism was also coming to an end. Many old Democrats were passing from the

37. Editorial from *People's Party Paper*, n.d., vol. 27, Watson Papers, UNC; pamphlet, *A Good Catholic*, reprinted from *People's Party Paper*, April 23, 1897, Thomas E. Watson Papers, Special Collections, Emory University Library, Atlanta; *People's Party Paper*, March 27, May 8, 1896.
38. Calhoun *Times*, April 21, 1892; Gracewood *Wool Hat*, February 3, 1894.

scene, and for the first time since Reconstruction a vacuum was forming in Georgia politics. Watson's strategy had been shrewd but untimely. Politicians knew that in a few years the ranks of the graybeards would be even thinner. Then the Populists and the urban middle class might again try to find a common destiny.

XI

Good-bye, Old Party, Good-bye

The old party is on the downward track,
  Good-bye, old party, good-bye.
Picking his teeth with a tariff tack,
  Good-bye, old party, good-bye.
With a placard pinned upon its back,
  Good-bye, old party, good-bye.
That plainly states, "I will never come back,"
  Good-bye, old party, good-bye.
  —"Good-Bye, Old Party, Good-Bye," by C. S. White, in
  Leopold Vincent, ed., *The Alliance and Labor Songster*, 1891

"My political career has forever ended," Tom Watson said after his campaign for the vice-presidency. Since his youth he had longed for success in politics, but after four defeats in four years, he was finally convinced he could never again hold public office. In the years that followed, Watson revived his law practice and finished writing a history of France. By 1904 he owned nine thousand acres and was worth $121,000. He fulfilled a twenty-year dream when he purchased Hickory Hill, a white-pillared manse just outside Thomson. There in baronial splendor Watson held forth, working on histories and biographies, writing editorials, and living the life for which he had always yearned—that of a gentleman.[1]

Still the "Sage of Hickory Hill," as Watson came to be called, could not forsake politics entirely. The Populist party had come to pieces in the election of 1896, and thousands believed that he was the only man who could restore the organization. Watson was uncertain if such a feat was possible. A feeling of hopelessness had fallen over party members. Watson was sure, however, that if the party was to be rebuilt, the fusionists had to be expelled and Marion Butler, the national chairman, had to be deposed. Most middle-of-the-roaders were of the same mind. They

1. Atlanta *Constitution*, March 16, 1892; Woodward, *Tom Watson*, 332–54.

agreed to meet in Nashville to decide upon a course of action. Watson quietly led the movement in Georgia, with thousands of the rank and file clamoring to join him. Still, many party leaders harbored reservations. They were disturbed by the vindictiveness of Watson's editorials about Butler, and they feared that he was turning the movement into an unseemly vendetta. Populists who had once been Republicans were likewise troubled by the idea of a midroad gathering, alarmed that the delegates might officially condemn fusion in the future. John Cunningham, the state party chairman, tried to delay the meeting. In the squabble that followed, Watson found a strange ally. His old foe, William L. Peek, joined him in demanding a state meeting. Rapidly the rank and file fell behind them, urging the ouster not only of Butler but also of Cunningham. Under pressure, Cunningham reluctantly called for a convention in Atlanta in early July, 1897.[2]

Soon it was obvious that Watson's feud with Butler had cost him much support. Many of his old cohorts—Mell Branch, Clarence Ellington, John Sibley, Seaborn Wright, and William Henning—failed to attend the gathering. Nor were the results of the meeting as decisive as expected. Although the convention selected delegates to attend the Nashville conference, it failed to order them to oust Marion Butler. Instead, it only condemned "fusion as practiced in the past"—hardly the ringing mandate that Watson had hoped for. Worse still, when the convention was about to deliver the customary endorsement of Watson, the unthinkable happened: a Populist opposed the resolution. As horrified delegates looked on, J. B. Osborne, the party's leading labor leader, bitterly denounced Tom Watson. Hastily, the embarrassed convention overruled Osborne, then went on to the task of picking at-large delegates. But again the unthinkable occurred: although Watson was selected with 145 votes, William L. Peek and James K. Hines were also named with 151 votes apiece. Possibly the most ominous aspect of the meeting was the poor attendance. Only seventy counties had sent delegates. Many seemed to believe the catastrophe of 1896 had cut the confidence and spirit from the movement. Few were as blunt as James Barrett. "The

2. *People's Party Paper*, November 13, 1896, July 9, 1897, November 19, 1898; Atlanta *Journal*, June 22, 23, 1897; Atlanta *Constitution*, June 22, 23, 1897.

populist party is dead," he told a reporter. "It's [*sic*] coffin was built at St. Louis and its interment will come in Nashville. It is gone and there is no hope."[3]

Under the shadow of this dismal prophecy, the Georgia delegation departed for Tennessee but without Tom Watson, who at the last minute decided not to attend. He had, however, apparently given his supporters instructions about a new third-party issue—anti-Catholicism. In his own district he had "espoused the cause of the American Protective Association," one Populist said.[4] Now Watson hoped the midroad convention would also embrace this philosophy. But when his supporters arrived at the meeting, nobody seemed interested in the idea, and it was soon dropped.

In many ways the Nashville meeting was a typical third-party gathering with the usual brawls, chaos, and bickering. At one point the chairman lost control of the convention, and in desperation he called William L. Peek to the chair. With an extraordinary flourish of parliamentary skill, Peek managed, in the words of one wag, to "reduce the number of delegates speaking from thirty-one to six." Nevertheless, when the pandemonium was over the delegates had virtually created a new party, having issued a manifesto, appointed a national committee, and endorsed the midroad philosophy. William L. Peek suddenly found himself a power in the infant organization. Because Georgia had the second largest delegation present, it was logical that the convention should appoint one of its members to the five-man executive committee. And because Tom Watson was absent, the delegates turned to Peek.[5]

With the preliminaries out of the way, Peek and his colleagues quickly prepared for the nomination of a national slate. Claiming to be the true Populist party, this organization was usually referred to as the "Middle-of-the-Road" People's party. In May, 1900, the party met in Cincinnati. Peek was elected as its permanent chairman, thus culminating his career as a Populist. But with Tom Watson still in retirement and refusing to run, the delegates were forced to field a weak ticket—Wharton Barker of

3. Atlanta *Journal*, June 22, 23, 1897; Atlanta *Constitution*, June 23, July 2, 1897.
4. Atlanta *Constitution*, July 5, 1897.
5. Hicks, *Populist Revolt*, 381–82; Atlanta *Constitution*, July 4–8, 1897; *People's Party Paper*, July 9, 1897.

Pennsylvania for president and Ignatius Donnelly of Minnesota for vice-president. The hopelessness of the midroad cause became apparent on election day. Not only did Barker fail to capture one electoral vote, but in the entire United States only 50,340 people supported him. Party strength was especially feeble in Georgia. Much to the anger of Populists, Tom Watson did nothing in Barker's behalf, and on election day the third-party candidate received only 4,568 votes.[6]

But the dissolution of the national People's party did not necessarily mean the death of the state organizations. Many wool-hat boys reminded their more skeptical brethren that reforms were still needed in Georgia. In December, 1896, Yancey Y. Carter, the Populist leader in the state senate, told a reporter that there were judges who were "worse than some of those . . . they send . . . to the chaingang." Carter darkly added, "Let not the senators ask me lest I give names." Sensing a bluff, the Democrats demanded the names of the guilty parties. To their chagrin, Carter accused the judge of the northern circuit, Seaborn Reese, of being drunk on the bench and profane in the presence of ladies. More titillating were his accusations against Judge Joel A. Sweat of the Brunswick circuit. Carter charged that Sweat had also been drunk in court, had once made an indecent suggestion to a girl, and later had an affair with a married woman. The Populist senator said that he was willing to produce more names. But by this time, the Democrats were too mortified to strike after the bait. All across the state, citizens demanded the prosecution of the accused jurists. Two days after Carter made his charges, the senate appointed a committee to investigate the accusations to see if there was enough evidence to warrant a bill of impeachment and trial.[7]

With the possible exception of Judge Sweat, Yancey Carter suddenly became the most talked-about man in Georgia. In every respect he was an impressive figure, at one convention being introduced as the "lion of the tribe of Judah." Even Democrats found him disarming and flamboyant. "He's an extraordinary type—a new type," one confessed. "We have never looked upon anything like him in our public life before." On

6. Hicks, *Populist Revolt*, 399–400; McKee, *National Conventions and Platforms*, 353; Diamond (ed.), *Guide to U.S. Elections*, 302.
7. Atlanta *Looking Glass*, December 2, 1896, quoted in Atlanta *Constitution*, December 8, 1896; Atlanta *Constitution*, December 16, 18, 1896.

the street Carter drew admiring glances. Immensely powerful, he possessed huge shoulders, a barrel chest, and a tangle of golden hair that encircled his head like a lion's mane. He was plainly a man not to be tampered with. Having started life in Georgia as a poor boy, Carter had read law and then had struck out for the West, where he joined the Texas Rangers. After the hardships of the plains, he returned to Elberton, Georgia, and became a schoolteacher. When drunks disrupted his classroom, Carter discovered the local stills and reported their whereabouts to the federal revenue agents. Thereafter, fearing for his life, he traveled with a bowie knife thrust into his trousers and pistols dangling from his belt. He was soon appointed a deputy marshal, a position he held for a number of years.[8]

But Carter was more than a man's man and a devil of a fellow. Having received little formal education, he studied constantly, trying to master the political and economic questions of the day. At least in a perfunctory way he read the works of Edmund Burke, Herbert Spencer, Thomas Jefferson, Patrick Henry, and Thomas Macaulay. Early in life he had made the unpopular choice of becoming a Republican; in 1892 he joined the Populists. Two years later he was elected to the legislature. When Charles McGregor retired in 1896, the Populist senators chose Carter as their minority leader. Without hesitation, "the lion of the tribe of Judah" predicted that someday he would be governor.[9]

Carter alleged that Seaborn Reese had been drunk during a trial and had used profanity in the presence of women—a crime in Georgia in the 1890s. Later, at a picnic, Reese was so intoxicated that he tumbled out of his chair. Judge Sweat had also been drunk in court at St. Simons Island. But Sweat's sexual escapades attracted the most attention. During the senate investigation, a girl testified that at Indian Springs the judge had suggested they "go to the woods and have a good time." When she rejected this proposal, Sweat replied that he would return with some money. At that, the young woman rushed to her stepfather, who began searching for the judge. The newspapers reported that Judge Sweat was last seen in Indian Springs hurrying to the train station while explaining

8. Griffin *News*, May 18, 1894; Atlanta *Constitution*, January 17, 1897.
9. Atlanta *Journal*, December 13, 1897; Atlanta *Constitution*, January 17, 1897.

to a friend that urgent business required his immediate departure. The girl's stepfather said he was later offered $300 not to press charges. On another occasion, Carter asserted, Sweat had had an affair with a woman whose husband was about to be tried in his court for murder. The judge declared a mistrial, and the man was eventually acquitted.[10]

When the committee hearing began, both sides produced scores of witnesses, and the press gave minute attention to every sensational revelation. Sweat became known as the "gay Jurist," his supposed mistress as the "lady in black." Both judges resolutely maintained their innocence. Sweat explained that he had been the unfortunate victim of circumstance. The woman seen leaving his hotel room had merely dropped by while he fetched his umbrella; he had offered nothing to the girl beyond, perhaps, some candies and fruits. "I yield to no man in my admiration and respect for ladies," the judge assured the committee. The charge that he was drunk during a trial at St. Simons Island also was untrue. Sweat noted, however, that he had been unwell on the day in question, and possibly spectators had mistaken his illness for intoxication. Another witness begged to differ: "He was so full he couldn't walk." Judge Reese maintained his innocence with as much vehemence as Judge Sweat. He had not been drunk on the bench; he had made no obscene gestures in court; and if he had indulged in profanity he was unaware that ladies were within earshot. "I yield to no man in respect for women," he declared. The investigation soon turned against Carter. Most damaging was an affidavit from Tom Watson, who said he had pleaded many cases before Judge Reese and had never known him to be drunk on the bench. And although there was an abundance of circumstantial evidence against Sweat, it was difficult to prove unconditionally that he had done anything improper. Eventually, a majority of the committee ruled that insufficient evidence existed for the impeachment of either judge.[11]

The results of the investigation did not harm the third party; most

10. Atlanta *Constitution*, January 17, 1897.

11. Atlanta *Looking Glass*, n.d., quoted in Atlanta *Constitution*, December 16, 1897; Atlanta *Constitution*, January 14, 1897; "Proceedings of the Special Committee Appointed by the Georgia House of Representatives, 1896, to Investigate the charges made by State Senator W. Y. Carter against Judges J. L. Sweat and Seaborn Reese of the Superior Court Bench," 7, 31, 47, 59, 66, 72, 112, 410, 594; typescript, Georgia State Department of Archives and History, Atlanta.

Populists undoubtedly expected the Democrats to exonerate Sweat and Reese. Nor had the investigation been simply an exercise in backwoods prudery. It had exposed Democratic corruption, kept the Populists in the public eye, and created a new third-party hero. Rumors flew that Yancey Carter would be the next Populist candidate for governor.

Yet beneath the surface Carter's ambitions were in trouble. Sometime in 1895 or 1896 he had had a mild falling-out with Tom Watson. The cause of the ill-feeling was unknown, but as time passed it flared frequently. Watson's affidavit had damaged Carter's case against Reese. In return, Carter had asked that the senate committee throw out Watson's testimony on the grounds that the Sage of Hickory Hill had failed to appear in person. "Mr. Watson is entitled to no more consideration than any other witness," Carter remarked coldly. The Carter-Watson feud again exploded in mid-November, 1897, when Watson venomously criticized Carter's opposition to a prohibition bill that was before the Georgia senate. Carter's position, Watson chided, was a betrayal of the third party's prohibition plank. Even more damning, the votes of Carter and two other Populist senators had prevented the passage of the bill. "We hereby apologize," Watson wrote. "We should have confessed that we were hypocrites. Hereafter let us not abuse democrats and republicans for violating campaign contracts. Let us keep our mouths shut about broken pledges." Carter replied with equal scorn, pointing out that before the third party endorsed prohibition he had promised his constituents that he would remain "wet" on the liquor question. Unimpressed, Watson demanded to know why Carter had served as chairman of the platform committee that had suggested the prohibition plank. "The anti-barroom bill is dead," Watson declared, "and Populist senators killed it." [12]

The Watson-Carter dispute was plainly destroying the prospect of a strong Populist campaign in 1898. Although Watson remained master of the party, Carter was gaining strength, especially among former Republicans. Also waiting for another chance at the gubernatorial nomination was William L. Peek. Now with three snarling factions, the Georgia Peo-

12. Atlanta *Constitution*, January 19, November 12, 1897; *People's Party Paper*, November 12, 1897.

ple's party seemed on the brink of self-mutilation. In an effort to bring harmony, some party leaders arranged a peace conference in Atlanta, after which a quiet fell over the wrangling Populists. In December, 1897, Watson announced that under no circumstances would he accept the nomination for governor. A day later Carter said that he, too, would not be a candidate. But Watson and Carter had no intention of leaving the field to Peek. With the Watson wing still talking about the nomination of Watson or Hines, Carter's supporters claimed that if nominated for governor the "lion of the tribe of Judah" would run. In addition, the party prohibitionists, although somewhat discredited by the defeat of 1896, hopefully whispered about the possibility of Seaborn Wright's candidacy.[13]

Thus with most prominent Populists bowing out of the gubernatorial race, the third-party state convention met in Atlanta on March 16, 1898. Reiterating that he would refuse the nomination, Tom Watson failed to attend. And without his dominating presence, for the first time the delegates were free to choose whomever they wished. Not surprisingly, they nominated Watson for governor. As the convention roared its approval, the old passion suddenly returned, one elderly Confederate veteran climbing onto a table to cheer for Tom Watson. Then, to placate all factions, the delegates nominated Peek for commissioner of agriculture, Ben Milliken (a Carter supporter) for comptroller-general, and Walter B. Hill, a prohibitionist, for chief justice of the state supreme court. The other members of the slate, which included a Republican and a Democrat, were also well-known and respected. It was the strongest ticket the Populists had ever fielded. The platform was in many ways similar to those of previous years. Planks condemned lynching, convict lease, and the granting of free railroad passes to politicians. There were also demands for free textbooks in grade schools and for the election of all public officials. A prohibition plank called for laws that would keep the "local prohibition already obtained and provide for the sale of intoxicating liquors, otherwise in barrooms under public control." Finally, the platform supported lower taxes, praised the Nashville convention, and endorsed the St. Louis demands. All in all, it was a typical set of Populist

13. Atlanta *Constitution*, December 11, 12, 1897.

principles with little that was novel. Its only surprise was the antisaloon plank, which the convention had emasculated so as to mollify those who believed prohibition had caused their defeat in 1896. Obviously, the delegates expected the ticket rather than the platform to be their main strength in the coming campaign. But everything depended on whether the Sage of Hickory Hill would accept the nomination.[14]

After a week of pondering, Tom Watson announced that he would not run for governor. "It is the unwritten law among Democrats of Georgia that I am not to hold office," he wrote in the *People's Party Paper*. "The time had been when political ambition was very strong within me and I looked forward to that field of honor, fame, and usefulness. It is no longer so." That announcement began the collapse of the Georgia People's party. Soon nearly every nominee on the state ticket had withdrawn. In desperation, the chairman called a new convention, but only a hundred delegates attended. Although Peek and Carter were willing to campaign for governor, the Watson wing refused. A month earlier, the Populists had nominated their strongest possible candidate. Now they seemed determined to pick their weakest. After some squabbling, the delegates nominated James Robert Hogan, a forty-eight-year-old farmer from Lincoln County. Hogan had few qualifications except that he was a devoted Watson man and was willing to run. These credentials won him the nomination, defeating Peek by two votes.[15]

It was difficult to imagine a more disastrous choice than Hogan. For six years he had served in the legislature, an able but colorless member. The most notable feature of his otherwise uneventful life was his choice of spouses. At the death of Mollie, his first wife, he married her sister, Emma. When Emma died, he proposed to the remaining sister, Lula. Except for that bit of panache, Hogan was an unremarkable man. His letter of acceptance was less than inspiring. "If I knew that I would be elected, then I would not desire the nomination," it read. With such a champion, even the optimistic Peek was discouraged and contributed little to the campaign. James K. Hines refused to run for Congress. The

14. Columbus *Enquirer-Sun*, March 15–17, 20, 1898; *People's Party Paper*, March 18, 1898; Atlanta *Constitution*, March 15, 17, 19, 1898.
15. *People's Party Paper* quoted in Savannah *Press*, March 24, 1898; Atlanta *Journal*, May 18–19, 1898; Atlanta *Constitution*, May 19–20, 1898.

old Populist façade of friendship toward the blacks also seemed to be crumbling. Party chairman Cunningham referred to them as "niggers" in his address to the March convention. Hines suggested that Democrats and Populists institute a white primary, with white people supporting the Democrat or Populist receiving the most votes. Amzon A. Murphy, a prominent Barnesville Populist, also called for the white primary in his district. Finally, the *People's Party Paper* continued to belabor the "rape circular," claiming that since 1896 rapes and lynchings in Georgia had increased fourfold. Earlier, when Governor Atkinson had suggested that prisoners be armed to protect themselves against lynch mobs, one Populist responded with an outraged letter. "No courts have made fewer mistakes than the lynchers for rape," it thundered.[16]

The Democrats compounded the third-party dilemma by nominating Allen D. Candler for governor. Candler, who had never lost an election in his life, had served in the legislature, in Congress, and as Governor Atkinson's secretary of state. Although he had been a railroad president and was a member of a prominent Georgia family, he also possessed qualities that appealed to the common man. During the Civil War, Candler rose from private to colonel and lost an eye in the process. "He is not pretty," one newspaper wrote. "He is a little short fellow who chews tobacco, has a vigorous flow of 'cuss' words, and has no frills on his language or his lingerie." But Candler reserved his profanity for private occasions. In public he seemed the soul of moderation, demanding that blacks receive equal justice and conceding that Populists had had good reasons for leaving the Democratic party in the early part of the decade. He argued, however, that the time had come for the wool-hat boys to return to the party of their ancestors. Affectionately known as "Uncle Allen" and the "One-Eyed Plowboy of Pigeon Roost," Candler appeared conservative, stable, and fatherly—a man who could bring peace to Georgia after the strife of the 1890s.[17]

16. Clinton J. Perryman, "History of Lincoln County, Georgia," 209–10, typescript, Georgia Department of Archives and History, Atlanta; *People's Party Paper*, November 19, 1897, March 8, September 17, 1898; Atlanta *Journal*, September 3, 1898; Savannah *Press*, October 15, 1898; Atlanta *Constitution*, September 1, 1898.

17. Chicago *Times-Herald*, n.d., quoted in Atlanta *Constitution*, June 18, 1898; Northen, *Men of Mark*, IV, 29–32; Cooper, *Story of Georgia*, IV, 663; Allen D. Candler, Biographical Data File, Georgia Department of Archives and History, Atlanta; Atlanta *Constitution*, July 22, August 21, 26, 1898.

Yet more obstacles blocked Hogan's path to the governor's mansion. All during his campaign a series of international events drew the attention of newspaper readers away from state politics. Otto von Bismarck and William Gladstone died, Empress Elizabeth of Austria was assassinated, the British fought the battle of Omdurman, the Fashoda crisis erupted, and new evidence was found that would bring about the second trial of Alfred Dreyfus. But these events were overshadowed by still another. Three weeks before Hogan's nomination, the United States declared war on Spain. Under the best of circumstances, few would have been interested in Hogan's humdrum campaign. Now the exciting news from the Philippines and Cuba drove any discussion of the gubernatorial race off the front page. One large newspaper, the Savannah *Press*, failed to mention Hogan's nomination, so enraptured was it by reports from the war. Many Populists were just as interested in the conflict, including Yancey Carter. In his typically swashbuckling manner, Carter declined to run for office. Instead, he organized a military company and was soon off to the war. In time Populists could read with pride that "Captain" Yancey Carter and his Georgians had landed with the invasion force near Santiago de Cuba.[18]

Like most Americans, Georgia Populists were anguished by the plight of Cubans. The *People's Party Paper* often carried items about oppression on the island. At the state convention Mell Branch had proposed a resolution demanding that the United States grant "belligerent rights to the Cuban forces, and, if necessary, to go further and give such suitable aid as may be necessary."[19] The resolution was unanimously endorsed. Populist enthusiasm for the Spanish-American War probably surprised some Democrats. For years the third party had complained about appropriations for the army, the navy, and the state militia. But rather than being pacifists, they simply objected to expensive peace-time armies that could be used against farmers. Nor was imperialism a motive for their endorsement of the conflict. Before the war no Georgia Populist seemed interested in acquiring overseas possessions, and few appeared concerned about overseas markets. Afterward, none gained a reputation as an impe-

18. Savannah *Press*, May 19, 1898; Atlanta *Constitution*, July 1, August 19, 1898.
19. *People's Party Paper*, March 18, 1898.

rialist, and at least two—Tom Watson and James Barrett—publicly decried the acquisition of the Philippines. Most third-party men had only
two reasons for supporting hostilities: they wanted to avenge the loss of
the U.S.S. *Maine*, and they wished to aid the embattled people of Cuba.

But once war had been declared, at least one Georgia Populist opposed
it. In an impassioned editorial Tom Watson asserted that the conflict was
unchristian, would raise taxes, and would ensnare the United States in
European troubles. The Sage warned that America might become an international "Don Quixote," intervening in all disputes. Nor could he
help but comment upon the blacks who were enlisting in the army: "The
employment of negro troops will immensely aggravate the race troubles,
and will be a tremendous step in the direction of Social Equality. Watch
. . . and see." [20]

Thus the third party was saddled with another liability—Tom Watson's opposition to a popular war. It soon became obvious that Hogan
had no chance and that Populists should concentrate on county and congressional races. The state executive committee advised all local party organizations to "take any stand" as long as it did not conflict with the state
platform. In the wiregrass country of southeastern Georgia, Populist
leaders embraced this advice with a vengeance. Two years before, the
wool-hat boys in that region had worked for William McKinley after the
withdrawal of the Populist electors. In return, the Grand Old Party had
given them a few minor positions in the post office. By 1898 the local
third-party leaders were again ready to make a deal. They pledged to
support a white Republican candidate for Congress after their new ally
promised to endorse a number of Populists running for the legislature
and local offices. Watson had always scorned such alliances, realizing that
the Democrats could then use the "Negro rule" argument with all its terrible effectiveness. But there was nothing he could do. For the first time,
Populists and Republicans had formally fused in at least part of Georgia. [21]

Watson's worst fears came to pass. Almost immediately, the Democratic press exploded with indignation, pointing to North Carolina,
where a similar union had occurred in 1894. The Atlanta *Constitution*

---

20. *Ibid.*, April 29, 1898.
21. *Ibid.*; Douglas *Breeze*, September 3, 1898; Atlanta *Constitution*, August 29, 1898.

claimed that the former slaves held a thousand offices in the Tar Heel State, including a seat in Congress. Such success had made them haughty with power. It was said that insolent blacks frequently insulted white people and that a white woman was never safe in the countryside. The Democrats charged that all these indignities were directly traceable to the Populist-Republican alliance. Georgia newspapers vied with each other to illustrate the horrors of life in "negro-ridden North Carolina." One weekly howled that white fusionists were "dirty Libertines"; another thundered that "carpetbaggery of thirty years ago was decency itself compared with populism and negro fusion of today." But the Atlanta *Constitution* won the prize for the most lurid description of what horrors fusion would visit upon Georgia: "The small farmers and the white laboring men will have the virtue of their daughters airily discussed by negro philosophers, and we shall have what modern balladists are pleased to term 'a hot time' in the rural regions." [22] The Democratic strategy worked with canny precision. Tom Watson and other third-party leaders refused to campaign in southeastern Georgia, and wiregrass Populists fled the party by the hundreds.

The *coup de grace* for the Populist campaign came in August when the *People's Party Paper* collapsed. For years it had been losing money. Although every effort was made to keep the newspaper alive until after the election, it was hopeless to continue publication. A laconic telegram to the party chairman announced its demise: "Will suspend publication. Say nothing[.] Advise further plans." But there were no further plans. On election day Allen Candler was triumphant, capturing 118,028 votes to Hogan's 51,191. Since Wright's campaign in 1896, the Populists had lost more than 34,000 supporters. The Democrats had also thrashed the People's party in the three congressional contests it had entered, the most successful Populist taking only 27.7 percent of the vote. The biggest disaster came in the races for the General Assembly. No Populists were elected to the senate and only twelve were sent to the house. The defeat of Mell Branch eliminated the third party's most talented legislator. [23]

22. Hicks, *Populist Revolt*, 391–92; Atlanta *Constitution*, September 4, 9, 1898; Columbus *Enquirer-Sun*, September 30, 1898.
23. Austin Holcomb to S. F. Carter, August 22, 1898, Box 3, folder 29, Watson Papers, UNC; Diamond (ed.), *Guide to U.S. Elections*, 404; Atlanta *Constitution*, October 7, 1898.

A dreary campaign had come to a dreary end. As usual there had been violence, the worst outbreak occurring at a nighttime debate in Chattahoochee County. The Democratic candidate was Thomas M. Adams; the Populist, William H. Bagley. After the debate, a black man named Jeff Davis spoke, challenging some previous statements made by the Populist. Abruptly, Bagley tried to strike Davis. Another black man intervened, only to have Bagley bludgeon him with a cane. Then, seeing Adams standing nearby, Bagley shouted, "You are the cause of all this trouble." Suddenly, shots rang out. "Oh, my God, I am a dead man," cried Adams as he fell to the ground. He died almost instantly with bullet holes in his head and chest. The identity of Adams's killer remained a mystery. Some claimed it had been Bagley; others said that someone else, trying to protect Davis, had committed the murder.[24]

Possibly the man most horrified by the slaying was an eyewitness, James "Jack" Gordy. Gordy, who had been campaigning as a Populist for county tax collector, was so sickened by the shooting that he withdrew. Both Bagley and Adams had been his cousins. "I am done with politics; somebody else can run in my place," Gordy said. But if Gordy had given up politics, he remained loyal to Tom Watson. In 1906 he named a newborn son Thomas Watson Gordy. And three-quarters of a century later, Jack Gordy's grandson, Jimmy Carter, would run for office claiming that he, too, was a populist.[25]

James R. Hogan's campaign for governor marked the last time the third party ever fielded a serious ticket in Georgia. In 1900 party diehards met and nominated John Humphrey Traylor of Troup County for governor. Traylor, who was seventy-six years old, fought a less than vigorous campaign against Allen Candler. Still he was able to capture 25,285 votes— an impressive figure considering the hopelessness of the contest. That year the Populists elected seven members to the house. In 1902 the party nominated James K. Hines for governor. Although Hines absolutely re-

---

24. Columbus *Enquirer-Sun*, August 27, 1898.
25. *Ibid.*, August 25, 1898; Harmon Zeigler, "Letters of Tom Watson to His Campaign Manager," *Georgia Historical Quarterly*, XLIV (1958), 274–79; David Kucharsky, *The Man from Plains* (New York, 1976), 30.

fused the honor, 5,566 citizens voted for him.[26] Hines's defeat was so convincing that Democrats could now look to the future, virtually certain that there would never be another Populist ticket in Georgia.

Many Georgians were mystified about what blighted the People's party. Almost all the old state issues still existed, yet for some reason they did not seem pressing enough to sustain the third-party organization. Tom Watson later argued that the conflict in Cuba was to blame. "The Spanish War finished us," he wrote. "The blare of the bugle drowned the voice of the Reformer."[27] He might also have mentioned the Populist-Republican fusion in the wiregrass country and his own refusal to accept the gubernatorial nomination in 1898. But there was even a more fundamental explanation for the demise of the party. Populism had been founded as an answer to national, not state, questions. Although Georgia possessed an abundance of problems in the 1890s, most of them could have been solved in the Democratic party, which already contained a reform wing. Neither party wished to address more fundamental difficulties like racism and lien law reform. Thus after 1896 Populism was largely superfluous in Georgia. It was this fact, not the "blare of the bugle," that finally silenced the party.

A body called the Georgia People's party existed until 1910, and in some ways it retained the regalia of a true political organization. An executive committee continued to function and occasionally hold meetings; earnest letters were exchanged discussing the possibility of reviving the organization; and every so often a farmer would run for office claiming to be a Populist—a practice that grew increasingly quaint after the turn of the century. But the People's party, as a political force, was nearly dead in Georgia.

Yet something remained. Many men still considered themselves "Pops," even when casting ballots in Democratic primaries; many still regarded themselves as reformers, even if their old party no longer nominated candidates. And many remembered with extraordinary fondness

26. Atlanta *Constitution*, April 11, October 18, 1900; Knight, *Georgia's Bi-Centennial Memoirs*, 407; Diamond (ed.), *Guide to U.S. Elections*, 404. For an account of the decline of the Populist party on the county level, see Furgeson, "Power Politics and Populism," 86–96.

27. *Watson's Jeffersonian Magazine*, October, 1910, p. 817.

the Sage of Hickory Hill and the clashes of the 1890s. They were a sizable group of voters who might be influenced by the right man. No one saw the possibilities better than Tom Watson. If the People's party, as a party, no longer existed, Watson realized it might still exist as something else. It was this realization that would change Georgia Populism from a working organization with many leaders, factions, and newspapers into something more monolithic. Watson was about to transform the party into a personality cult.

His opportunity came in 1904. Since William Jennings Bryan's unsuccessful campaign for the presidency in 1896 and an equally unsuccessful bid in 1900, there had existed a growing movement within the Democratic party to run a more conservative candidate. This stirring gave Populists across the country reason for optimism, and they soon formulated a scheme to rejuvenate their own organization. First, they planned to hold an early national convention and nominate a strong reform candidate. If the Democrats then selected a conservative, some believed that Bryan and his followers might bolt and join the third party.

With such hopes, the Populists met on July 4, 1904, in Springfield, Illinois. It was a disappointing meeting with only two hundred delegates present. Many agreed that the strongest candidate they could pick was Tom Watson, but there was no guarantee that the Georgian would accept the nomination. It was widely known that Watson, claiming to be through with politics, had refused to run for governor of Georgia in 1898. Hope for his candidacy finally expired when a delegate produced a letter from the Sage of Hickory Hill saying that he did not desire the nomination. But shortly before the balloting, word swept the hall that Watson would accept. Although nobody seemed to know the origin of the rumor or if it contained any truth, the convention nominated Tom Watson for president and Thomas H. Tribbles of Nebraska for vice-president. Then the delegates went home, still having heard nothing from Hickory Hill.[28]

Meanwhile, the Democrats were meeting in St. Louis. Just as the

28. Atlanta *Constitution*, July 3–6, 31, 1904; Hicks, *Populist Revolt*, 402; Woodward, *Tom Watson*, 257–58; Brewton, *Watson*, 291.

Populists had hoped, the party conservatives tried to wrench control of the convention by nominating for president Alton Brooks Parker, the chief justice of the New York Court of Appeals. In response, the silverites nominated the New York newspaper publisher, William Randolph Hearst. Parker had little difficulty winning the nomination on the first ballot. But shortly after his victory, the judge sent the convention a telegram saying that he supported the gold standard. The message stated that if this was unacceptable another candidate should be chosen. Such a position was clearly a repudiation of the Democrats' principal plank since 1896. After considerable debate, the bewildered delegates at last agreed to retain Parker, comforting themselves in the knowledge that the platform made no mention of the money question.[29]

The predictions of third-party strategists had unfolded with nearly supernatural precision. All that remained was to see if Bryan or Hearst would secede from the Democratic party and if Watson would consent to run for president. For a week and a half after his nomination, nothing was heard from Watson, who was undoubtedly waiting to learn what Bryan and Hearst would do. Soon it became obvious that neither Democrat planned to bolt. Still, letters and telegrams continued to speed to Hickory Hill imploring the Sage to become the Populist candidate. Finally, on July 30 Watson sent word to the party chairman that he would accept the nomination.

Why, after eight years of political retirement, did Watson suddenly return to politics in such a forlorn endeavor? He hoped the party might be resuscitated, although he had no illusions about his chances for victory. "With me," he explained later, "the only question was: [Did] . . . a sufficient number of old line Populists want this fight made. In reaching a conclusion upon that subject, I was guided by the evidence of general discontent with what had been done at the Democratic convention." It was also possible that Watson accepted the nomination to promote the sale of his various publications. Since March, William Randolph Hearst had been urging the Sage to come to New York and serve as one of his editors. Nor was it altogether surprising that just after the election Wat-

29. Atlanta *Journal*, August 21, 1904.

son announced the creation of *Tom Watson's Magazine*, financed not by
Hearst but by another New York publisher.[30]

Whatever Watson's motives, he was soon barnstorming the country,
alternately denouncing Parker and the Republican presidential candidate, Theodore Roosevelt. His campaign began in Lincoln, Nebraska;
then he spoke in New York, Atlanta, Kansas City, and Chicago. This
tour differed in some respects from those of earlier days. A blatant racism
had crept into Watson's speeches. Arguing that the South had a right to
know where Parker stood on the race issue, the Sage posed a number of
questions to the Democratic candidate. Would Parker refuse to dine with
Booker T. Washington? Would he refuse to appoint blacks to political
office in the South? Did he favor the integration of schools in New York?
Watson produced a letter in which Parker referred to a black as "my dear
[sir]"—"just as though [he] . . . had been a white man," Watson declared. And while campaigning in Georgia, Watson called for the elimination of black voters. Such action was necessary, Watson argued, because the "men who control" continued to bribe them and crush reform.
The Sage offered his aid to any progressive Democrat who would work
for disfranchisement.[31]

Despite Watson's efforts, the results of the election were unspectacu-
lar; Roosevelt was easily triumphant, and Watson received only 114,051
votes across the nation. More heartening was his tally in Georgia, where
he found 22,635 supporters.[32] Possibly it was this showing that convinced him of the resiliency of Populism in his home state. Certainly it
was a sobering revelation to Georgia Democrats who had thought, just
two years before, that they had seen the last of the People's party. It was
still unlikely the Populists would ever again nominate a serious state
ticket, but with more than 22,000 voters seemingly at his command,
Tom Watson was again a force in state politics.

Many Georgians wondered why Watson, who had courted black voters
in the 1890s, had suddenly called for their elimination at the beginning of
the twentieth century. Although this seemed like an extraordinary meta-

---

30. Watson quoted in Woodward, *Tom Watson*, 350; see also *ibid.*, 365–66; Brewton,
Watson, 295–303.
31. Atlanta *Constitution*, September 2, 1904; Woodward, *Tom Watson*, 371.
32. Diamond (ed.), *Guide to U.S. Elections*, 302.

morphosis, in reality it was not. Since 1898 a number of his colleagues
had advocated the white primary. Moreover, expediency and not compassion had been the Populists' motive for their earlier alliance with
blacks. By 1904 it was obvious that such a union could never again be
forged. But blacks remained, at least in theory, the potential arbiters of
state politics. In 1904, twenty-four thousand Republican votes were cast
in Georgia, and so Democratic leaders could still shout the old shib-
boleths about "Negro rule." Arguing that this issue was the only reason
why Democratic conservatives remained in office, Watson advocated the
final elimination of the black balance of power.[33] Rather than the product
of monstrous racism, this demand was more likely the result of Watson's
desire for influence. During this time, the Sage's castigations against
blacks were still reasonably moderate, at least when compared with his
later outbursts.[34] Watson simply wanted to eliminate the black balance of
power and replace it with his own. Most Populists agreed. "In my feeble
way I am doing all I can to make this a white mans government," Peek
assured Watson. Four years later, when the Democrats included in their
state platform a demand for the white primary, the third party passed a
resolution congratulating them on an idea the Populists had long advocated. And if anyone continued to think the People's party had any concern for blacks, this belief vanished in 1908, when the state voted in
favor of an amendment to the constitution disfranchising blacks in
Georgia. Although twenty counties objected to the proposal, all the old
Populist counties voted in the affirmative. "I expect to dominate this
state for the next ten years," Watson exclaimed after the contest.[35]

But it took time to eliminate the black man from Georgia politics. At
least one important faction, the conservative Democrats, was wary of the
idea. When they selected Clark Howell to run for governor in the Democratic primary of 1906, Howell argued that the disfranchisement of
blacks might also mean the disfranchisement of thousands of illiterate
whites. He also claimed that blacks were so inconsequential in state poli-

33. *Ibid.*, 282; Woodward, *Tom Watson*, 370–71.
34. Compare *Tom Watson's Magazine*, June 1905, p. 396, and Woodward, *Tom Watson*, 432–33.
35. Peek quoted in John Michael Mathews, "Studies in Race Relations in Georgia, 1890–1930" (Ph.D. dissertation, Duke University, 1970), 116–17; Atlanta *Constitution*, July 10, 1908; Atlanta *Journal*, July 9, 1908.

tics that their formal elimination was unnecessary.[36] Watson thought this an absurd and dangerous view, and he set to work finding a reform-minded Democrat who would oppose Howell. With the encouragement of James K. Hines, he eventually decided upon Hoke Smith, the former owner of the Atlanta *Journal*.[37] It was a peculiar choice because in the 1890s Smith had been a champion of the gold standard. In other ways, however, Watson found Smith's views acceptable. In the past, Smith had called for election reform, sterner railroad regulation, an end to child labor, and, more recently, black disfranchisement by means of a literacy test. But the most appealing aspect of the Howell-Smith schism was that Watson and his 22,000 followers now seemed to hold the balance of power in Georgia. On election day Smith was victorious, capturing 104,796 votes to his opponents' 70,477. Whether correctly or not, Watson took credit for the triumph. "WE WHIPPED THEM!" his newspaper blared.[38]

Once in office, Smith went about the work of trying to please his benefactor. It was no mean task. He constantly asked for Watson's advice on bills, appointments, and policy. A natural reformer in his own right, Smith proposed or supported many reform measures, including legislation for statewide prohibition. He also strengthened the railroad commission and appointed James K. Hines the commission's special attorney. Finally, under Smith's leadership, the literacy test was added to the state's election laws. This legislation, along with the poll tax, assured the disfranchisement of 95 percent of Georgia's blacks. No administration in the state's history had accomplished so much in so short a time. "Governor Smith has done well," wrote Watson, in a benediction to the governor's first two years in office.[39]

Such a congenial alliance seemed to promise almost anything for Smith

36. Atlanta *Constitution*, January 10, 1906.

37. Atlanta *Constitution*, January 10–12, 14, 1906, September 3, 1910; Atlanta *Journal*, January 12, 1906; Grantham, *Hoke Smith*, 139; Woodward, *Tom Watson*, 374; Brewton, *Watson*, 307; Alfred Edward Hicks, "Watson and Hardwick in Georgia Politics: A Study in Political Personality and Reform Tension" (Senior honors thesis, Trinity College, 1967); Josephine Newsome Cummings, "Thomas William Hardwick: A Study of a Strange and Eventful Career" (M.A. thesis, University of Georgia, 1961).

38. Grantham, *Hoke Smith*, 154; Woodward, *Tom Watson*, 383. Besides Smith and Howell, there were also a number of minor candidates in the contest.

39. Grantham, *Hoke Smith*, 160–61, 165–66, 168; Jack Temple Kirby, *Darkness at the Dawning: Race and Reform in the Progressive South* (Philadelphia, 1972), 27–28, 142; John

and Watson; in fact, the Sage predicted that Georgia would one day elect Smith to the United States Senate. Yet the partnership was to explode over what at first appeared to be a minor difference. In the 1890s a man named Arthur Glover had served as one of Watson's bodyguards, and the Sage believed Glover had saved his life during the dangerous campaign of 1892. In October, 1906, Glover murdered his mistress after discovering she was being unfaithful to him. The next year Glover stood trial, was convicted, and was sentenced to be hanged. Watson promised the condemned man that he would personally ask Governor Smith to commute his sentence to life imprisonment. When Smith refused, Watson called him "cold-blooded and selfish." Glover was a "cracked-brained" lunatic, the Sage insisted, and to send him to the gallows would be murder. Refusing to change his mind, Smith allowed Arthur Glover to be executed in late January, 1908.[40]

Watson's defense of Glover had spoken well for the Sage's compassion and loyalty to his followers. Glover was indeed a "cracked-brained" lunatic, who believed, among other things, that he was John the Baptist. Twenty-five witnesses testified that Glover was mentally ill, suffering from delusions, depression, and probably schizophrenia. But there were other reasons why Watson believed the sentence should have been commuted. The trial had been a burlesque of proper legal proceedings, at one point the wife of the jury foreman shrieking, "Hang the defendant!" And when the prosecuting attorney delivered his final arguments, he included an observation that was completely irrelevant and completely damning: "Glover was a Tom Watson man." Rather than a crackbrained defense of a crackbrained man, Watson's actions were rational and compassionate. As for Arthur Glover, even his deranged and illiterate mind saw truths that eluded Hoke Smith. "It is my past Political life that is what they are after me so hot about," he wrote. "It is not the Woman I have killed or the crime I have comited. They has not punished others with the gallows that has comited crimes more shocking."[41]

Dittmer, *Black Georgia in the Progressive Era, 1900–1920* (Urbana, 1977); *Watson's Jeffersonian Magazine*, September, 1907, p. 847.

40. Woodward, *Tom Watson*, 386–69; Grantham, *Hoke Smith*, 185–86; Hicks, "Watson and Hardwick," 128.

41. Hicks, "Watson and Hardwick," 104, 111; Atlanta *Constitution*, May 2, 1907.

For Watson the last straw came when the Democratic executive committee, which Smith controlled, changed the rules governing party primaries. In the future the candidate with a majority of votes would receive
the nomination for governor. Watson believed this move was a deliberate
attempt to steal power from the countryside. He noted that under the
former county-unit system, no county had more than three votes at the
state nominating convention. Therefore, urban counties with their large
populations were underrepresented and rural counties were overrepre-
sented. In a blind rage, Watson wrote to Joseph M. Brown, asking if he
would oppose Smith in the next election. Brown agreed. It was an extraordinary entente. "Little Joe" Brown—who was the son of the old triumvir, Joseph E. Brown—was a millionaire, a railroad owner, and an enemy of reform. Yet with the aid of Tom Watson and the Panic of 1907,
Brown was victorious in the Democratic primary of 1908.[42]

For many, Watson's actions were inexplicable. While thousands of old
Populists rallied to Brown, thousands more were dumbfounded by the
Sage's defection. "You have lost some of the truest & bravest Populists
that ever walked Gods green Earth," one wrote to the Sage. The sorriest
loss came when James K. Hines refused to abandon Smith. During the
general election, Yancey Carter announced his candidacy as an independent in a vain effort to capture the disaffected Smith supporters and put a
reformer in the governor's mansion. Carter won only 11,746 votes, and
Brown was elected overwhelmingly.[43]

Watson surely had mixed feelings after the triumph of "Little Joe" in
1908. In one respect his grandest dream had been realized: in his own
mind at least, he was now the undisputed arbiter of state politics. Still he
must have had doubts. His claims of dominion over Georgia's public affairs were based on the considerable number of Populists he could command. In 1906 there had been no reason for concern because he had carried almost all the old Populist counties for Smith. But in 1908 only half
had followed his orders and shifted to Brown.[44] Most humiliating was the

42. Woodward, *Tom Watson*, 392. See also Watson, "The Gubernatorial Campaign in
Georgia," *Watson's Jeffersonian Magazine*, July, 1908, 359–62; Frances Beach Hudson,
"The Smith-Brown Controversy" (M.A. thesis, Emory University, 1929); Grantham, *Hoke
Smith*, 187–93; Woodward, *Tom Watson*, 393–95, 400; Atlanta *Constitution*, May 23, 1908.
    43. Woodward, *Tom Watson*, 394; Diamond (ed.), *Guide to U.S. Elections*, 404.
    44. Atlanta *Constitution*, August 26, 1906, June 8, 1908.

vote of Watson's own McDuffie County. In both elections the Sage's neighbors had sided with his enemies.

Equally depressing was Brown's reign as governor, which proved as conservative as many had feared. Watson must have realized that he was largely responsible, and by 1910 he had had enough of Brown. Even so, he could not bring himself to support Hoke Smith, who had again announced his candidacy for governor. Watson promised, however, that he would make no statements about the contest. He remained aloof, while James K. Hines attempted to swing the Populists to Smith. On election day, Smith won the Democratic nomination, 96,638 votes to Brown's 92,469.[45]

Watson was shaken by the results, now realizing that Smith could indeed become governor. In a turnabout that astounded Georgia, the Sage then announced that he was supporting Brown in the general election. But old Populists appeared deaf to Watson's wishes, and on election day Hoke Smith easily defeated Joe Brown. Watson's power in Georgia had seemingly dissolved. Even more terrible for the Sage was the realization that the vast majority of his followers had gone over to his enemies. Only three of the old Populist counties had voted for Brown.

The mental strain this revelation placed on Watson was immense. Hiring men to guard his house at night, he became obsessed with the fear of assassination. "I never was more conscious in my life of having reached a crisis," he wrote. Soon strange letters and pronouncements were issuing from Hickory Hill. The Sage warned that if Smith had him murdered, the Populists would avenge the killing. "It is closing in on you," a wire from Watson threatened Smith. "I give you one more chance to save your wife and son. Resign by two o'clock today, or your crimes will be known to all the world." Smith elected not to resign, and Watson let it be known, without a respectable grain of evidence, that the governor-elect had "ruined more than one pure girl."[46]

But in the midst of his troubles Watson saw a way to restore his past glory. In the Tenth Congressional District Congressman Thomas W. Hardwick was running for reelection. If there was anywhere in the state

45. Brewton, *Watson*, 321–22; Grantham, *Hoke Smith*, 202–203.
46. Quoted in Woodward, *Tom Watson*, 410, 413–14.

Watson still retained influence, it was in the "terrible" Tenth. Thus the Sage began what was in many ways the most desperate struggle of his career. If he could defeat Hardwick, he would prove that he was still a force in Georgia affairs.

Hardwick and Watson had once been friends. Hardwick sponsored one of the first disfranchisement bills to appear before the state legislature, and in 1906 he helped convince the Sage to support Hoke Smith for governor. Their friendship, however, cooled after Watson endorsed Brown two years later. Still they remained on fairly good terms until 1910, when Watson asked Hardwick to have Charles McGregor appointed to a federal position. Hardwick and McGregor were old political enemies, and Hardwick sent Watson a message saying that it would be impossible for him to honor the request. "Why we parted company," Watson wrote in the margin of the letter.[47] He then let it be known that he was supporting Hardwick's opponents in the congressional race, one of whom was a member of the Augusta ring. If the parallels to the Glover case escaped Watson, they eluded no one else.

All of this occurred before the defeat of Brown. Now Watson was fighting for his political life. The contest rapidly degenerated with each side indulging in name-calling and mudslinging. As the campaign progressed, Hardwick's popularity swelled, and soon he was boasting that he would capture all the old third-party counties. The situation became so bleak that late in the contest Watson found he was begging his followers to save him: "Now, [Hardwick] . . . says I have lost out with the old Pops in the Tenth district and they are going with him against me. Now, boys, will you stand by me? I appeal to you. If Hardwick is reelected I will be considered in disgrace. Don't put that cup to my lips. Stand by me."[48]

But the boys refused. On election day Hardwick easily won the primary. Still Watson would not drink from the cup of disgrace. There remained one last hope—the general election. Watson convinced Charles McGregor to run against Hardwick in a final attempt to win the wool-hat boys. It did no good. At the polls Hardwick captured 75 percent of the

47. Hicks, "Watson and Hardwick," 157.
48. Quoted in Woodward, *Tom Watson*, 410.

vote. "The world is plunging hellward," the Sage exclaimed after the defeat.[49] For his world, at least, it was true.

What happened to the Populists after the demise of their party in 1910? For most of the leaders their association with Populism ruined any chance for later political success. Such party fathers as William Peek, Mell Branch, John West, and James and John Sibley gave up politics. H. W. Reed, who was treasurer of the national party and Watson's assistant during the campaign of 1896, traveled to Mexico in 1900, bought several gold mines, and died there in about 1902.[50] Only a few later attained public office. In 1923 Charles McGregor was elected state pension commissioner, a position he held until his death in October, 1924. Clarence Ellington served as ordinary of McDuffie County from 1898 to 1909.[51] James Hogan, Mark Irwin, and Seaborn Wright were later elected to the Georgia legislature. Although Wright was considered a possible prohibition candidate for president in 1908, only three Populist leaders won later statewide prominence. In 1920 Tom Watson was elected to the United States Senate, and two years later James K. Hines was appointed associate justice of the Georgia Supreme Court. When the Sage died in 1922, Rebecca Latimer Felton was selected to fill out his term. Serving for only two days, Mrs. Felton had the distinction of being the first woman United States senator.[52]

In the years that followed, most third-party leaders retained an interest in reform, many cheerfully joining with the latter-day Georgia progressives. James K. Hines vigorously aided in the election of Hoke Smith in 1906 and was crucial in convincing Tom Watson to do the same. When Watson betrayed the reform movement by endorsing Joe Brown, Hines refused to desert Smith. In 1907 Smith appointed Hines special attorney to the Georgia Railroad Commission, and for fifteen years Hines helped

---

49. Diamond (ed.), *Guide to U.S. Elections*, 712; Watson quoted in Woodward, *Tom Watson*, 411.

50. *People's Party Paper*, May 28, 1897; Atlanta *Constitution*, July 13, 1902.

51. Charles E. McGregor File, Georgia Department of Archives and History, Atlanta; Atlanta *Constitution*, October 15, 17, 1924; McCommons and Stovall, "History of McDuffie County, Georgia, 1870–1933."

52. Harris (ed.), *Supreme Court of Georgia*, 239–49; Woodward, *Tom Watson*, 473; Talmadge, *Felton*, 140–49.

lead the fight for lower freight rates. As a private citizen and member of the legislature, Seaborn Wright also joined with Georgia progressives. Besides his stand on temperance, Wright championed child labor laws, ballot reform, and the regulation of lobbyists. While serving as members of the legislature, Mark Irwin and James Hogan likewise supported reform legislation. In particular, Irwin struggled for bills that would require the rotation of judges and put solicitors-general and county officials on salaries. Rebecca Latimer Felton later struggled for prohibition, woman suffrage, prison reform, and better schools. Finally, such latter-day progressives as Walter B. Hill, Thomas B. Felder, and Hooper Alexander had been Populist allies in the 1890s.[53]

Many rank-and-file Populists clung to the reform tradition with as much passion as their leaders. In 1906 they overwhelmingly supported Hoke Smith for governor. Two years later, when Watson threw his support to Brown, probably half refused to abandon Smith. During the second Brown-Smith contest, even more Populists voted for Hoke Smith, and in the general election only a handful backed "Little Joe."[54] In these elections, a majority of the old Populist counties usually voted for Hoke Smith, the progressive candidate, indicating the loyalty Populists felt for reform and that Tom Watson had no magical grip on the rank and file. Most loved Watson dearly, but they loved reform even more.

And finally what of Tom Watson? Was he, like other party leaders and the rank and file, a link between Populism and progressivism? To a large extent he was. His publications, which were among the most reform-minded in the country, vigorously supported child labor laws, railroad legislation, and other changes.[55] Watson's endorsement of Hoke Smith in 1906 was vital in bringing into existence Georgia's first truly progressive administration. Yet how can this action be reconciled with Watson's

53. Grantham, *Hoke Smith*, 165–66; *Leaders in the Georgia General Assembly, Session 1913–1914* (N.p., n.d.), no pagination; Talmadge, *Felton*; Carroll *Free Press*, August 10, 1894; Winder *Jackson Economist*, July 20, 1899; Atlanta *Constitution*, April 10, 1900.

54. Of the nineteen Georgia counties having a strong Populist heritage, only McDuffie voted against Hoke Smith in 1906. Two years later, nine of these counties voted for Smith and nine for Brown. (In Oconee County there was a tie.) In the Democratic primary of 1910, twelve voted for Smith and seven for Brown; in the general election, sixteen voted for Smith and three for Brown. See Atlanta *Constitution*, August 24, 1906, June 8, 1908, August 26, 1910; Atlanta *Journal*, October 7, 1910.

55. Atlanta *Journal*, January 12, 1906; Watson, *Life and Speeches*, 182–87.

seemingly irrational support of Brown in 1908 and Hardwick's opponents in 1910? In the final analysis such acts cannot be reconciled. But they occurred not because Populism was irrational but because Watson was irrational.

Although many people were baffled by what appeared to be a serious change in Watson's personality, those who knew him well could not have been too surprised. Indeed, no drastic transformation in the Sage's nature ever took place. From his boyhood to his days as a Populist, he was a profoundly troubled individual. His youth had been pleasant, his mother allowing him ample time for games and reading. Yet even during this period, a darker Tom Watson often surfaced, displaying wild anger and gratuitous violence. In high school he was remembered "for his readiness to draw a knife"; in college Watson "had to have" a weekly fight. On one occasion he fell to arguing with his brother while working near a circular saw. Becoming enraged, Watson grabbed a sledgehammer and smashed it into the whirling blade until the machine was demolished. When he was twenty-five, Watson shot a lawyer during an argument.[56]

These outbursts might be dismissed as boyish mischief or the hotheadedness common to young southerners of his day. But as Watson matured he could never gain control of his temper and sarcasm. As long as his fury was aimed at the enemies of the farmer, it could be put to good use. Frequently, however, it turned against his friends and colleagues. Although everyone knew there was no love between Watson and Yancey Carter, few realized the extent of Watson's anger. "If I had [had] a bomb in my hand I could have thrown it under his feet," the Sage exclaimed after a meeting with Carter. When Carter voted against the prohibition bill that was before the Georgia senate in 1897, Watson saw a chance to even the score. But instead of fighting his battle in private, he risked tearing the party to pieces with a public statement. Apparently realizing that the Sage might lose control of himself, at least one party leader attempted in vain to dissuade him. In a venomous article, Watson portrayed Carter as the worst kind of hypocrite.[57]

A similar quarrel erupted with James Barrett. At the contested election

56. Brewton, *Watson*, 62–63, 152; Woodward, *Tom Watson*, 20, 96–98.
57. Atlanta *Journal*, June 22, 1897; *People's Party Paper*, March 20, 1896, November 12, 19, 1897.

hearings between Watson and Black in 1896, a witness described Barrett's cruelty at the Florence stockade during the Civil War, even claiming that Barrett had poisoned the drinking water of federal prisoners. When Barrett refused to answer the charges, Watson penned a sarcastic editorial. Later Barrett denied the accusations. "You harped upon the poisoning as if I was a second Beatrice Cenci," Barrett wrote to Watson. The Sage publicly replied that in his "mental confusion" Barrett had mistaken Cenci for Lucrezia Borgia. Shortly afterward, Barrett engaged in a fist fight with a Democrat in which several inaccurate punches were thrown. Watson recounted the fracas in his newspaper, observing that Barrett had chosen a "scrawny, feeble, weevil-eaten" opponent. "Nothing could have been more lady-like," he sneered.[58]

Watson's battles with Carter and Barrett were the only ones to gain public notice. They were not, however, the only ones to be fought with party officials. After pledging his loyalty to Watson—"I assure you that though you may have abler supporters you will never have one more devoted"—William Henning, the editor of the *Wool Hat*, felt compelled to add, "Your words of mock are painful. You might reserve your shafts of sarcasm for your enemies." On another occasion Watson's poisonous gibes lost the *People's Party Paper* its most faithful worker, Lulu Pearce. Complaining to Watson that she could never get a "civil reply, not to mention a business one," she resigned in 1895. "I have submitted to insults from you. I have done this because I was willing to receive slights on my own account if I could prevent any harm being done the paper. But when you question my honor and truthfulness you are going too far." The precise cause of the rift was unknown. But in an age and region that prided itself upon chivalry, Watson was not above aiming his barbs at women. "[Your] personal remarks I will not take," Pearce declared. "I am a woman and cannot help myself, but I have a few protectors who will not broch [brook] an insult to me."[59]

As the years passed, Watson continued to antagonize his associates. Early in the Populist crusade, Peek, Hines, and Ellington had serious quarrels with the Sage. Later Cunningham, Osborne, and probably

---

58. *People's Party Paper*, March 27, 1897.
59. W. J. Henning to Thomas E. Watson, October 15, 1895, Box 2, folder 15, Watson Papers; Lulu M. Pearce to Thomas E. Watson, June 1, 1895, Box 2, folder 13, *ibid.*

James L. Sibley joined the ranks of his enemies. "[Watson doesn't have] a kind word for any of our leaders," one Populist observed. "Ellington, who used to be one of his chief lieutenants[,] doesn't go to his home, Peek doesn't go there, Cunningham doesn't go there." Indeed, save for the "amiable, lovable" John T. West, this Populist could think of no third-party leader with whom Watson was on good terms. But even the "lovable" John West was not immune to Watson's wrath. In 1907 he wrote an icy letter to Warren A. Candler, the former president of Emory College, telling him that Watson had lied about how he had voted during an earlier election. "Mr. Watson sets himself up as a censor of other people's conduct," West wrote, "and seems to overlook the fact that his own record is very much subject to criticism." [60]

For the purposes of this study it is unnecessary to find the cause of Watson's mental torments. Yet they certainly existed during his Populist days. As a leader of the third party, he demonstrated much of the same personality traits, if in a less exaggerated form, that he did in later years. He was a reformer but one who had no love for blacks and who distrusted Catholics. He was also a man who found it almost impossible to maintain friendships—except, of course, for those with the anonymous wool-hat boys who thronged his rallies. Watson himself realized something was wrong. "I have imagined enemies where there were none: been tortured by indignities which were creatures of my own fancy," he wrote at age twenty-six. A year later he confided to his wife: "The better part of me is poisoned." [61]

In July, 1910, Thomas E. Watson announced his return to the Democratic party. It was surely time. Ever since the election of 1898 the Georgia People's party had slowly ceased to be a political organization. Now, with most of the old leaders and ideals gone, it was no more than a personality cult. Gone, too, was that great army of 95,000 Populists who had rallied to the faith in 1894. Still it would be inaccurate to say that the Sage had completely lost his following. When Watson endorsed Joe

60. Atlanta *Journal*, June 22, 1897; John T. West to Warren Akin Candler, July 23, 1907, Box 14, in Warren Akin Candler Papers, Special Collections, Emory University Library. See also West's letter in the Atlanta *Constitution*, May 11, 1911.
61. Quoted in Woodward, *Tom Watson*, 17.

Brown during the general election of 1910, about 17,000 citizens followed him in what everyone knew was a hopeless cause. Some of these voters were probably not Populists; nevertheless, Watson still wistfully referred to them as "the faithful 17,000." His description was apt. There did remain a body of voters who would support Watson no matter how outlandish his views became. Although the majority of Georgia Populists were rational, "the faithful 17,000" represented what a later generation would dub "the lunatic fringe." For them the Sage of Hickory Hill was not simply a man. In the 1890s, Tom Watson had often been described as an agent of God. In one home his magazines were neatly stacked beside the Holy Bible, and by the time of Watson's death in 1922, for a few at least, he had become a deity. One old Populist, writing to Watson's daughter in 1927, was still grieved by the Sage's passing. "I must live out the years that are mine," he declared, "thinking only of Hickory Hill and America's Master, who once lived there,—to me HE must be there forever. Yes HE is there. Many were the time, when HE used to write to me." [62]

But before Watson returned to the Democratic party there was one last rising of Georgia Populism. In early April, 1908, a convention met in St. Louis and selected the party's last national ticket: Thomas E. Watson for president and Samuel W. Williams of Indiana for vice-president. Watson never clearly explained why he accepted the nomination, although he murmured the old clichés about the need for a southern candidate, white supremacy, and a party devoted to the ideals of Thomas Jefferson. Watson's reason probably was to test his strength in Georgia. Confining his campaign almost totally to his home state, he sallied forth from Hickory Hill, making forty speeches in late summer and early fall. Watson had no illusions about his influence on national affairs. "I am a political nonentity," he declared during one address. On election day this assessment was borne out. Across the country he collected a mere 28,537 votes; in Georgia only 16,687. [63]

---

62. Grantham, *Hoke Smith* 204n.; U.S. Congress, House, *Watson vs. Black*, 670, 713; private interview conducted by the author, May, 1975; *Watsonian*, May, 1927, pp. 172–73.
63. Hicks, *Populist Revolt*, 402–403; Thomas E. Watson, "Why I Am Still a Populist," *American Review of Reviews*, September, 1908, pp. 303–306; *Watson's Jeffersonian Magazine*, November, 1908, p. 673; Diamond (ed.), *Guide to U.S. Elections*, 302.

Despite his defeat, Watson's last presidential campaign captured much of the spirit of old-time Populism. When word of his nomination spread, many of his disciples stirred with the passion of the 1890s. Letters of encouragement flowed across Watson's desk—from Marietta: "You deserve to have every man in the South, Bro. Watson"; from Adel: "I am greatly interested in your race for President of the United States. My father, who now sleeps beneath the willow, was for you"; and from Brinson: "I was among the first to go to the Pops after the party was organized, and, if I live, will be the last to go away from them. The boys are holding their own down here and we intend to give you the county." [64]

For the last time a Populist convention was to be held in Atlanta, where the third party would select electors and formally notify Watson of his nomination. On July 8 trains roared into the capital, disgorging the party faithful, who filled several Atlanta hotels. The next day a thunderstorm pummeled the city, as if heaven itself opposed this last gathering of the Populist party. Still five thousand people hurried out into the tempest and down Ponce de Leon Avenue to the meeting place, the St. Nicholas Skating Rink. Once inside, they wiped the rain from their faces and clothing, shed their coats, and unfurled their banners. An organist kept them happy by playing "Dixie." The same spirit and resolve prevailed as in Populist conventions of old. But no one bothered to ask what had become of the old party leaders who were now strangely absent—William L. Peek, Mark Irwin, Clarence Ellington, Seaborn Wright, Mell I. Branch, James R. Hogan, John D. Cunningham, and Yancey Carter. The party was in the hands of different men. J. A. Bodenhauer, the anti-Semite who had once edited the Dallas *Herald*, served as party secretary. Likewise, the delegates were different. They were not the wool-hat boys who had rallied in the 1890s, first to reform and then to Tom Watson. Instead, they were the true believers, the "faithful 17,000." They would be loyal to Watson to the end and make his name holy in the backwoods of the South.

Abruptly, a hush fell over the throng. For a moment the rain, drumming on the roof, echoed throughout the hall. An old Populist named "Blue" Fred Wimberly mounted the stage to introduce their chief. His

64. *Watson's Jeffersonian Magazine*, November, 1908, p. 738.

speech was like those heard a hundred times before, a pouring forth of rhapsodies to the Sage of Hickory Hill. "May God bless and preserve our Tom," Wimberly cried, "the leader of our people, the redeemer of our Israel." Suddenly the redeemer appeared. A slender man with a gaunt face and a shock of red hair that tumbled down over his brow strode to the center of the stage and slowly bowed his head. A roar exploded from the multitude, which quickly turned into a strange, hypnotic chant: "Tom Watson! Tom Watson! Tom Watson!"[65]

65. Atlanta *Constitution*, July 10, 1908; Atlanta *Journal*, July 9, 1908.

Bibliography

PRIMARY SOURCES

MANUSCRIPT COLLECTIONS

Duke University Library, Manuscripts Department, Durham, North Carolina
Middleton, James. Papers.
Emory University Library, Special Collections, Atlanta, Georgia
Candler, Warren Akin. Papers.
Fort, Tomlinson. Papers.
Watson, Thomas E. Papers.
Georgia Department of Archives and History, Atlanta, Georgia
Contested Election Hearings and Legislative Investigations
"G. W. Burnett vs. J. C. Camp: Contested Election from Douglas County—Evidence for Contestant [1892]." Typescript.
"G. W. Burnett vs. Columbus Blair, T. R. Whitley vs. Bion Williams, Contested Election Cases, Douglas County 1894." Typescript.
"A. O. Blalock vs. W. M. Cook, Contested Election, Fayette County, 1894." Typescript.
"Proceedings of the Special Committee Appointed by the Georgia House of Representatives, 1896, to Investigate the Charges made by State Senator W. Y. Carter against Judges J. L. Sweat and Seaborn Reese of the Superior Court Bench." Typescript.
"L. F. McDonald and W. P. Cosby vs. Henry L. Peeples and J. F. Espy, Contested Election Case, Gwinnett County, 1894." Typescript.
County Tax Records

Bartow, 1892	Hall, 1892
Bibb, 1892	Hancock, 1892
Carroll, 1892	Hart, 1892
Clark, 1892	Jackson, 1892
Cobb, 1889	Lincoln, 1892
Columbia, 1892	McDuffie, 1892
Cowetta, 1892	Macon, 1892
Douglas, 1892	Monroe, 1892
Floyd, 1892	Putnam, 1892
Fulton, 1892	Richmond, 1892
Gwinnet, 1892	Rockdale, 1892

Sumter, 1892   Warren, 1892
Taylor, 1892   Worth, 1892
Papers, Letter Books, and Biographical Data Files
    Atkinson, William Y. Letter Books.
    Candler, Allen D. Biograpical Data File.
    McGregor, Charles E. Biographical Data File.
    Northen, William J. Papers.
    Peek, William L. Biographical Data File.
    Wright, Seaborn. Biographical Data File.
Miscellaneous Manuscripts
    McCommons, W. C., and Clara Stovall. "History of McDuffie County,
        Georgia, 1870–1933." Typescript.
    Perryman, Clinton J. "History of Lincoln County, Georgia." Typescript.
University of Georgia Library, Manuscripts Division, Athens, Georgia
    Brown, Joseph E. Papers.
    Camak Family. Papers.
    Evans, Lawton B. Papers.
    Felton, Rebecca Latimer. Papers.
    Smith, Hoke. Papers.
University of North Carolina Library, Southern Historical Collection, Chapel
    Hill, North Carolina
    Black, James C. C. Papers.
    Butler, Marion. Papers.
    Graves Family. Papers.
    Watson, Thomas E. Papers.

NEWSPAPERS

Atlanta *Constitution*, 1880, 1882, 1890, 1891, 1892–98, 1900, 1902, 1904, 1906,
    1907, 1908.
Atlanta *Journal*, 1891, 1892–98, 1904, 1906, 1908.
Athens *Banner*, 1889.
Augusta *Chronicle*, 1892–98.
Bainbridge *Democrat*, November 19, 1892, November 8, 1894.
Blakely *Early County News*, August 30, 1894.
Calhoun *Times*, 1892–93.
Carnesville *Enterprise*, 1891–93.
Carroll *Free Press*, August 10, September 14, 1894.
Columbus *Enquirer-Sun*, 1892–96, 1898.
Conyers *Hale's Weekly*, 1892, 1894.
Conyers *Living Issues*, 1894.
Conyers *Solid South*, 1886, 1892.
Dahlonega *Signal*, 1892–94.
Dallas *Herald*, 1893–94, 1896.
Dawson *News*, 1891–92, 1894.
Douglas *Breeze*, 1896, 1898.

Gracewood *Wool Hat*, 1892–94.
Greensboro *Herald-Journal*, 1894.
Griffin *News*, 1894, 1896.
Jackson *Herald*, 1894.
Jefferson *Jackson Herald*, 1894–96.
Knoxville *Crawford County Herald*, May 27, 1892.
Macon *Telegraph*, 1891–92.
McDonough *Henry County Weekly*, June 3, 1892, May 12, 1893.
National Economist, 1891–92, 1896.
New York *World*, August 4, 1896.
People's Party Paper, 1892–98.
St. Louis *Globe-Democrat*, 1896.
Sandersville *Herald and Georgian*, April 7, 1892.
Sandersville *Middle Georgia Progress*, 1894.
Savannah *Press*, 1892–98.
Southern Alliance Farmer, 1892.
Sparta *Ishmaelite*, 1892–93, 1896.
Washington *Chronicle*, 1892.
Winder *Jackson Economist*, March 2, July 20, 1899.

PUBLIC DOCUMENTS

FEDERAL

Congressional Record. 52nd Cong., 1st Sess.
Contested Election Case of Thomas E. Watson vs. J. C. C. Black. 1896.
Contested Election Case of William H. Felton vs. John W. Maddox from the Sixth Congressional District of the State of Georgia. 1895.
House Reports. 53rd Cong., 2nd Sess., No. 1147, pp. 1–6.
House Reports. 54th Cong., 1st Sess., No. 1743, pp. 1–6.
House Reports. 54th Cong., 1st Sess., No. 2892, pp. 1–4.
U.S. Congress. House. *Testimony Taken by the Joint Select Committee to Inquire into the Condition of Affairs in the Late Insurrectionary States: Georgia.* 42nd Cong., 2nd Sess.
U.S. Department of Agriculture. *Yearbook of the United States Department of Agriculture, 1901.* 1902.
U.S. Department of Commerce and Labor. Bureau of the Census. *Thirteenth Census of the United States, Abstract of the Census, Supplement for Georgia.* 1913.
U.S. Department of the Interior. Census Office. *Abstract of the Eleventh Census, 1890.* 1895.
———. *Compendium of the Eleventh Census, 1890.* 1895.
———. *Report on Manufacturing Industries in the United States at the Eleventh Census, 1890.* 1895.
———. *Report of the Statistics of Agriculture in the United States at the Eleventh Census, 1890.* 15 vols. 1895.
———. *Report on Statistics of Churches in the United States at the Eleventh Census, 1890.* 1895.

The War of the Rebellion: A Compilation of the Official Records of the Union and Confederate Armies. 130 vols. Washington, D.C., 1880–1901. Ser. II, Vol. VIII.

STATE OF GEORGIA

Department of Agriculture. *Georgia Historical and Industrial.* Atlanta, 1901.
The Code of the State of Georgia. Atlanta, 1882.
Comptroller-General. *Report of the Comptroller-General.* Atlanta: 1892, 1893, 1895, 1896.
General Assembly. *Georgia Laws: Acts and Resolutions of the General Assembly of Georgia.* 1881, 1892–97, 1903.
————. Joint Committee on Railroad Leases. *Majority and Minority Reports, with Exhibits of the Joint Committee on Railroad Leases.* 1891.
————. *Majority and Minority Reports, with Exhibits of the Joint Committee on Railroad Leases.* 1891.
————. *Manual of the Georgia General Assembly, 1892–93.* 1892.
————. House. *Journal of the House of Representatives of the State of Georgia at the Session of the General Assembly.* 1883, 1892–97.
————. Senate. *Journal of the Senate of the State of Georgia.* 1887, 1892–97.
Division of Pensions and Records. *Roster of the Confederate Soldiers of Georgia, 1861–1865.* 6 vols. Hapeville, 1955–64.

BOOKS AND ARTICLES

Allen, E. A. *Lives of Weaver and Field and Achievements of the People's Party.* N.p., 1892.
Appleton's Annual Cyclopaedia and Register of Important Events, N.s., XVIII. 1893.
Avery, I. W. *The History of the State of Georgia from 1850 to 1881.* New York, n.d.
Brief Biographies of the Members of the Constitutional Convention, July 11, 1877. Atlanta, 1877.
Cozart, A. W., and Jno. J. Strickland, "Memorial of James Alexander Binceer Mahaffey." In *Report of the Thirty-seventh Annual Session of the Georgia Bar Association, May 22–29, 1920.* Atlanta, 1920.
Felton, Rebecca Latimer. *"My Memoirs of Georgia Politics."* Atlanta, 1911.
Georgia General Assembly, 1880–1881. Atlanta, 1882.
Georgia State Gazetteer, Business and Planters Directory, 1886–87. Savannah, 1886.
Georgia State Gazetteer and Business Directory for 1896. Atlanta, 1896.
Goss, Warren Lee. *The Soldier's Story of Captivity at Andersonville, Belle Isle, and Other Rebel Prisons.* Boston, 1868.
Ham, H. W. J. *Representative Georgians.* Savannah, 1887.
Hammond, M. B. *The Cotton Industry: An Essay in American Economic History.* New York, 1897.
Hines, James K. "Herschel V. Johnson." In *Report of the Forty-First Annual Session of the Georgia Bar Association, May 29–31, 1924.* Macon, 1924.

Kellogg, Robert H. *Life and Death in Rebel Prisons*. Hartford, 1866.
Leaders in the Georgia General Assembly, Session 1913–1914. N.p., n.d.
Link, Arthur S., ed. *The Papers of Woodrow Wilson*. 23 vols. Princeton, 1967.
Loyless, Thomas W., ed. *Georgia's Public Men, 1902–1904*. Atlanta, n.d.
McElroy, John. *Andersonville: A Story of Rebel Military Prisons*. Toledo, 1879.
Maxwell, John L. *Hand Book of Augusta*. Augusta, 1878.
Northen, William J., ed. *Men of Mark in Georgia*. 7 vols. Atlanta, 1907–12.
Post, Charles C. *Congressman Swanson*. Chicago, 1891.
———. *Driven from Sea to Sea; or Just Campin'*. Chicago, 1884.
———. *Metaphysical Essays*. Boston, 1895.
———. "The Sub-Treasury Plan." *Arena*, V (February, 1892), 342–52.
Sherman, William T. *Memoirs of General William T. Sherman*. 2 vols. New York, 1875.
Southern Historical Association. *Memoirs of Georgia*. 2 vols. Atlanta, 1895.
Vincent, Leopold, ed. *The Alliance and Labor Songster*. 1891; rpr. New York, 1975.
Watson, Thomas E. "Governor Hoke Smith." *Watson's Jeffersonian Magazine*, September, 1907, pp. 47–48.
———. "The Gubernatorial Campaign in Georgia." *Watson's Jeffersonian Magazine*, July, 1908, pp. 359–62.
———. "The Honest Ignorance of the Average Southern Democratic Editor." *Watson's Jeffersonian Magazine*, October, 1910, pp. 816–22.
———. "Is the Black Man Superior to the White?" *Tom Watson's Magazine*, June, 1905, pp. 392–98.
———. *Life and Speeches of Thomas E. Watson*. Thomson, 1911.
———. "The Negro Question in the South." *Arena*, XXXV (October, 1892), 540–50.
———. *The People's Party Campaign Book. Not a Revolt; It Is a Revolution*. Washington, D.C., 1892.
———. *Political and Economic Handbook*. 5th ed. Thomson, 1916.
———. *Sketches: Historical, Literary, Biographical, Economic, etc.* Thomson, 1912.
———. "Why I Am Still a Populist." *American Review of Reviews*, XXXIV (September, 1908), 303–306.

SECONDARY SOURCES

BOOKS

Argersinger, Peter H. *Populism and Politics: William Alfred Peffer and the People's Party*. Lexington, 1974.
Arnett, Alex Mathews. *The Populist Movement in Georgia: A View of the "Agrarian Crusade" in the Light of Solid-South Politics, Economics and Public Law*. 1922; rpr. New York, 1967.
Baker, Pearl. *A Handbook of History, McDuffie County, 1870–1970*. N.p., n.d.
Banks, Enoch Marvin. *The Economics of Land Tenure in Georgia*. New York, 1905.

Billings, Dwight B., Jr. *Planters and the Making of a "New South": Class, Politics, and Development in North Carolina, 1865–1900* Chapel Hill, 1979.

Bonner, James C. *Georgia's Last Frontier: The Development of Carroll County.* Athens, 1971.

Brewton, William W. *The Life of Thomas E. Watson.* Atlanta, 1926.

———. *The Son of Thunder: Epic of the South.* Richmond, 1936.

Brooks, Robert Preston. *The Agrarian Revolt in Georgia, 1865–1912.* Madison, 1914.

Buck, Solon J. *The Agrarian Crusade: A Chronicle of the Farmers in Politics.* New Haven, 1921.

Burnham, W. Dean. *Presidential Ballots, 1836–1892.* Baltimore, 1955.

Cash, W. J. *The Mind of the South.* New York, 1941.

Coleman, Kenneth, ed. *A History of Georgia.* Athens, 1977.

Coletta, Paolo E. *William Jennings Bryan.* 3 vols. Lincoln, 1964–69.

Conway, Alan. *The Reconstruction of Georgia.* Minneapolis, 1966.

Cook, James F. *Governors of Georgia.* Huntsville, 1976.

Cooper, Walter G. *The Story of Georgia.* 4 vols. New York, 1938.

Cooper, William J. *The Conservative Regime: South Carolina, 1877–1890.* Baltimore, 1968.

Coulter, E. Merton. *Georgia: A Short History.* 2nd ed. Chapel Hill, 1947.

DeCanio, Stephen J. *Agriculture in the Post-bellum South: The Economics of Production and Supply.* Cambridge, 1974.

Diamond, Robert A., ed. *Congressional Quarterly's Guide to U.S. Elections.* Washington, D.C., 1975.

Dittmer, John. *Black Georgia in the Progressive Era, 1900–1920.* Urbana, 1977.

Dowell, Spright. *A History of Mercer University, 1833–1953.* Macon, 1958.

Durden, Robert F. *The Climax of Populism: The Election of 1896.* Lexington, 1965.

Eaton, Clement, *The Mind of the Old South.* Rev. ed. Baton Rouge, 1967.

Faulkner, Harold U. *Politics, Reform and Expansion, 1890–1900.* New York, 1959.

Fite, Gilbert C. *The Farmer's Frontier, 1865–1900.* New York, 1966.

Flippin, Percy Scott. *Herschel V. Johnson of Georgia: States Rights Unionist.* Richmond, 1931.

Friedman, Lawrence J. *The White Savage: Racial Fantasies in the Postbellum South.* Englewood Cliffs, N.J., 1970.

Gaither, Gerald H. *Blacks and the Populist Revolt: Ballots and Bigotry in the "New South."* University, Ala., 1977.

Gaston, Paul M. *The New South Creed: A Study in Southern Mythmaking.* New York, 1970.

Gilbert, Stirling Price. *A Georgia Lawyer: His Observations and Public Service.* Athens, 1946.

Glad, Paul W. *McKinley, Bryan, and the People.* Philadelphia, 1964.

Goodwyn, Lawrence. *Democratic Promise: The Populist Moment in America.* New York, 1976.

Grantham, Dewey W., Jr. *Hoke Smith and the Politics of the New South*. Baton Rouge, 1958.

Griffith, Louis Turner, and John Erwin Talmadge. *Georgia Journalism, 1763–1950*. Athens, 1951.

Hackney, Sheldon. *Populism to Progressivism in Alabama*. Princeton, 1969.

Harper, Roland M. *Development of Agriculture in Georgia: A Series of Four Articles from the Georgia Historical Quarterly*. University, Ala., n.d.

Harris, John B., ed. *A History of the Supreme Court of Georgia*. Macon, 1948.

Hart, Roger L. *Redeemers, Bourbons, and Populists: Tennessee, 1878–1896*. Baton Rouge, 1975.

Hicks, John D. *The Populist Revolt: A History of the Farmers' Alliance and the People's Party*. Minneapolis, 1931.

Higgs, Robert. *Competition and Coercion: Blacks in the American Economy, 1865–1914*. Cambridge, 1977.

———. *The Transformation of the American Economy, 1865–1914*. New York, 1971.

Howell, Clark, ed. *History of Georgia*. 4 vols. Chicago, 1926.

Johnson, Michael P. *Toward a Patriarchal Republic: The Secession of Georgia*. Baton Rouge, 1977.

Kinzer, Donald L. *An Episode in Anti-Catholicism: The American Protective Association*. Seattle, 1964.

Kirby, Jack Temple. *Darkness at the Dawning: Race and Reform in the Progressive South*. Philadelphia, 1972.

Klein, Maury. *The Great Richmond Terminal: A Study in Businessmen and Business Strategy*. Charlottesville, 1970.

Knight, Lucian Lamar. *Georgia's Bi-Centennial Memoirs*. 3 vols. N.p., 1932.

———. *A Standard History of Georgia and Georgians*. 6 vols. Chicago, 1917.

Koenig, Louis W. *Bryan: A Political Biography of William Jennings Bryan*. New York, 1971.

Kousser, J. Morgan. *The Shaping of Southern Politics: Suffrage Restriction and the Establishment of the One-Party South, 1880–1910*. New Haven, 1974.

Kucharsky, David. *The Man from Plains*. New York, 1976.

McGill, Ralph. *The South and the Southerner*. Boston, 1963.

McKee, Thomas Hudson. *The National Conventions and Platforms of all Political Parties, 1789 to 1905*. N.d.; rpr. St. Claire Shores, Mich., 1970.

McLaurin, Melton Alonzo. *Paternalism and Protest: Southern Cotton Mill Workers and Organized Labor, 1875–1905*. Westport, Conn., 1971.

McMath, Robert C., Jr. *The Populist Vanguard: A History of the Southern Farmers' Alliance*. Chapel Hill, 1975.

Martin, Roscoe C. *The People's Party in Texas: A Study in Third Party Politics*. Bureau of Research in Social Sciences, Study No. 4. Austin, 1933.

Mathews, Mitford M., ed. *A Dictionary of Americanisms on Historical Principles*. 2 vols. Chicago, 1951.

Murray, Paul. *The Whig Party in Georgia*. The James Sprunt Studies in History and Political Science. Chapel Hill, 1948.

Nevins, Allan. *Grover Cleveland: A Study in Courage*. New York, 1933.

Nixon, Raymond B. *Henry Grady: Spokesman of the New South*. New York, 1943.

Noblin, Stuart. *Leonidas LaFayette Polk: Agrarian Crusader*. Chapel Hill, 1949.

Palmer, Bruce. *"Man Over Money": The Southern Populist Critique of American Capitalism*. Chapel Hill, 1980.

Phillips, Ulrich Bonnell. *Georgia and States Rights*. Washington, D.C., 1902.

———. *The Life of Robert Toombs*. New York, 1913.

Range, Willard. *A Century of Georgia Agriculture, 1850–1950*. Athens, 1954.

Ransom, Roger L. and Richard Sutch. *One Kind of Freedom: The Economic Consequences of Emancipation*. Cambridge, 1977.

Raper, Arthur F. *Tenants of the Almighty*. New York, 1943.

Roark, James L. *Masters Without Slaves: Southern Planters in the Civil War and Reconstruction*. New York, 1977.

Rowland, Ray, and Helen Callahan. *Yesterday's Augusta*. Seeman's Historical Cities Series, No. 27. Miami, 1976.

Saloutos, Theodore. *Farmer Movements in the South, 1865–1933*. University of California Publications in History, Vols. 63–65. Berkeley and Los Angeles, 1960.

Schwartz, Michael. *Radical Protest and Social Structure: The Southern Farmers' Alliance and Cotton Tenancy, 1880–1890*. New York, 1976.

Scott, Anne Firor. *The Southern Lady from Pedestal to Politics, 1830–1930*. Chicago, 1970.

Shadgett, Olive Hall. *The Republican Party in Georgia from Reconstruction Through 1900*. Athens, 1964.

Shannon, Fred A. *American Farmers' Movements*. Princeton, 1957.

———. *The Farmer's Last Frontier: Agriculture, 1860–1900*. New York, 1945.

Simkins, Francis Butler. *Pitchfork Ben Tillman, South Carolinian*. Baton Rouge, 1944.

Sobel, Robert. *Panic on Wall Street: A History of American Financial Disasters*. London, 1969.

Stovall, Pleasant A. *Robert Toombs: Statesman, Speaker, Soldier, Sage*. Richmond, 1892.

Talmadge, John E. *Rebecca Latimer Felton: Nine Stormy Decades*. Athens, 1960.

Tankersley, Allen E. *John B. Gordon: A Study in Gallantry*. Atlanta, 1955.

Thompson, K., ed. *Touching Home: A Collection of History and Folklore from the Copper Basin, Fannin County Area*. Blue Ridge, Ga., 1976.

Trelease, Allen W. *White Terror: The Ku Klux Klan Conspiracy and Southern Reconstruction*. New York, 1971.

Watkins, Floyd C., and Charles Hubert Watkins. *Yesterday in the Hills*. Chicago, 1963.

Weiner, Jonathan M. *Social Origins of the New South: Alabama, 1860–1885*. Baton Rouge, 1978.

Wigginton, Eliot. *The Foxfire Book*. Garden City, 1972.

Williams, Alfred B. *Hampton and His Red Shirts: South Carolina's Deliverance in 1876*. Charleston, 1935.

Williams, T. Harry. *Romance and Realism in Southern Politics*. Athens, 1961.

Woodward, C. Vann. *Origins of the New South, 1877–1913*. A History of the South, Vol. IX. Baton Rouge, 1951.

————. *The Strange Career of Jim Crow*. 2nd ed., rev. London, 1966.

————. *Tom Watson, Agrarian Rebel*. New York, 1938.

Wright, Gavin. *The Political Economy of the Cotton South: Households, Markets, and Wealth in the Nineteenth Century*. New York, 1978.

ARTICLES AND PAPERS

Bacote, Clarence A. "Negro Proscriptions, Protests, and Proposed Solutions in Georgia, 1886–1908." *Journal of Southern History*, XXV (1959), 471–98.

Bonner, James C. "The Alliance Legislature of 1890." In *Studies in Georgia History and Government*, edited by James C. Bonner and Lucien E. Roberts, pp. 151–71. Athens, 1940.

Brooks, R. P. "Race Relations in the Eastern Piedmont Region of Georgia." *Political Science Quarterly*, XXVI (1911), 193–221.

Clark, Thomas D. "The Furnishing and Supply System in Southern Agriculture Since 1865." *Journal of Southern History*, XII (1946), 24–44.

Crowe, Charles. "Tom Watson, Populists, and Blacks Reconsidered." *Journal of Negro History*, LX (1970), 99–116.

Derrill, Robert. "Joseph E. Brown and the Convict Lease System." *Georgia Historical Quarterly*, XLIV (1960), 399–410.

Edmond, Horace P., Jr. "A Brief History of the Democratic Party in Georgia." *Atlanta Historical Bulletin*, XV (Fall, 1970), 44–51.

German, Richard H. L. "The Augusta Textile Strike of 1898–1899." *Richmond County History*, IV (Winter, 1972), 35–48.

Hicks, John D. "The Sub-Treasury Plan: A Forgotten Plan for the Relief of Agriculture." *Mississippi Valley Historical Review*, XV (1928), 355–73.

Holmes, William F. "The Demise of the Colored Farmers' Alliance." *Journal of Southern History*, XLI (1975), 187–200.

Lee, Georgia Watson. "The McGregor Case." *Watsonian*, II (January, 1928), 404–11.

McMath, Robert C., Jr. "Mobilizing Agrarian Discontent: The Rise of the Farmers' Alliance in Georgia." Paper presented at the annual meeting of the Southern Historical Association, Atlanta, 1973.

Murray, Dorothy Haynie. "William John Henning: The Man—the Publisher." *Richmond County History*, II (Winter, 1970), 7–12.

Parsons, Stanley B., Karen Toombs Parsons, Walter Killiae, and Beverly Borgers. "The Role of Cooperatives in the Development of the Movement Culture of Populism." *Journal of American History*, LXIX (1983), 866–85.

Reid, Joseph D. "Sharecropping as an Understandable Market Response: The Post-Bellum South." *Journal of Economic History*, XXXIII (1973), 106–30.

Reznick, Samuel. "Unemployment, Unrest, and Relief in the United States During the Panic of 1893–97." *Journal of Political Economy*, LXI (1953), 324–45.

Roberts, Derrell. "Joseph E. Brown and the Convict Lease System." *Georgia Historical Quarterly*, XLVI (1960), 399–410.

224 Bibliography

Smith, Robert W. "*The People's Party Paper* and Georgia's Tom Watson." *Journalism Quarterly*, XLII (1965), 110–11.

Thompson, William Y. "Robert Toombs and the Georgia Railroads." *Georgia Historical Quarterly*, XL (1956), 56–64.

———. "The Toombs Legend." *Georgia Historical Quarterly*, XLI (1957), 340–44.

Turner, James. "Understanding the Populists." *Journal of American History*, LXVII (1980), 354–73.

Ward, Judson C., Jr. "The New Departure Democrats of Georgia: An Interpretation." *Georgia Historical Quarterly*, XLI, (1957), 227–36.

Wooster, Ralph. "The Georgia Secession Convention." *Georgia Historical Quarterly*, XL (1956), 41–52.

Zeigler, Harmon. "Letters of Tom Watson to His Campaign Manager." *Georgia Historical Quarterly*, XLIV (1958), 274–79.

DISSERTATIONS AND THESES

Adams, Olin Burton. "The Negro and the Agrarian Movement in Georgia, 1874–1908." Ph.D. dissertation, Florida State University, 1973.

Bacote, Clarence Albert. "The Negro in Georgia Politics, 1880–1908." Ph.D. dissertation, University of Chicago, 1955.

Bonner, James Calvin. "The Gubernatorial Career of W. J. Northen." M.A. thesis, University of Georgia, 1936.

Brown, Marsha G. "The People's Party Paper: A Consideration in the Light of Recent Controversy." M.A. thesis, Emory University, 1968.

Callaway, James E. "The Early Settlement of Georgia." Senior thesis, Princeton University, 1935.

Cummings, Josephine Newsome. "Thomas William Hardwick: A Study of a Strange and Eventful Career." M.A. thesis, University of Georgia, 1961.

Flynn, Charles L., Jr. "White Land, Black Labor: Property, Ideology, and the Political Economy of Late Nineteenth Century Georgia." Ph.D. dissertation, Duke University, 1980.

Furgeson, Jim Alan. "Power Politics and Populism: Jackson County, Georgia, as a Case Study." M.A. thesis, University of Georgia. 1975.

Hahn, Steven Howard. "The Roots of Southern Populism: Yeoman Farmers and the Transformation of Georgia's Upper Piedmont." Ph.D. dissertation, Yale University, 1979.

Hamilton, William B. "Political Control in a Southern City." Honors paper, Harvard University, 1972.

Hicks, Alfred Edward. "Watson and Hardwick in Georgia Politics: A Study in Political Personality and Reform Tension." Senior honors thesis, Trinity College, 1967.

Hudson, Frances Beach. "The Smith-Brown Controversy." M.A. thesis, Emory University, 1929.

Jones, Alton DuMar. "Progressivism in Georgia, 1898–1918." Ph.D. dissertation, Emory University, 1963.

Jones, George L. "William H. Felton and the Independent Democratic Movement in Georgia, 1870–1890." Ph.D. dissertation, University of Georgia, 1971.

Mathews, John Michael. "Studies in Race Relations in Georgia, 1890–1930." Ph.D. dissertation, Duke University, 1970.

Quillian, Bascom Osborne, Jr. "The Populist Challenge in Georgia in the Year 1894." M.A. thesis, University of Georgia, 1948.

Reddick, James Lawson. "The Negro and the Populist Movement in Georgia." M.A. thesis, Atlanta University, 1937.

Saunders, Robert M. "The Ideology of Southern Populists, 1892–1895." Ph.D. dissertation, University of Virginia, 1967.

Shaw, Barton C. "The Wool-Hat Boys: A History of the Populist Party in Georgia, 1892 to 1910." Ph.D. dissertation, Emory University, 1979.

Shipp, Mauriel. "The Public Life of William Yates Atkinson." M.A. thesis, University of Georgia, 1955.

Ward, Judson Clements, Jr. "Georgia under the Bourbon Democrats, 1872–1890." Ph.D. dissertation, University of North Carolina, 1947.

Werner, Randolph Dennis. "Hegemony and Conflict: The Political Economy of a Southern Region, Augusta, Georgia, 1865–1895." Ph.D. dissertation, University of Virginia, 1977.

Wynne, Lewis Nicholas. "The Alliance Legislature of 1890." M.A. thesis, University of Georgia, 1970.

———. "Planter Politics in Georgia, 1860–1890." Ph.D. dissertation, University of Georgia, 1980.

Index

Adams, Thomas M., 196
Adamson, William C., 174n
Agriculture
—cotton: post–Civil-War decline in
price of, 7–8, 9, 14, 22, 25, 35;
during Panic of 1893, pp. 103–105,
113
—crop values in Tenth Congressional
District, 163
—tobacco, 164
—fertilizer, 9, 19, 27, 42
—fruit, 42–43, 97
—superstitions, 13–14
Alexander, Hooper, 208
Allen, William V., 145
Alliance and Labor Songster, 92
American Fruit Growers Association, 173
American party, 165, 166, 180
American Protective Association, 121–22,
185
Anarchism, 58, 171
Andersonville Prison, 64
Anti-Catholicism, 3, 121–22, 143, 185
Antisemitism, 3, 178–81
Anti-trust legislation, 134, 135
Army, U.S., 109, 193
Arnett, Alex Mathews, 4
Atkinson, William Yates: early career, 67,
111, 125–26; race for governor in 1894,
pp. 112–16; opposes lynching, 136–38;
race for governor in 1896, pp. 155–57;
mentioned, 73, 134–35, 174
Atlanta, Ga., 1, 6, 7, 17, 18, 29, 70, 75,
82, 107, 108, 111, 124, 125, 132, 134,
142, 150, 153, 154, 167, 171, 178, 184,
190, 200, 213
Atlanta *Constitution*: editorial philosophy,
7; endorses Evans, 110; denounces
Populist-Republican fusion, 194–95;
mentioned, 20, 25, 28, 29, 30, 50, 60,
66, 119, 132, 159, 179
Atlanta *Journal*: editorial philosophy, 7;

exposé on General Weaver's war record,
69; lampoons black Populist delegates,
109; endorses Evans, 110; mentioned,
66, 127–28, 147
Augusta, Ga.: Populist kills deputy sheriff
in, 71; anti-Catholicism in, 121–22;
strike of 1898, p. 153; strike of 1886,
pp. 167–68; mentioned, 18, 39, 64, 73,
75, 94, 111, 132, 151, 154, 163, 164,
169, 170, 172, 181
Augusta *Chronicle*, 37n, 80, 180
Augusta Ring: opposes Alexander Stephens, 166; Patrick Walsh and, 180;
mentioned, 121, 206
Augusta *Tribune*, 49

Bacon, Augustus O., 73, 174n
Bagley, William H., 196
Banking: National Banking Act, 8; failures
during Panic of 1893, p. 103; Populist
oppose banks of issue, 109, 127, 143
Barker, Wharton, 185
Barrett, James: nominated for commissioner of agriculture in 1892, p. 59;
Civil War record, 64; accused of war
crimes, 64–66; opinions of blacks, 83;
nominated for commissioner of agriculture in 1894, p. 108; advises workers
to blow up wheel at Sibley Mill, 153;
growing knowledge of his Civil War
record, 154; his opinions on women,
178; denounces purchase of Philippine
Islands, 194; falling out with Watson,
209–10; mentioned, 167, 173n, 176,
184–85
Bartlett, Charles L., 79, 174n
Bell, John, 165
Berner, Robert L., 32, 174n
Black, James C. C.: 1892 congressional
race, 71, 72, 75, 76; 1894 congressional
race, 118; 1895 congressional race,